Life Is with Others

Life Is with Others

Selected Writings on
Child Psychiatry

Donald J. Cohen, M.D.
Edited by Andrés Martin, M.D., M.P.H.,
and Robert A. King, M.D.

Yale University Press
New Haven and London

Set in Adobe Garamond and Stone Sans by The Composing Room of Michigan, Inc.

Printed in the United States of America.

Library of Congress Cataloging-in-Publication Data

Cohen, Donald J.
   Life is with others : selected writings on child psychiatry / Donald J. Cohen ; edited by Andrés Martin and Robert A. King.
      p. ; cm.
   Includes bibliographical references and index.
   ISBN-13: 978-0-300-11466-9 (cloth : alk. paper)
   ISBN-10: 0-300-11466-4 (alk. paper)
   1. Child psychiatry.
   [DNLM: 1. Child Psychiatry—Collected Works. 2. Autistic Disorder—Collected Works. 3. Psychoanalytic Theory—Collected Works. 4. Tourette Syndrome—Collected Works. WS 5 C678L 2006] I. Martin, Andrés.
   II. King. Robert A., 1943– III. Title.
   RJ499.C593 2006
   618.92′89—dc22

                                                                    2005031948

A catalogue record for this book is available from the British Library.

The paper in this book meets the guidelines for permanence and durability of the Committee on Production Guidelines for Book Longevity of the Council on Library Resources.

10 9 8 7 6 5 4 3 2 1

To Phyllis,
to Matthew, Aviva and Hannah,
to Rebecca, Max, Ariela, Gabriela and Jacob Donald,
to Rachel, Allan, Sarah and Danya,
to Joseph,
and to the extended Yale Child Study Center family,
through all of whom Donald lives on.
מדור לדור
From Generation to Generation

Contents

Foreword, by Peter Fonagy, xi

Preface, xv

Acknowledgments, xxv

Two Introductions

A Memoriam to a Scientist and Visionary in Service of the World
James F. Leckman 3

Life Interrupted . . . but More than Memory Remains
Martin Peretz 8

Part I **A Life in Science Revisited**

1 Into Life: Autism, Tourette's Syndrome, and the Community of
Clinical Research (2001) *Donald J. Cohen* 15

2 A Lifetime of Research on Autism (2001) *Donald J. Cohen* 28

Part II **Understanding Other Minds: Autism**

3 Desire and Fantasy: A Psychoanalytic Perspective on Theory of Mind and
Autism (1993) *Linda C. Mayes, Donald J. Cohen, and Ami Klin* 49

4 Experiencing Self and Others: Contributions from Studies of Autism to the
Psychoanalytic Theory of Social Development (1993) *Linda C. Mayes and
Donald J. Cohen* 65

Part III **The Thin, Translucent Veil: Tourette's Syndrome**

5 The Self Under Siege (1999) *Donald J. Cohen and James F. Leckman* 83

Part IV **Hardworking Road Show: Play and Child Analysis**

6 Enduring Sadness: Early Loss, Vulnerability, and the Shaping of Character
(1990) *Donald J. Cohen* 107

7 Playing and Therapeutic Action in Child Analysis (1993) *Linda C. Mayes
and Donald J. Cohen* 128

8 The Development of a Capacity for Imagination in Early Childhood (1992)
Linda C. Mayes and Donald J. Cohen 142

Part V **No Safe Haven: Aggression, Violence, and Trauma**

9 The Social Matrix of Aggression: Enactments and Representations of
Loving and Hating in the First Years of Life (1993) *Linda C. Mayes and
Donald J. Cohen* 159

10 Child Development and Adaptation to Catastrophic Circumstances
(1996) *Steven Marans, Miriam Berkman, and Donald J. Cohen* 179

Part VI **Under Commodious Wings: Research and Mentorship**

11 The Immorality of Not Knowing: The Ethical Imperative to Conduct
Research in Child and Adolescent Psychiatry (1994) *Ami Klin and
Donald J. Cohen* 207

12 Research in Child Psychiatry: Lines of Personal, Institutional, and Career
Development (1986) *Donald J. Cohen* 225

Postscript: Inner Life *Matthew Isaac Cohen* 242

Notes, 249

Bibliography, 251

List of Contributors, 268

Index, 269

Foreword

Only a handful of individuals in child psychiatry might deserve the accolade of genius: Donald Cohen is one of them. His remarkable intellect spanned the entire breadth of the specialty, from molecular biology at one end to psychoanalysis at the other. His research contributions to the understanding of Tourette's syndrome and autism are well known, as are his writings about philosophical issues in child psychiatry, including his attempts at integrating knowledge of the mind-brain relationship with knowledge on psychosocial causation. But most of us would lack the capacity even to review his works, simply because we would not be able to muster the expertise to approach the subtlety and complexity of writing in as many fields to which he made seminal contributions.

The ideas presented in the pages of this book remain major concerns, particularly of psychodynamic child psychiatry, and Donald's solutions are probably still the best ones we have. His success in developing psychoanalytic scholarship in the context of a psychobiological program of research was rooted in his integrative capacity—one that the chapters of this book so beautifully illustrate. The value of the pre-

sent volume is precisely in bringing together key articles crossing the major domains of Donald's broad interests. Because his work was spread across so many
fields, it is not easy to get an immediate sense of the depth and breadth of his
contributions. A remarkable achievement of the present collection is that it offers an encompassing vista of Donald's major intellectual and scholarly contribution without seeming incoherent or fragmented on the one hand, or repeti-
tious on the other. Reading the book cover to cover, the reader comes away with
a sense of some of the key lessons for the discipline of psychodynamic developmental psychopathology that was Donald's trademark—and the brainchild of
this great mind of child psychiatry.

   I will select a few examples to entice the reader. The article on enduring sadness (Chapter 6) represents the clearest exposition of Donald's view of psychoanalysis. The article not only summarizes his position in relation to the writings
of Hans Loewald in particular, but also includes some of the best examples of
Donald's own clinical and intellectual virtuosity. The two individuals described
in the article are both overwhelmed with sadness and depression. Donald recognized the major challenge that depression represents for the mental health
profession. Far from being a problem solved by a judicious combination of
medication and cognitive behavior therapy, in a significant proportion of individuals depression turns out to be complicated and relatively unresponsive to
treatment. Antidepressants may bring about only a relatively small degree of
change in mood relative to placebo (Moncrieff and Kirsch, 2005). Cognitive
behavior therapy, although undoubtedly effective in effecting change in a
significant number of individuals treated, is not immune from the problems
of relapse (Roth and Fonagy, 2004). Donald aimed the developmental psycho-
anaytic approach, integrating genetics, early experience, and a therapeutic
intervention, toward initiating a process of self-understanding. I highlight this
article because of the remarkable intellectual achievement of integrating a formulation of depression as a failure of the modulation of aggression with patterns of caregiving and unconscious fantasy. The article is about not being able
to make use of the "nutrients of caregiving," the vulnerability that ends up pre-
disposing an individual to potentially a lifetime of sadness. It is also a deep
meditation on the shaping of character and the arduous work needed by therapist and patient alike in order to alter deeply ingrained habits of thought, feeling, and action.

   In this and other articles included in the present volume, Donald laid out his
framework for psychodynamic developmental psychopathology, which was
undoubtedly his guiding intellectual reference. The developmental approach

to psychopathology, masterfully embodied in the two-volume textbook he jointly edited with Dante Cicchetti (Cicchetti and Cohen, 1995c), is a tradition that has become the dominant perspective of child psychiatry. In those volumes and in many of the articles in this collection, Donald was able to bring together the intrapsychic perspective of someone steeped in psychoanalysis and individual clinical work with children, with the broad overview of a scholar for whom all findings about the biology, sociology, and psychology of development fit within a single frame. He preserved the intrapsychic perspective in retaining a focus on the developmental unfolding of representation, most clearly outlined in Chapter 7 of this book. In this article and in the one on imagination that follows it (Chapter 8), Donald generated a compelling model of how traditional psychoanalytic formulations about affect regulation dovetail with discoveries from developmental science concerning the emergence of the capacity for the representation of mental states. The collaborative work with Linda Mayes reproduced in the current volume (Chapters 3, 4, and 7–9) allows the reader to see another aspect of one of the great constructivist developmentalists at his most creative. Mayes and Cohen were pioneers in perceiving the relevance of the theory of mind construct for an understanding of self-development out of the social context of parent-child relationships. They were also the first to apply this framework to clinical issues of autism and child analysis.

The article on aggression (Chapter 9) presents a developmental model from the same perspective of psychodynamic developmental psychopathology, again considerably ahead of its time. It brings together the developmental perspective afforded by observation with the intrapsychic perspective that the psychoanalytic situation has the potential to create. Chapter 10 applies these theoretical constructs and through the innovative Child Development/Community Policing project addresses the gritty realities of urban trauma. As we confront war, terrorism, and trauma at an unprecedented worldwide scale, this line of work appears particularly prescient today. Along similar lines, the article on the immorality of not knowing (Chapter 11) makes a moving case for research in child psychiatry that is perhaps even more relevant today than when it was originally penned in the mid-1990s.

The final article (Chapter 12) gives meaning to the entire volume by expressing Donald's attitude on mentorship. Much of what is included in this book is the product of collaborations between Donald and his mentees, many of whom have become world-class scientists. This lends credence to the privileged position that Donald gave to mentorship in this chapter. He applied the developmental viewpoint as rigorously to that of the scientist moving forward in her career as he did to the child coming to terms with limitations in his genetic or psychosocial heritage.

The reader will admire much in this volume, in terms of wisdom, insight, and practical clinical description, but perhaps nothing is more admirable than the productive collaborations Donald established with a group of remarkably talented child mental health professionals who share the credit for the outstanding intellectual quality of this work.

In the first of two semiautobiographical articles included in this book (Chapter 1), delivered in 2001, Donald wrote about the joy of offering himself as a teacher and a doctor to be "metabolized" by students and patients so that his thoughts and attitudes could become internalized by others and thus immortalized. There is something immensely painful yet poignant in Donald, so close to death, speaking about outlasting his physical existence through his teaching and the care he offered his patients. There can be few scholars in any discipline whose direct contact with others reached quite so many people. While Donald was able to be relatively neutral in his analytic technique, he was anything but in his personal dealings with students and colleagues. He had "wisdom" in the most traditional sense of the term. He looked at life and saw that which others could not readily detect, therefore being able to point people in directions that seemed clear to him but hazy to all those who did not share his extraordinary clarity of vision. There was no inherent limitation to the scope of his wisdom. He could see and solve problems in high science as readily as in social issues, from youth violence and city policing, through psychiatric consultation and care, to administrative and organizational issues at government, university, and family and even individual levels. In addition to the creativity of his writings, Donald was a consultant par excellence. Those who had the benefit of his wisdom did not always like the advice he gave when they first heard it but on most occasions would see its appropriateness in time, whether they decided to follow his counsel or reject it. To all those who did not know him personally (and to the many who did), this book offers a singular opportunity to benefit from Donald's knowledge and insight. I encourage you to sit down with him now, to listen attentively, and to think carefully about his words—lest you miss out on the gentle human concern that permeated his conversations and that emanates so powerfully from these pages.

Peter Fonagy

Preface

The transfer of knowledge from teacher to pupil could be seen as the most crucial issue in any tradition, psychiatry and Judaism alike. The Hasidic structure of master and *hasid* placed this relationship at the very center of religious communal life. In *Tales of the Hasidim, Early Masters,* Martin Buber (1947) described the Maggid, Dov Baer of Mezritch, the Hasidic master-teacher par excellence in the following terms: "Disciples live with their master just as apprentices in a trade lived with theirs, and "learn" by being in his presence, learn many things for their work and their life both because he wills it, or without any willing on his part. That is how it was with the disciples of the Maggid . . . the will to teach was the mainspring of his existence" (p. 18). Donald [was] an embodiment of Buber's ideal teacher, and we are blessed to have gained from him. (Greenberg, 2001)

Donald Cohen's contributions to the field of child psychiatry were prolific and prodigious. This selection of articles attempts to distill what was unique and most distinctive about his work. The volume's title is a variation on *Life Is with People,* the name of the classic study of the *shtetl* written by two sociologists (Zborowski and Herzog, 1995 [1952]). *Life Is with Others* is the title that Donald himself had chosen—but then discarded—for his last speech, eventually finalized in print as *Into Life*, after the last two words in Franz Rosenzweig's *The Star of Redemption* (1971 [1930]). *Into Life* (Chapter 1 in this volume) proved to be the perfect title for a valedictory speech in which Donald reiterated his life-affirming engagement and took his leave, not capitulating to the expected and ultimately anticlimactic victory of his illness. But the discarded title, *Life Is with Others*, serves now to effectively bind this collection of his works. Indeed, if a summary word was to be sought for his work, or a fundamental essence of his life identified (unfair and fruitless as such a reductionistic pursuit might be), the term *social* would surely top the list.

Donald was an immensely social being for sure: he was deeply rooted, connected, and committed to his family, friends, colleagues, and community, remaining engaged across long stretches of time and distance through lively and regular communication. He took delight in building connections, putting people he knew in touch with each other and serving as *shadchen,* or matchmaker, to scores of friendships, scientific collaborations, and yes, even to marriages. His social life had the vibrant immediacy, density, and realistic texture of the *shtetl,* while paired with a much further and universal reach. For Donald was social in many ways other than *being* social: he was intrigued, troubled, excited, and propelled forward by social phenomena from his earliest days: "The thread between the awkward concerns of a bookish childhood—in large part spent observing an ethnically expressive, extended family, as well as a richly populated fantasy world—and a career in child psychiatry may seem easy enough to follow from this end. It was not so clear when this life was lived forwards" (Chapter 12).

To begin with, there was the breadth and depth of Donald's conceptual perspective. It may appear as serendipity that Donald was able to find and make use of so many diverse mentors, in the flower of their own scientific maturity, to master new fields still in their formative stages: social operant conditioning with Ogden Lindsley; neurochemistry with Daniel X. Freedman and Malcolm Bowers; infant development with William Kessen and Peter Wolff; child policy and cognitive developmental psychology with Edward Zigler and Julius Richmond; and psychoanalysis with Hans Loewald, Sally Provence, Samuel Ritvo, and Albert Solnit. Although luck and chance no doubt played a role, Donald had a keen intuitive eye for the methodologies he needed for what he wanted to study, and the capacity to engage his teachers deeply, both challenging and learning from them (Chapters 1, 2, and 12). As Pasteur once put it, "Chance favors only the prepared spirit."

Where others may have been daunted or paralyzed by what seemed a bewildering Tower of Babel of theoretical views and approaches, Donald was able to develop his own bridges and syntheses between these diverse paradigms. While he had a deep respect for scholarship of all sorts and an immense appreciation for any *chiddush* (what Talmudic scholars call a novel insight or new approach to a topic), it was his human immersion in caring for patients as a physician that gave the moral seriousness and center to his intellectual inquiries. On the wards, in Boston or New Haven, Donald talked with his patients and their families with the same intensity, engagement, and focus with which he and Ogden Lindsey used to argue psychology late into the night at Metropolitan State Hospital, but this time with mortal stakes. He saw being a doctor as conferring the unique privilege of being present at the crucial moments of pain, anguish, grief, birth, and death, as well as the heavy responsibility of trying to alleviate suffering and of providing hope even when one could not cure.

When Donald returned to Yale in 1972 from Washington, D.C., the disorders he chose to study—autism and Tourette's syndrome—were to shape much of his subsequent career (Chapter 1). The choice of these disorders was multidetermined. In those days, these appeared to be rare but desperate conditions that blighted the lives of children so afflicted and their families. Despite the work of a few pioneers—Leo Kanner and Edward Ritvo in the field of autism, Arthur Shapiro in the area of Tourette's—these were "orphan" conditions, poorly understood but little studied in either the large state or private hospitals that were the bulwarks of academic psychiatry, or in the consulting rooms of private-sector dynamic psychiatry.

Philosophically, these were also deeply compelling disorders that raised profound questions about basic aspects of the human condition that we usually take for granted. In autistic individuals, the usually innate capacity to see other people as agents with feelings, motives, and perspectives like our own somehow failed to develop or was terribly truncated, while at the same time the autistic individual's inner world remained opaque to his or her family and clinicians, despite their best efforts at empathic understanding. The problem of others' minds, or, borrowing the title of one of Donald's books, of *Understanding Other Minds* (Baron-Cohen et al., 2000), was a classical philosophical conundrum from René Descartes on and one that Donald had studied with the British analytic philosophers in Cambridge. How can we know that minds other than our own exist? Autistic individuals posed an all-too-terrible real-life example of what it meant to be trapped in the isolation of a solipsistic vacuum (Chapters 1–4).

In a different way, individuals with Tourette's syndrome (TS) also challenge the notions of our everyday language of psychology. We like to think of ourselves as being the sovereign authors of our intentions and actions and the thinkers of our thoughts. But the person with TS feels driven to perform acts or voice utterances experienced as senseless, repugnant, or unwanted, yet at the same time that urgently clamor for expression. These actions are at once longed for and resisted, wanted and unwanted, voluntary and involuntary, and indeed call into question the validity of these usual dichotomies. Obsessional thoughts and compulsive urges press on the individual with TS, leaving him or her to struggle continually as to what to accept or claim as "me" or to repudiate as "not-me." For the clinician-scientist in Donald, TS provided a powerful heuristic through which to bridge "the thin, translucent veil between psychological and biological processes in childhood" (Cohen, 1991b) (Chapters 1 and 5).

Not surprisingly, these disorders and the anguish they caused those affected engaged Donald deeply. From the first, Donald attempted to bring a multiplicity of theories, investigational techniques, and interventions to bear on these complex disorders, with the focus always being how better to understand and help patients and their families. This patient-focused approach to these chronic disorders had several consequences.

First, it meant a pragmatic scientific approach that made use of whatever methodologies and collaborators were at hand to shed light on the patient's condition. This led to some of the first applications to children of the techniques for studying neurotransmitter regulation that were advancing the field of adult psychiatry and to which Donald had been exposed at the National Institutes of Health. Other approaches adapted from the world of adult biological psychiatry involved neuroendocrine protocols, psychophysiological paradigms, and genetic studies. The burgeoning complexity of these new and potentially useful techniques soon outstripped Donald's personal expertise (extensive though it was), and he enlisted other promising young researchers with competencies in these areas to share his interest in these conditions. This collaborative team approach, centered on patient care, was to become the model for clinical research at the Yale Child Study Center (Chapters 1 and 12). It remains best epitomized in the autism and TS/Obsessive Compulsive Disorder clinics at the center, which under the respective batons of Fred Volkmar and James Leckman continue today as child psychiatry exemplars worthy of emulation.

Second, Donald treated both his patients and his patients' families as his collaborators, often over many, many years. Rather than taking an oracular "doctor knows best" stance (or an implicitly parentogenic view of the child's condition), Donald tried to share what was known and not known and where the promising leads for further understanding or help lay. Because families sensed Donald's long-term commitment both to them and to understanding their child's condition, many were eager to collaborate in research as, over the years, promising new hypotheses or methods became available. For example, in the earliest days of neuroimaging, pneumoencephalography was one of the few crude methods available for studying the living patient's brain. This technique, arduous for all concerned, involved introducing air into the cerebrospinal fluid space and then positioning the patient to use it as a contrast medium to reveal brain structure. Yet parents were willing to have their autistic children participate in such difficult research, not out of any false hopes of a messianic breakthrough, but because they came to share Donald's belief in the imperative of long-term programmatic research efforts to advance our understanding of the serious neuropsychiatric disorders of childhood: "[The] research in which I have been engaged has been in tune with the spirit and methods of the times . . . But its tone has been set most clearly by its center: clinical concern about children and their families, and a fascination with their inner lives. For young clinical investigators (and tiring older ones), having a belief in their value as clinicians is extremely important; it helps them survive the failures, competition, and aggression of science, and to maintain a sense of personal integrity in the process of doing and reporting their work" (Chapter 12).

Occasionally there *were* discoveries that changed patients' lives for the better. Studies of the autonomic nervous system suggested to Donald and his colleagues the theoretical possibility that clonidine, a modulator of adrenergic system functioning used to treat high blood pressure, might be of help in TS. A landmark clinical trial confirmed this hypothesis, and although many years of further study and refinement were to follow, the successful use of clonidine in TS was one of the first theory-driven psychopharmacological interventions for children, and a welcome alternative to the often cognitively blunting high doses of neuroleptics that were the standard treatment at the time.

The obduracy of these disorders and the level of multidisciplinary effort that needed to be sustained over the decades led Donald to think much about how to identify, shape, and nurture the young clinical researchers such efforts required (Chapter 12). Even within Donald's lifetime, advances in molecular biology, neuroimaging, and genetics required such intensive postgraduate training to be mastered as to threaten to make the physician-clinician-researcher obsolete. Under the leadership of one of Donald's closest colleagues, James Leckman, the Child Study Center developed a two-year fellowship providing research training for child psychiatrists, psychologists, and others interested in child mental health; over its three decades of operation, the training program has produced several generations of productive child psychiatric clinical researchers.

Beyond the requisite training in research methods, Donald was ever mindful of what sorts of mentorship and emotional, financial, and institutional support young clinical researchers needed. He emphasized the importance of the child psychiatric researcher's core identity as a clinician and the fruitfulness of immersing oneself in clinical phenomenology as a means of finding vital questions to study. Drawing on his own experiences of having been mentored by giants and of having mentored in turn a legion of young researchers, Donald described the developmental trajectory along which clinical research careers were shaped, as well as the normative crises that challenged them. What he once wrote about one of his mentors became his own essence: "At the time, Dr. [Daniel X.] Freedman was a brilliant young researcher, bubbling with ideas about neurochemistry, drugs, psychosis, hallucinations, LSD, psychoanalysis, schizophrenia. The leftovers were enough to fuel several careers. He never stopped working or talking, and I attached myself to his office and laboratory and came under those commodious wings, which have sheltered five or six generations of students through residencies and into full-blown careers" (Chapter 12).

Together with his own mentor and predecessor as director of the Yale Child Study Center, Albert Solnit, Donald saw the center as an institution that outlived any one individual and provided a vehicle for transmitting values and nurturing a community of clinician-scholars, over the various phases of their own individual development, during the many years required to advance knowledge. Beyond providing continuity of space, funding, and administrative support, this institutional milieu, which shared many of the complexities of family life, had to help negotiate the tasks of separation and individuation, of bringing in new blood from the outside, and of managing sibling rivalries, oedipal resentments, and the timely relinquishment by aging faculty of power and opportunity to younger colleagues.

While in the Public Health Service in Washington, Donald held down, as usual, at least two jobs: one as a research associate at the National Institute of Mental Health, the other as special assistant to Edward Zigler in the White House's Office of Child Development, writing federal day-care legislation and other child policy initiatives. This experience gave Donald an insider's view of how child social policy is made, as well as thwarted. (President Nixon vetoed the developmental day-care legislation on which Donald and Edward Zigler worked, proclaiming that he was preventing "the sovietization of the American family.") On returning to Yale, Donald became involved in the many innovative and socially progressive programs implemented at the Child Study Center by Albert Solnit, James Comer, Barbara Nordhaus, Jean Adnopoz, and other colleagues: school reform, court custody consultation, foster care reform, family support programs, early day care, and public child mental health.

In his last decade, Donald's scope and vision grew even larger. As president of the International Association of Child and Adolescent Psychiatry and Allied Professions (1992–1998), he traveled around the world—to Italy, Korea, Japan, China, Germany, Uruguay, Gaza, Brazil, and Egypt—leaving a wake of ever more friends, colleagues, and students. He saw concern for the world's children as *the* one great force for peace: that regardless of politics or nationality, all parents wanted their children to grow up healthy and secure and could find common cause in that endeavor.

Israel had a special place in Donald's heart, and there too he launched the field of scientific child psychiatry, built institutions and collaborations, and trained a whole generation of young clinical researchers. With the outbreak of the first Gulf War and the Scud missile attacks on Tel Aviv, Donald was immediately on the phone with Nathaniel Laor and other Israeli colleagues, planning mental health interventions for exposed children and families. Since, in Donald's mind, evaluation was always a key component of any intervention, this collaboration also included a longitudinal follow up (now entering its second decade) of exposed families.

Although increasingly engaged internationally with issues of children exposed to political violence, Donald was also aware of the toll of violent crime on children and families in New Haven, then in the grips of a drug-related crime wave. *No Safe Haven* was the title that he chose for a series of epidemiological studies that under the leadership of Mary Schwab-Stone documented the extent of this epidemic (Schwab-Stone et al., 1999 and 1995). But he provided more than titles and scientific documentation to all-too-well-known facts: he facilitated intervention. Together with Steven Marans and other colleagues at the Child Study Center, and Nicholas Pastore, a visionary New Haven chief of police, Donald put together an innovative mental health–police partnership to provide around-the-clock on-site mental health services and training for police in dealing with children and families exposed to urban violence (Chapter 10). As with other pilot projects, Donald was able to draw on the Child Study Center's Associates, a dedicated group of private philanthropists organized by

Irving B. Harris, to provide seed money. Now in its second decade, the Child Development/Community Policing project has been replicated nationally, led to the formation of the National Center for Children Exposed to Trauma, and culminated with the Donald J. Cohen National Child Traumatic Stress Initiative, introduced to Congress in late 2001.

Alongside the fertile challenges of autism, Tourette's syndrome, and trauma, other areas of investigation occupied Donald throughout his lifetime. He was drawn to psychoanalysis by many considerations (Chapters 3 and 4, and 6–9), not least his own two personal analyses, the first with Suzanne van Amerongen, a distinguished Boston child analyst, and the second with Hans Loewald, a profound émigré analytic thinker who had studied with and subsequently repudiated Heidegger. Empirically and clinically, psychoanalytic work, especially with children, provided a wealth of phenomenological data about the individual mind and its attempts to understand and represent itself on multiple layers: "If all psychoanalysis, with people of every age, shares qualities with the creation of a dialogical play, the players of child analysis create and act out the stage instructions as well as the speeches. At the end, the actors must recognize the unique ontological status of the analytic drama—its transitional status between the world of true lovers, friends, teachers, students, parents and children, and the world of memories and wishes (Loewald, 1960; Loewald, 1979). The actors in the children's theater know that they have been closer than those in adult analysis to building and rearranging palpable stage props and scenery; they have served together, as coach and apprentice, in a hardworking road show" (Cohen, 1980a).

Psychoanalysis also provided a developmental and affective perspective that complemented more cognitivist and behavioral approaches by trying to understand how desire, attachment, aggression, and envy were shaped in the unfolding context of the parent-infant dyad and later relationships. The importance psychoanalysis gave to early bodily experiences and the vicissitudes of early physical care (and its miscarriages) in shaping later character style appealed to Donald as shedding light on various forms of character pathology (Chapter 6) and psychosomatic disorders (Chapters 1, 5, and 12).

As an observer of children and a working analyst, Donald appreciated the creative ways in which play and fantasy gave form to longings and fears while helping to transmute and tame them into wellsprings of our vitality. His own creativity, and that of Linda Mayes, resulted in a fruitful collaboration of articles documenting such transformations (Chapters 3, 4, 7, 8, and 9). Donald was always wary of grand metapsychologies; he preferred the more experience-near concepts with which the analyst and patient attempted to make sense of the hard, daily slogging of analytic work. In place of the elaborate hydraulics of classical libido theory, in which "the object" appears as a mere after-the-fact contingency, Donald preferred Loewald's account of how the caretaker shapes the infant's physical rhythms, longings, and affects from the very onset. For better or for ill, the mother's reactions and responses to the infant, as well as the fantasies and imaginings she constructs of the infant in relation to her, become deeply constitutive of the infant's own emerging sense of self.

This "constructivist" view of how the child's self emerged in the matrix of mother-infant interaction did not deny the importance of biological or genetic factors. Although the spectrum of autistic disorders represented one extreme "experiment of nature" derailing development, Donald took it for granted that one of the tasks of developmental psychopathology was to uncover the ways different constitutional traits (in both parent and child) interacted over time to color development: "Individuals with autism have inborn errors of metabolism: they cannot make use of others from the start; those with early failures of internalization have acquired errors of metabolism: they cannot make use of the nutrients of caregiving later for enrichment of self and development of higher levels of representation of aggression" (Chapter 6).

The interactional perspective also resonated with Donald's more general philosophical and religious predilections. In his Sterling lecture (Chapter 1), he recounts his struggles with Descartes, for whom the mind and body were deeply divided and for whom the existence of other minds remained a hypothesis to be proved. Donald rejected the notion of an infantile tabula rasa or a Skinnerian account in which the infant stumbles into the world of language and social interaction through fortuitous reinforcements. Instead, he preferred the perspectives of Ludwig Wittgenstein and Noam Chomsky, who saw language as rooted in a human "speech community" with a shared form of life, from which the human infant was evolutionarily programmed to extract an understanding of language in all its shared meanings and usages, if only given the average expectable immersion in early social interaction with caretakers and other interlocutors.

In this sense, self and language are intrinsically shaped by others from the very onset. Although we may have our most private intimate thoughts not shared with others, this private communion with ourselves is not where we begin; rather it is the fruit of a lifetime of conversation and interaction with others that gives us the tools of language and meaning. (For Loewald [1978a], "consciousness" had the root of con-scire—a knowing together).

If we are born, "thrown into the world," in a particular body with a particular genetic makeup, it is also out of the particular family, in a particular culture, in a particular historical moment that we shape who we are to become. Donald was deeply impressed by the way family and culture shaped our intimate grammar of relating, the rituals that mark our collective lives and life cycles together. The community of shared meaning in which Donald was most natively at home was that of Ashkenazic Judaism, which for him provided a shared form of life that made it possible, as Rosenzweig saw it, "to live a life at once fully reconciled to human finitude and open to the experience of transcendence within it" (Lila, 2002). But he was also a citizen of the world, intrigued by how each culture provided its members transmittable forms of meaning for understanding the joys and sorrows of life.

Although Donald's loss is unredeemable for those close to him, this volume attempts to present the fruit of what he gave us: "The great surprise is birth, Being, and the improbability of lives such as ours, suffused with friendship, communication, and the shared pursuit of knowledge, wherever it may lead" (Chapter 1).

Robert A. King
Andrés Martin

Acknowledgments

Soon after Donald Cohen's untimely death in 2001, members from two of the institutions that he had so loved and nurtured during his lifetime—the Yale Child Study Center and the Yale University Press—planned a publication collecting some of his major works on child psychiatry. Even though most of his extensive writings are easily accessible in medical libraries and online (an estimated 493 papers and 13 books at a recent, but not definitive, count), we believed that bringing a representative sampling of them into a single volume would interest and engage readers anew. Such a collection would provide the vehicle for his contributions to reach another generation of clinicians and scholars, and allow for a condensed and synthetic overview of a career unparalleled in contemporary pediatric mental health by its breadth, depth, and influence.

We are indebted to Tina Weiner, Jonathan Brent, and Keith Condon of Yale University Press for their commitment to seeing this work through to publication. And we are grateful to David Rosen, John Schowalter, and Lawrence S. Cohen for shepherding it through and supporting its editors from the start. We thank William W. Hallo for his scholarly aide on Franz Rosenzweig, and Wendy Israel, Mary Gray Leary, Megan Waal, and Nisha Baat for their help in preparing the manuscript.

One of Donald's twelve pieces included in this collection (Chapter 2) appears for the first time in print here. The remaining eleven, as well as James Leckman's introduction, are reprinted with the permission of the respective authors and copyright owners. Except for minor changes made to ensure clarity or limit redundancy, the pieces are reproduced unaltered.

Donald J. Cohen's unpublished manuscripts and files are stored in the Yale University Library Archives (accession number 2003-A-024).

Two Introductions

A Memoriam to a Scientist and Visionary in Service of the World

James F. Leckman

Psychiatry begins and ends with our patients—with their diseases and dysfunctions, their biographies and aspirations—which, as a clinical medical science, we must systematically study. Doing that, we will borrow from and pose problems for all the life sciences. New knowledge about how cells and biological systems acquire, code, and exchange information challenges all of medicine. (Freedman, 1992)

What fascinated me most was how intimate relationships and the desire for being with the other precede the rest of cognitive development, and that this social motivation moves these other achievements forward, including meta-representation and theories about other minds. This intuitive, deeply encoded social orientation is first expressed in the mother's arms and then forms the basis for all future I-Thou relationships. (Cohen, 2001a)

Donny Cohen, the son of Joseph and Rose from Chicago, Ill, of Moshe and Molly from Berditchev, Ukraine, and Mashie and Avrum

First appeared in *Archives of General Psychiatry* 59:183–184 (2002). Copyright © 2002, American Medical Association. All rights reserved.

from Bialystok, Poland, died early in the morning of October 2, 2001, in New Haven, Conn. Born to and beloved by a family of Chicago bakers, Donald was a rare human being: intellectually gifted yet down-to-earth; playful yet busy envisioning and building a better world; filled with knowledge but always ready to listen, to be taught, and to find solace despite the hardships of life.

By all accounts, by the age of 4 or 5 years Donald was already an expert psychologist, reflecting on the workings of his mind and the minds of his parents, capable of moving from past dialogues to write the scripts of imaginary plays, knowing the difference between saying and meaning. By the age of 8 years, he had moved on to experiment on his younger brother, Howard, and to interview socially dysfunctional adults and publish verbatim accounts in his school newspaper.

By age 17 years, Donald had become a philosopher, absorbing the epistemologies of Aurelius, Augustine, Rene Descartes, and Ludwig Wittgenstein on how we come to know the mind and intentions of the other. Was it simple observation, a reflex mechanism of the sentient brain, or something to do with the profundity of ordinary language and the density and intensity of interpersonal dialogues?

Donald had immense erudition, but he was dissatisfied with these philosophical accounts. They neglected the earliest moments of parent-child reciprocity. He wanted to know the hows and whys of the shifts in our hedonic homeostasis and how these tides of love enriched our lives with others, our internal sense of well-being, and our relationship with God. Following 4 years at Brandeis University (Waltham, Mass), where he met Phyllis, his wife and lifelong companion, and many of his dearest friends, Donald moved on to Johns Hopkins University (Baltimore, MD), to the University of Cambridge (Cambridge, England), to Yale Medical School (New Haven), to Boston Children's Hospital (Boston, Mass), to the National Institute of Mental Health (NIMH), and to the Office of Child Development in what was then the US Department of Health, Education and Welfare (Washington, DC). During these peregrinations, he pursued his abiding interests in child development, pediatrics, genetics, neuroscience, psychoanalysis, Jewish mysticism, and social policy. Donald's mentors included many of the great figures of psychiatry, psychoanalysis, and child development of the 20th century: Drs Daniel X. Freedman, William Kessen, Ed Zigler, Hans Loewald, Sally Provence, Samuel Ritvo, and Albert J. Solnit.

In 1972 at age 32 years, Donald returned to Yale to join the faculty at the Child Study Center. At the time, he was thought by "very exacting people to know just about everything" (Peretz, 2001).

My first encounter with Donald occurred a couple of years later. I was a fledgling Clinical Associate in the intramural Adult Psychiatry program at the NIMH. Thanks to Elliot Gershon, MD, I was off to central Connecticut with Eleanor Dibble, DSW, to interview and collect blood specimens from members of a bipolar kindred. Eleanor had worked closely with Donald during his days at NIMH and insisted that we stop by the Child Study Center in New Haven to say hello. I remember a bright young man surrounded by an eager group of research assistants who took the time to discuss his interests in autism and something called "Gilles de la Tourette syndrome," an obscure neurological condition characterized by tics and obscenities. I recall his fascination with the sensory urges associated with Tourette syndrome and how these unwanted urges altered the patients' sense of self. He was interested in my background in philosophy and genetics as well as the time I had spent in Egypt, Lebanon, Jordan, and Israel.

I eventually came to New Haven to complete a residency in psychiatry. From those years, I remember most his class on child development and the extended interviews with children and parents that took place with 15 or so residents and other trainees in the same room. These were bravura interviews that seamlessly explored the emerging competencies of the child as well as the images, indeed the portraits, of the child that were to be discovered in the mind of the parent. He also taught us, in these compassionate mental vivisections, that the child's self-portrait is powerfully fashioned by parental imagoes, and the fearful consequences when those images are not idealizing.

In 1983, Donald became the Director of the Yale Child Study Center. Under his leadership, the center became internationally recognized for its multidisciplinary programs of clinical and basic research, particularly in the areas of autism and Tourette syndrome. Like his mentor and friend Danny Freedman, Donald was committed to the concept that clinical work enriches and is enriched by research, and that authentic clinical investigation is respectful of the complexity of children's inner experiences and the multiple determinants of their adaptive functioning.

His effective leadership in the worlds of autism and Tourette syndrome has been instrumental in encouraging physicians to listen to patients and their families and for educators, health care providers, and parents to work together to further research and clinical care.

Donald's academic achievements were formidable. He published more than 400 articles and chapters and more than a dozen books. In addition, he served as President of the International Association of Child and Adolescent Psychiatry and Allied Professions from 1992 to 1998. Donald was also elected a member of the Institute of Medicine of the National Academy of Sciences. He greatly enjoyed his role as a Training and Supervising Psychoanalyst at the Western New England Institute of Psychoanalysis (New Haven). He has received numerous awards, including an honorary degree in 1997 from Bar-Ilan University in Ramat Gan, Israel, as well as the Blanche Ittleson Award for child psychiatric research and a Special Presidential Commendation from the American Psychiatric Association. Other awards came in the past year for his contributions to research in autism (Cure Autism Now) and Tourette syndrome (Tourette Syndrome Association Award) as well as the Ruane Prize for Child and Adolescent Psychiatry Research from the National Alliance for Research on Schizophrenia and Depression.

Donald's devotion to both Yale Medical School and the Yale community had a global impact. From his close ties with the Dean, the President of the University, the New Haven Mayor, the Superintendent of Schools, and the Chief of Police, he helped to fashion community-based programs that have now been replicated across the country. Donald's leadership in studies of the effects of violence and trauma on children and families in the United States and abroad has created a worldwide network of collaborators in Italy, France, the Netherlands, the United Kingdom, Germany, Russia, Turkey, Israel, Egypt, Brazil, Chile, China, Taiwan, Japan, and Korea.

Donald especially loved the nation of Israel. He was home when he was in Jerusalem. He loved staying at Mishkanot Shaananim, built by Moses Montefiore in the Yemin Moshe neighborhood just outside the Jaffa Gate of the Old City. He established programs of research and clinical service and took special joy in fostering the development of gifted young Israeli physician-scientists. Although he was a passionate Zionist, he loved Israel so much that 3 years ago he convened the first meeting of the Middle East Child Psychiatric Association at Sharm el Sheikh, with representatives from Iran, Iraq, Jordan, Lebanon, Egypt, and Israel. He was committed to forging closer ties with the Palestinian people through contacts and visits with various psychiatrists, psychologists, and social service agencies in Gaza and the West Bank. When will we find another like him?

Donald's greatest joy during this past year, indeed the past several years, was to see his grandchildren growing up around him, to be a *zaydie*—a special, enchanting figure in their young lives. He frequently would come into the center a little late or leave just a bit early to be his playful self with Max, Ariela, and Gabriela and to see the world through their eyes and, yes, to have them see themselves reflected in his loving gaze.

In closing, let me say a few words about the past year. What we discovered was Donald's courage in facing the frailties of the body. He did not slow down; he did not give up. He sought to live in the moment. As Martin Peretz of the *New Republic* so poignantly said, "[L]ife kept interrupting his dying" (Peretz, 2001). He sought to do his work and to prepare us for a future without him, or rather, a future where he is very much within us.

Donald never wrote his treatise, his *Philosophical Investigations* or his *Star of Redemption.* In the end, he ran out of time for that. He will be remembered most for his dedication, his intelligence, his smile, his self-deprecating humor, and for his extraordinary gifts as an organizer, physician, teacher, mentor, and friend. He taught us the power of idealization: to look beyond our limitations to what can be achieved through teamwork and sustained effort. His life was his treatise. It was a privilege to know him—so many hours, so many ideas, so much love. Let us rejoice in the life of this remarkable man by redoubling our efforts—moment by moment—to improve the lives of children in the years to come.

Life Interrupted . . .

but More than Memory Remains

Martin Peretz

I remember a sentence from a letter Donald Cohen wrote me while he was a young Fulbright scholar at Trinity College, Cambridge: "Everyone here thinks Trinity is a great college because Isaac Newton studied at it." Do not misunderstand the words. Donald was not someone hostile to tradition or indifferent to the past. No one I know had more respect for old ways that had sustained themselves through time. In fact, the immemorial had a prima facie call on Donald's imagination. In many ways, his own head was focused on the past. His relationship to God was steeped in antique texts that he not only knew but, as his piety instructed, studied again and again. In fact, he himself was taken with that very man Newton's pious obsession with those very same texts . . . and what he had made of them.

Donald gave me many books during our friendship of forty-odd years, and I still remember the first, when we were both undergraduates. It was *The Last Trial,* by Shalom Spiegel, a scholar of exquisite learning, who had studied, through poetry and the literature of prayer, the bloody historical emanations—over centuries and particularly during the Crusades—of God's command to Abraham to offer his son Isaac as a sacrifice. Donald actually gave me the book twice. Thinking that I knew the languages of the past as well as he did (he usually assumed that his friends were as erudite as he was), he first gave it to me in Hebrew and then again almost in solace for my ignorance, perhaps ten years later, when *The Last Trial* came out in English.

Donald collected antiquities, mostly from the Land of Israel; it was not a lavish collection but a choice one, fueled by the enthusiasm of one of his sons, a young friend of mine, Joseph. Donald looked often at his (and Joseph's) pieces and fondled them, marveling at their beauty, at their strength and at their millennial survival. The past spoke to him not only through words, but through clay and stone, image and representation. And, of course, he also knew a lot about these pieces.

And, of course, he was loyal to the past. He read Yiddish, a language that, when mentioned at all, is usually characterized as "dying." His reading of Yiddish was, then, virtually an act of private defiance, and he would sometimes mention to me a scattered piece of evidence of its resilience. Yiddish was also simply a quotidian part of his life. At our last conversation before he died, we parsed two poems, written just after the Second World War, by Jacob Glatstein. We struggled with their contradictions. In one, "My Brother Refugee," the poet declares,

> The God of my unbelief is magnificent,
> how I love my unhappy God,
> now that he's human and unjust.
> How exalted is this proud pauper
> now that the merest child rebels
> against his word.

These lines led us into a discussion of the role of irony in Jewish literature, in the Jewish world. The second poem, "Dead Men Don't Praise God," was altogether without irony, but rather was an intricate threnodic verse, a lamentation on history as immanence itself, which ended thus:

> [W]e received the Torah on Sinai
> And in Lublin we gave it back.
> Dead men don't praise God.
> The Torah was given to the living.

Did the poet really believe this was the end? Donald did not.

The past was also the very stuff of Donald's professional life: the genetic origins of the healthy and why others are predisposed to illness; the place of mem-

ory, real and imagined, in one's psychic life and particularly in the psychic life
of his patients (and of their families, friends, and associates as well) and of people catastrophically on the edge; the social etiology of violence and conflict,
both individual and communal. But what Donald grasped most firmly was the
mind of a troubled child. There was a magic to his grasp—in the interpretation, of course, and in the treatment, but also in his sheer feeling. Psychopharmacology, yes, of course, an answer to be tried, and used with increasing confidence. OK, he did not possess magic. But he had a secure and palpable
instinct—part historic, part prophetic—about how to reach a distressed youngster. I know some of these youngsters, now grown. Believe me.

Donald's stretch was so large that I could hardly absorb the facts of it all. His
sway originated at Yale, and it is not surprising that his clinical work at the
Child Study Center somehow perambulated into a once experimental, even
daring, now permanent and practical program with the New Haven Police Department. But his sway went out in concentric circles virtually everywhere, to
affect and ease lives wherever there were clinicians he had touched. Even in be-
nighted Saudi Arabia, there are acolytes of Donald Cohen, and in China, too.

So what was it that led him to make that testy little remark about Trinity
College? There was something extremely smug about the cultural life of
Oxbridge Britain in the sixties, something stubbornly antediluvian, and it offended Donald. (Now that the country has experienced a severe and extended
brain drain from its universities, especially to the United States, in the sciences,
but not only in the sciences, the U.K. intelligentsia is a bit chastened, less
haughty.) Donald also observed in his letter to me that English students saw a
reading assignment as a bit of an imposition, preferring facile talk—and facile
writing—to real study and research. Donald's observations had not a touch of
arrogance to them. He was disappointed, and he made from this experience a
personal code of honor: the laurels of the institution you work in or for are not
your own. You have to earn your own medals. Which, of course, he did.

Still, there was nothing grand about Donald. But there was also nothing
falsely modest about him either. He knew how large were his achievements and
how wide his sway. Nonetheless, when I once suggested to him that he was of a
Jewish type that could be traced to Maimonides (or the Rambam, as he is sometimes called acronymically), the twelfth-century Jewish thinker whose life was
lived from Spain to Provence to Morocco to Egypt and finally to Palestine,
Donald protested that the comparison was absurd, pretentious, in fact. Now, it
is true that Maimonides was a greater thinker than Donald; but Donald was a
greater doctor, although Maimonides was the chosen physician among many

Muslim royals. But Donald was not just a traditional Jew with a Yale Jewish study group that would discuss his thoughts. His deepest Jewish thoughts went into his thinking about the treatment of troubled youngsters, and three or four times, right before Passover, I called him to discuss the disconcertingly sterile child psychology of the Haggadah's discussion of the four sons, the "wise" one, the "wicked" one, the "dumb" or "stupid" one, and the "one who does not know how to ask." I told him that, with gentiles at our seder, I was inclined to leave out the entire disquisition. I could not cope. But each time, he retaught me a transformational gloss. All his glosses were transformational, and they came from the soul of one who was both child psychiatrist and thinker. As it turned out, under Donald's tutelage, I coped rather well.

There is a long tradition of Jewish physicians being Jewish philosophers, and the legacy comes down to the present day. Yehoshua Leibovitz, the late and highly controversial (even pugnacious, perhaps even inflammatory) Israeli philosopher and physician is a case in point. Sigmund Freud was an earlier and more revolutionary instance, whose Jewish thinking was based on instinct rather than on real learning, but shrewd instinct it was. Another Jewish physician and thinker (and medical historian), Sherwin Nuland, a colleague of Donald's at the Yale Medical School—for some unexplained reason they were not really friends—makes the point that the only novelty in Maimonides' work was "the attention he paid" in books like *Discourse on the Explanation of Fits* and *The Regulation of Health* "to the emotional life of his patients and his proposition that mental states influence disease." This, of course, was at the essence of Donald's work, and was, in a way, its very subject.

We once discussed whether people with mortality staring them in the face should be given hope. Donald, like Maimonides, was absolutely clear that they should, even if the physician was reasonably clear that hope was misplaced, perhaps a stark delusion. One reason Donald thought this was that he was not sure that hope or faith might not actually extend the life of a patient even if it could not cure a disease. Hope of transcending diseases of the mind was certainly something that Donald deployed, as we can see in some of his articles, not only because it made the life of patients and their families more tolerable, but because it was in a way part of the cure.

Which brings me to Donald's last year and months. He had absolute clarity about his own grim condition and was still more than brave in undergoing truly debilitating and even horrifying medical procedures that may have worked for others, at least anecdotally. He did such at the National Institutes of Health, and came out on a relative high, only to be told—he had already intuited it himself—the bad news. After one of these psychological roller coasters, we sat in his garden, chatting, and, as I remember it, he received a continuous stream of phone calls: two from his mother, who had forgotten that she had already called and was calling, in any case, to ask him why he had not called her, which he had; one from a younger colleague at the Yale Child Study Center asking advice about a particularly nettlesome case; another from Israel about dealing with some youngsters who had survived a suicide bombing. He took these calls patiently and attentively. He knew he had not long to live. I had already said to him that he actually "didn't look so bad." To which he replied: "I know. And I also look better than my x-rays."

I'm not a doctor. But I had heard here and there from people who had been "cured" of cancer or cured themselves by diet, by self-imaging, by one or another of dozens of extra-medical therapies that suffuse the imperiled patient underground. Donald would not allow himself the luxury of such hope. It was frustrating for me . . . and for others. But it was honest to him. He had lived a life with science, knew its promise and its limits. He could not abjure this element of his secular faith.

No more than he could abjure his faith as a Jew. Some years after he had given me *The Last Trial,* he gave me *The Star of Redemption,* by the German Jewish philosopher Franz Rosenzweig, a book that begins with a meditation on the fear of death. I fear death, and I feared Donald's death. But I do not think Donald feared his own death. He conscientiously prepared his family and his friends for it. I think he prepared himself, as well. And, in some nonliteral way, he was sure that in death he would be reunited with all those who had been at Sinai.

Part One **A Life in Science Revisited**

Chapter 1 Into Life: Autism, Tourette's Syndrome, and the Community of Clinical Research (2001)

Donald J. Cohen

A great deal of our mental energy is devoted to understanding the life that we are leading. From the moment of birth throughout the course of development, from infancy to old age, our reflections, conscious and unconscious, naturally dwell on the most intimate human activities—the forming, sustaining, repairing, and terminating of our closest relationships. Surely, nothing is more compelling than this process—falling in love, taking in and being taken in by the other, and then, at one point or another, surviving as the other leaves, or saying goodbye as we move on.

Much of the cortex evolved for these purposes—to look outward at the vicissitudes of our relationships—with joy or dismay—and to look inward at the wishes and urges that arise in our personal depths—with wonder and surprise. Our observations of the social world and introspection of our inner world are necessary to navigate the changing social sea and to find some degree of satisfaction.

Special Dean's Lecture in Recognition of the Sterling Professorship. Delivered at the Child Study Center, Yale University; New Haven, Connecticut, February 27, 2001. First appeared in print in *Israel Journal of Psychiatry and Related Sciences* 38: 226–234 (2001). Copyright © 2001, Gefen Publishing House. All rights reserved.

These capacities also make us vulnerable—from early in life—to experiencing and recognizing conflicts between our desires and perceptions and the desires and perceptions of others, as well as conflicts within ourselves between competing desires and between wishes and values. These conflicts become represented in feelings and fantasies; as they provoke anxiety and suffering, their resolution helps move development forward.

By age 4 or 5 years, children are expert psychologists. Their meta-representational capacities allow them to reflect on the workings of their own minds and the minds of their parents. They can move beyond current realities to write scripts of imaginary plays, they know the difference between saying and meaning, they know when they are being deceived, and they can fool others. From what they see and guess, from bits of family gossip, from their intuitive understandings, they develop motivational theories of sex and aggression and spin their own family romance.

These phenomena—the gratification and pains of forming, sustaining, repairing, ending and understanding relationships—have been at the core of my own mental life from childhood and at the heart of my research.

What are the preconditions for the process of humanization in the context of social relations? What must the infant bring into the world and what must the world offer to the child, for the formation of the intimate relationships that shape the biology of the central nervous system and the tone of experiences forever? How do genetic and constitutional vulnerabilities, developmental miscarriages, psychiatric disorder, and persistent trauma block the process of forming and sustaining relationships—at the very first stages of socialization, as in autism, or, later, when developing trust and friendships in the school years. Most recently, I have been preoccupied with the distortions of these capacities for relationship that arise because of trauma of growing up in zones of war.

My first course in philosophy in college was the same year as the publication of Ludwig Wittgenstein's *Philosophical Investigations.* My teachers and I thus could experience together the thrill of studying this text that canonized an approach to philosophy that emerged only during the 1950's. The *Investigations* turned philosophy away from formalization, first principles, analytic certainty and the search for truth on any other ground outside of a community of shared meanings.

At the start of the *Investigations,* Wittgenstein quotes a famous passage from Augustine's *Confessions* about a child learning to speak. The child, according to Augustine, observes his elders naming objects and, at the same time, moving towards and using them; he recognizes the adults' intentions from their behavior.

In showing the limitations of this traditional account in which language seems to be learned like any other skill, Wittgenstein revealed the profundity of ordinary language and the density of the simple activities of daily living and thinking. He showed the virtuosity displayed in talking with each other and in dealing with misunderstandings by thinking together about each other's thinking.

It takes talent and motivation for real dialogue to occur—for you to know what I am thinking is on your mind, as I go on talking and trying to make sense, myself, of who I am and what I have just said. A child gets the hang of this thinking about her mind and the mind of others not by being taught, but by living a certain kind of life, a child's life, immersed in her specific language community.

I was forever influenced by Wittgenstein's way of doing philosophy, but I also felt then that he was missing the first, dramatic act in the developmental play—the affectionate substrate of social salience that forms the preconditions for becoming interested in others. What fascinated me most was how intimate relationships and the desire for being with the other precedes the rest of cognitive development, and that this social motivation moves these other achievements forward, including meta-representation and theories about other minds.

This intuitive, deeply encoded social orientation is first expressed in the mother's arms and then forms the basis for all future I-Thou relationships. Hans Loewald, my second psychoanalyst, described this process of differentiation from the mother-child matrix not only in the formation of the self and agency, but also in the origin of desires; my first psychoanalyst, Suzanne van Amerongen, made this process meaningfully alive for me. Once in place for a young child, the grammar of relationships becomes the code for understanding that Augustine's elders are indeed intentional agents, and not just usable and effective things in motion.

At that point in the intellectual world of the 1960's—and my own personal world—there were two major streams of thinking about what appeared to be fundamental processes in development—and I was attracted to both.

One side emphasized powerful, environmental forces—operant conditioning and the contingencies of behavioral control. My first scientific publication—my college thesis—described a novel method for studying operant conditioning of social behavior. I focused on the analysis of the social life of one boy—a youngster named Justin—and his friends in a highly controlled, operant conditioning paradigm that examined mutuality and competition.

In this experimental, Skinnerian world, the inner experiences of the child are epi-phenomena. Boys and girls just like rats and pigeons behave predictably because the same contingencies operate across all forms of behavior. I loved this simplicity and my earliest papers—I take pride that they are now classics, forty years later—were among the first to develop these paradigms for children. Years later, the young Ed Zigler and I still argued about their limitations. He was a cognitivist and was of course right.

The other stream of thinking was at the opposite pole—a view argued by Chomsky that language—and thus all those linguistic concepts that underlie social life—simply grows out of the organism. Like leaves on a tree, concepts express genetic programs waiting to unfold with sunshine and water. How intriguing this theory was. It appeared also to provide a neurobiological platform for Wittgenstein's sense that language emerges, rather than is taught.

There was a real tension between these two poles—the rigorous study of the behavioral surface and the fascination of the internal psychological landscape, however it may be described theoretically. This tension also has been reflected in the history of the Child Study Center—in the break between the eras of Arnold Gesell—a Chomsky precursor—and Milton Senn—a devoted interactionist. Even today, we still struggle to reconcile the empirical accounts of external behavior with the phenomenology of experience.

When I finished college three careers loomed ahead, each reflecting different poles and a resolution—psychology graduate school in Skinner's pigeon laboratory at Harvard; philosophy graduate school to study theory of mind in Cambridge, England; and as resolution of the conflict, medical school with the sense of keeping all options available.

I started first in philosophy (with acceptances to medical school and psychology graduate school in pocket). At Cambridge, I tried to make sense of the competing models of mind by studying Descartes' mechanistic, reflex physiology—the precursor of the Skinnerian point of view—from the perspective of Wittgenstein's philosophy of mind. I learned that once split, the domains of internal and external can only with difficulty, and perhaps not even then, be reintegrated; rather, the challenge, it seemed to me, is to avoid the original epistemological sin of dividing body and soul. Instead, we need always to remind ourselves that internal and external world, mind and body, behaviorism and cognitivism, psychology and neurobiology reflect abstractions and can distort the wholeness of natural phenomena. Splitting is the source of much philosophical mischief. The more I recognized this, the more I knew that I was made for medical school. I wanted desperately to learn from and be with real, whole people. And I felt, too, that medical school would allow for the expression of my desire to care for others, a motivation that I have felt with increasing clarity as a religious motivation.

At Yale Medical School I felt intellectually at home. I discovered the beauty and calling of clinical medicine—the special, privileged position that is offered to us to study whole persons, children and adults, in their most private lives, because of our commitment to offer care and reduce suffering. The Fitkin wards in Yale-New Haven Hospital held the same magical attraction as the Cambridge University Library stacks—a world of minds and bodies to be investigated. I remained fascinated by the same basic questions—the neurobiology and development of children's relationships—and two great teachers—Daniel X. Freedman and William Kessen—opened new vistas.

I entered medical school just months after the publication in 1961 of Danny Freedman's classic paper on hyperserotonemia in autism. Elevated blood serotonin is the first and most widely replicated biological finding in autism. Danny became my research mentor and then great booster, my counselor at each phase of my career. For decades now, George Anderson and I have continued Danny's work on the neurochemistry of serotonin in autism; our research serves, in a way, as a daily memorial for Danny, whose students were his children.

The role of serotonin in the CNS—its impact on arousal, sensitivity, and inhibition—can serve as an example of the paradigmatic search for biological correlates of basic behavioral processes. The transmission of a research area from generation to generation is an example of the community of clinical scholarship here.

In Bill Kessen's group, I joined the leading young developmentalists of the generation. My research focused on the study of the child's first self-soothing capacities—the ways in which a newborn's sucking reduces arousal and distress. Studying hundreds of babies during circumcision—perhaps an ethnic predisposition must have been at work—I showed the psychologically traumatic nature of the surgery but also the God-given capacity of babies to calm as they suck on breast or pacifier. Studying how such self-regulatory systems emerge and are modulated within families was an organizing theme during the next years, as I cared for babies whose arousal could not be modulated by themselves or others.

During my training in pediatrics, I had the privilege of caring for such children—children whose pain was not tranquilized by what they could do or elicit from their parents. I have always been rather squeamish, but I was magnetically pulled to children with deformities, to physically unattractive children, and children in misery—children whose relationships are most challenged and who require more than is possible from ordinary devoted parents.

At the Boston Children's Hospital, I developed a clinic for children with intractable eczema who could not escape the incessant demands of their itchy skin; they tore themselves apart with angry scratching. Furious at their own bodies and inconsolable, these pathetic children became isolated and drew into their own bodies and minds. Overwhelmed by their inability to soothe their child, parents became depleted and sad, and they averted their gaze from their child's blighted face.

A child's first mirror is the eyes of his parents. Parents who cannot idealize their child as the fairest in the world, who see their deformed or defoliating child as an indictment or worse, provide the child with a horrifying image that the child will internalize as his self-portrait. As I learned to see through the child's skin lesions and see the whole child, not just the eczema, I could guide parents in this process of re-engagement.

In the intense furnace of clinical engagement with these families in crisis, I learned a great deal about clinical epistemology—of how and what we can learn as clinicians by becoming immersed in situations of extreme emotional arousal and intimacy. These situations cannot be studied in the laboratory but they are the essence of authentic clinical work. Because of the relationships we are allowed to establish, we can join with child and parents as they are pushed to the limits of endurance and beyond. In this clinical context, we can examine the varieties of suffering, from infancy throughout the life cycle; the breakdown of internal coherence; and the capacities of the psyche for coping, repair and restitution when sustained by holding and knowing relationships. In such engagement, we are working at the borders between clinical medicine and what the Jewish and Christian traditions call the service of the heart—our personal, hands-on comforting of others.

All life is shaped by accidents, sometimes good. I had the accidental providence of being in Washington for my Public Health Service when Edward Zigler became the first director of the Office of Child Development. As his Special Assistant, I learned from him about growing up poor, social policy based on science, and being a citizen. Ed also re-introduced me to Albert Solnit, and the two of them brought me back to Yale University. When I auditioned for my position at Yale, I shared my dream about a new integration of neuroscience and psychology to inform clinical care.

Another remarkable accident was meeting Bennett Shaywitz during our very first week on the faculty of the medical school. For the next decade, we worked daily to realize the new field of developmental neuropsychiatry.

It was not an accident, though, that I focused on autism and the spectrum of children whose first years of life are burdened by inborn limitations in the capacity to fall in love. Their troubles are at the core of my long-standing fascinations. I had met some children with autism in my training and I was the advocate for the National Society during my years in Washington. At Yale, I decided to devote myself to understanding the disorder at each level—from biology to life course.

Autistic children cannot enter into the richness of family give and take; they do not acquire the forms of exchange that distinguish us as social animals; and they are deaf to the nuances and fun of ordinary language. They cannot engage in imaginative play and are poor at reading minds; they are also too honest—they are easily fooled and cannot tell lies. They are not good psychologists.

What causes such a condition? And, given the unbelievable stress of raising such a child, what keeps parents committed over decades of unrequited love?

Over the years, my colleagues and I have used each new scientific methodology to answer these questions, with each method revealing facets of normal and atypical development and raising further questions. Today, the remarkable power of neuroimaging provides new paradigms for understanding the neurobiological basis for social expertise and the availability of compensatory methods for navigating the social world when normal, intuitive processes are derailed. We can study autistic children's language, social relations, development, neurobiology, and genetics to a degree that we barely dreamed of at the start of this research program. We can even look through the eyes of an autistic child and see the world as he sees it—not filled with loving, interactive people, but with interesting objects and things instead.

We now believe that there are complex interactions between underlying brain systems and environmental provisions that subserve social salience and the integration of seeing, knowing, appreciating, and engaging in the social world. When all goes well, a good enough brain meets a good enough caregiving world, and children get the knack for peek-a-boo and lap play during the first year; shared social activities at dinner and on the floor during the second; meta-representation and theory of mind in the third year of life; imaginative play in the fourth; and the increasingly rich give and take of living together—the forms and language of society—that make mature relationships possible and gratifying.

For autistic children, these neurobiological pathways are often visibly disrupted from the first days or months of life. Yet, while most autistic children are stopped in their social development before reaching first base, the establishment of social relations and a sense of self is not an all or none affair. Some children with autism slowly acquire these skills, sometimes with the painful awareness of their terrible, insurmountable disabilities; and there are children with other complex, developmental neuropsychiatric disorders whose social relations become burdened by the specific features of their illness. Many of these conditions also reflect the impact of interactions between constitutional, presumably genetic vulnerabilities and environment; these disorders provide natural models for exploring fundamental questions of development.

My first interest in tics must have been aroused early in my childhood, when I recognized tics all around me. And then, as I finished my residency in psychiatry, I was sitting at coffee with a friend who for many years had been my peer confidant. We were reflecting on our plans. John was about to start his career as a psychoanalyst devoted to humanistic therapies. I said that I had a different goal—to pursue a narrow phenomenon to its roots. "What kind of phenomenon?" he wondered. Somewhere, from my unconscious, I quickly said "tics." I was genuinely surprised by my spontaneous, unplanned answer. I had never thought about Tourette's before that moment. What if we could learn everything about a simple tic, I asked—where did it come from, what made someone vulnerable, what neurons and neurochemicals were involved, how did it get expressed or held back? How did other children feel about a child with tics, and how did their feelings make a child feel about himself? In a few moments, from my unconscious, I outlined a program of research.

Thus, years later, when I first saw children with Tourette's syndrome in the middle 1970's, the intellectual and emotional soil was prepared. Here were children to compare to those with autism. Both had stereotypies, their problems originated in the developmental years, and they seemed to involve abnormalities in neurochemical modulation. Yet, unlike those with autism, the children with tics are fully aware that their symptoms cause their parents terrible pain and lead to their own social isolation.

These children suffer an excruciating sense of the loss of self-control—of the capitulation to inner impulses that hover between consciousness and the preconscious. Like young philosophers, they develop theories about what is voluntary and what is involuntary, what is psychological and what is neurological; they know there is a broad, indeterminate domain in between these contrasting categories; and they think about the mysterious leap from body to mind, mind to body, inside themselves. They also long to be in the mainstream of society—and with real courage and the use of all their talents, including their psychological sensitivities, they often achieve their goal.

With my closest colleague James Leckman, I have had the privilege of engaging over decades with children and adults with Tourette's syndrome. When we first started, TS was considered exotic, rare and devastating. Today, it is recognized in every school and community, with many milder variants. From the work in the Center, Tourette's syndrome has become the model neuropsychiatric disorder for developing and exploring each component of the contemporary model of developmental psychopathology.

Today, investigators throughout the world are exploring ideas developed within our research group—including the structure of symptomatology and natural history, genetic transmission, neurochemistry, neurobiology, treatment, and role of specific brain circuits that subserve the integration of intention, planning, execution and monitoring of thoughts and actions.

I have grown up with some of my childhood TS patients, who now return to introduce their fiancés, review their own lives, and think about their future families. Sometimes they return with their own children, who may also have a tic or two. We can offer more effective guidance and treatment when this occurs, sustained by our enduring relationships.

In the 1970's, I cared for a young boy, Steven, whose non-stop head banging, spitting, eye gauging, spasms, yelling and swearing excluded him from family and school. As we met together several times a week over several years, he allowed me to understand a life tormented by destructive urges in which he killed whatever he loved, pushed away whoever came close. He was the first child to receive clonidine for TS and thus helped open a new era of research and treatment.

And then I had the fortune of beginning to care for Bruce, who, for twenty years, has been my steady companion in understanding TS. He gives me permission to use his name, although in publications he is called Abe, a name I chose to reflect his role as forefather of much of what we have learned about the inner experience of TS.

Bruce came to me tied to a chair because of his self-mutilation and he begged for help. He felt caught between two bulls inside of his mind and head that tore at each other and fought to the death; these competing forces lurched him first in one direction and then in another. He was thus frozen in obsessions, compulsions and complex dystonic and destructive movements. In rare moments of peace, his sadness, warmth and empathy showed through.

I have learned more about the concept of intentional action from this clinical work than had I stayed at Cambridge to earn my PhD studying the concept of intention, as I had planned. After twenty years of seeing each other two or three times a week, Bruce and I celebrated his 40th and my 60th birthday together, appreciating the mutuality of decades of clinical investigation.

The pursuit of clinical research is a family affair. We study children in their families, and we become part of the family. Our clinical careers, too, are lived in families. Those of us who are fortunate to find places such as the Child Study Center start off with an advantage because we can enjoy the groves planted by our predecessors. We can also take pleasure in helping plant those trees that hopefully will nourish those who follow us.

This community of clinical scholars inspires us with confidence and sustains us, when our work or care goes badly. Albert Solnit's idealization of our competence has become integrated in our self-representations, along with Sally Provence's warmth, Samuel Ritvo's nonjudgmental regard, and our entire familial, internal entourage. Our minds are shaped within this community, and we shape those with whom we form relationships.

At the end, after relationships have been formed, sustained, repaired, ripened, internalized and then re-externalized, we hope to find the strength to say goodbye. Ending is not as sweet as first love, but termination is a natural phase of therapy and of life, and it is inevitable. Saying goodbye is essential for children to leave home and form their own families; for false-starts and disappointing relationships to be left behind in order for there to be space for fresh beginnings; and for the bereaved survivors to get up from mourning and resume relationships and life's adventures.

For clinical researchers, endings too must fall under the beam of rigorous, tough-minded scrutiny. The genes that underlie attachment also must have their suppressors, to allow for detachment, just as the brain circuitry involving relationships must have its buffers when relationships in the real world fade and exist only in imagination.

As teachers and doctors, we offer ourselves to be metabolized by students and patients, and we enjoy seeing our thoughts and attitudes become internalized and thus immortalized. We do not know which student will carry what part of us into his future. Danny and Bill Kessen could not have known what an enduring presence they have been for me, nor will I know which student or colleague—perhaps the most quiet in the group—will make my work and my beliefs a part of himself or herself. We know that only through risking ourselves in true encounters—in family and in our teaching—is there any hope for surviving, at least in part.

Franz Rosenzweig's *The Star of Redemption* (1971 [1930]) is the most important text of Jewish philosophy of the 20th century and a deep influence, along with the work of Martin Buber, on my religious sensibility. It begins with a stark statement that I used to believe as a matter of faith: "The beginning of philosophy,"

Rosenzweig writes, "is the fear of death." I no longer feel he was quite right. I fear that he has given too much, undeserved credit to Thanatos, to Death.

I have learned from our research and clinical work, and in my own bones, that philosophy can be fed from a sweeter well, a more caring source—from Eros and its earthly representative, our first and continually replenished capacities for loving. From this point of regard, Death seems predestined, dull and not a surprise. The great surprise is birth, Being, and the improbability of lives such as ours, suffused with friendship, communication and the shared pursuit of knowledge, wherever it may lead. In experiencing and thinking about such phenomena, we use our highest capacities for sublimation and symbolization—true achievements of development that are supported by a religious tradition and a living community of transcendent meaning.

The process of self-understanding—the task to which so much of our mental energy is directed, throughout life—goes on from moment to moment, epoch to epoch. Its product is an increasingly nuanced self-portrait—including thoughts, feelings, motivations, actions, reactions, memories—that is tested in lived experience. When this self-understanding proves trustworthy, we feel more certain in knowing who we are and with whom we are living, we can make wiser decisions with recognition of consequences, and we are not so easily surprised. Our theory of our own minds and minds of others becomes more reliable, a firmer basis for expectation. Yet, the story of a life—this rich construction built of feeling-filled memories—remains, at least in part, tentative and open to renovation. Its tone and narrative arc depend not only on what has transpired in the inner and outer worlds, as felt and seen by the person, but also on the moment in time it is created.

At this moment, two forces—each, in their own ways, unexpected and yet predictable—impress themselves on my personal history.

The first: Some months ago a powerful character knocked abruptly on my door and has cast a pervasive shadow backward on the story as well as towards the future—threatening a premature end of the story and its teller. I have been forced to recognize the fate that is intrinsic to being human—the ultimate vulnerability that neither intelligence nor will can overcome. This shock, this tectonic shift in my world has yielded a resonance to my life-review.

The second, from an opposite direction: The award of the Sterling Professorship has felt like an act of grace. Many professors at Yale, before and now, have earned this distinction surely as much as I, without the pleasure of being called to this chair. It is a blessing, then, to have been selected. Since self-regard is an important developmental achievement, this honor, too, must be expressed for the story to be truthful. Indeed, I take healthy, narcissistic delight in the recognition of becoming Sterling. The recognition fulfills my childhood fantasies of becoming a teacher of teachers in a community of scholars. I have been wonderfully lucky to have been able to share in the creation in the real world of these dreams.

One cannot fully know how such conflicting, powerful forces will achieve their final integration in self-understanding. Each summons in a different direction. Yet, one hopes that in the darkest moment, it will be possible to stand alongside Job in expressing, as he did at the time of his ultimate distress, "Yet will I trust in him" (13:15). Such an expression, when it is possible, is not an act of a solitary person, but a faithful relationship between an I and an engaged Thou—from the start to the end of social life.

The end of *The Star of Redemption* is an ecstatic crescendo. After confronting what can and cannot be known, Rosenzweig imagines reaching a divine sanctuary of truth, above whose gate is the sign: *Walk humbly with thy God.* Nothing more is required than a wholly present trust in this relationship, in the capacity for honest relationship. "Whither do the wings of the gate of this sanctuary open?" Rosenzweig asks us. "You do not know?" He then provides the simple yet powerful answer: the engagement with others in the fullness of relationships is the foundation which sustains us in facing life and enduring suffering, the motivation for development from birth until the very end: "*Ins Leben.*" The gate opens into Life: *l'chaim.*

ACKNOWLEDGMENTS

The Sterling Professorship recognizes the scientific and clinical work of the faculty and staff of the Child Study Center during the last nine decades, and especially the commitments of many individuals who have worked so closely with me over the last thirty years.

Advances in the study of early social development and autism have been central to the work of several generations within the Center—first, Sally Provence, and then myself, J. Gerald Young, Rhea Paul, George Anderson, David Pauls, Sara Sparrow, Linda Mayes, and those now at the cutting edge of creating the field of clinical, developmental social neuroscience—Ami Klin and Robert Schultz. Under the baton of Fred Volkmar, today's research program on autism is a scientific opera company that is peerless.

The remarkable achievements concerning Tourette's syndrome and associated disorders are the work of several generations of brilliant investigators and clinicians who have joined James Leckman and me and have devoted their careers to this program—Robert King, David Pauls, Bradley Peterson, Lawrence Scahill, Paul Lombroso, Flora Vaccarino, Mark Riddle, and many others, all equally appreciated.

The Associates of the Child Study Center, convened and led by Irving B. Harris, have provided the Center with the resources to maintain our primary missions of research, patient care, and education. Their vision and trust have allowed young faculty to pursue new ideas and for all of us to follow emerging concepts, wherever they may lead. Mr. Harris also has presented us with a personal model of authentic concern for knowledge and for children.

In this context of joy, I wish to acknowledge my beloved Phyllis, whom I met in college and who has shared this journey throughout, and our children, children-in-law and grandchildren who teach us about the primacy of relations. Also, I am fortunate in having family and friends—Howard Cohen and David Rosen, individually, and as standing for precious others—who have been a constant presence.

To President Richard Levin for his gracious act in naming me to the Sterling Professorship, to Dean David Kessler and Deputy Dean Carolyn Slayman, and to colleagues and co-workers in the Child Study Center (Shana Wildstein, my administrative assistant, as well as many others not mentioned explicitly) who have sustained me and have brought us to this time, I wish to express deepest appreciation as we all move from strength to strength.

Chapter 2 A Lifetime of
Research on Autism (2001)

Donald J. Cohen

I am thrilled by the recognition of receiving the Lifetime Award for Research on Autism. Having one's narcissism reinvigorated is a special opportunity that maturity allows us to receive with increasing grace. Also, this award allows me to reminisce and express appreciation to the many individuals and organizations that have sustained my research on autism and my clinical care for children and adults with autism over the decades.

In a special way, it is suitable that this award is for lifetime involvement with autism. For me, this is almost literally true. My very first publication about autism was in 1948, when I was a third-grade student in the Gregory School in Chicago. At that time, my best friend Michael Potashnik and I decided to publish a school newspaper. (Parenthetically, I became editor of school newspapers in grammar school,

Speech posthumously delivered by videotape on the occasion of the presentation of the Lifetime Award for Research on Autism. International Meeting for Autism Research, sponsored by Cure Autism Now, the National Alliance for Autism Research, and the M.I.N.D. Institute. San Diego, California, November 2001.

high school, and then in college; writing has always brought me pleasure and has made scientific publication a multidetermined delight).

Even at age 8, I was curious about relationships and thought about thinking, especially how we think about each other. This was the context of my first formal interview. Michael and I often went to the Garfield Park Conservatory, a wonderful institution available to youngsters in Chicago. We would wander through the rooms filled with tall tropical trees and exotic flowers, taking in the beauty and the misty, musty smells. I became especially aware of one man who would always be standing quietly and watering the plants; he patiently did his job with a sense of calm and a gentle smile. For the newspaper, I thought he would be the ideal person to interview, and he consented. The interview was then published in our school newspaper and constitutes one of the earlier reports, though less widely circulated than that of Kanner and Asperger, on the central phenomena that still intrigue our field. Let me quote the full article, published in 1948, at this time as an historic, pioneering study, and as the documentation of the launching of a lifetime career in autism research. This is the verbatim interview: "I was a shy and frail child. Therefore I decided to become a gardener." This early report on a socially dysfunctional adult identifies constitutional factors, shyness, and possible biological correlates, frailty, with long-term prognosis in a career that was socially isolated: the gardener represents an optimistic adaptation to an underlying disability in social orientation.

This pioneering research report also exemplifies my preoccupation as an observer of relationships—an early sign of what has become a persistent, scientific curiosity. For this area of study, my broad and buoyant ethnic family provided substantial raw material. We were a closely knit family with grandparents, aunts, uncles, and cousins; our household constantly was filled with guests, friends, and family for meals and holidays. A quiet participant observer like me had multiple opportunities for trying to figure out who was related to whom, which people cared for the others, what uncle or aunt or cousin was odd, but yet part of the group. With the guidance of a revered Eastern European grandfather and uncle, I also felt deeply connected with family histories that went back generations: I was intrigued by the transmission of traditions from the early 18th century to the very moment in which we were celebrating the same events in our house. For me, holidays and family activities reenacted a history that stretched back many centuries. This interest in human relationships filled my imagination—about how children are born into families, how parents love their children, how children express their needs, how children grow up, and how families change, in the course of generations of birth, maturation, marriage, and old age.

To study the happiness as well as the grief of family life became a favorite intellectual hobby and later developed into a deep interest in history and particularly social history. In those days, and in our particular ethnic world, children were included in everything from large family meals to celebrations of bar mitzvahs and weddings, to going to funerals and sitting with relatives during the period of mourning. This ecology has tremendously diminished and perhaps doesn't exist for any of us in the way it did just a short time ago; those of us who experienced this density of social phenomenology were no doubt enriched by a range of internal representations and theories that shaped our internal world in a particular way and focused us on people, especially what it means to be a person in a rich context of people.

This is particularly reinforced for those of us who became junior psychologists and the confidants of parents or relatives who recognized our interests in understanding them, their biographies, and the relationships between them and other relatives. For me, it was further reinforced by a strong current in our family life of interest in politics and the growing recognition of the devastation of the Holocaust, which destroyed the home cities of both my father's and mother's families of origin, Bialystock and Berditchev. Growing up under this umbrella of tremendous protection within the family was thus tempered by the increasing realization of the destructiveness and danger to which families are exposed.

At age 8, with the creation of the state of Israel, I became a young Zionist and collected food and clothes, which could be shipped to the newborn state. This provided a further sense of being part of an extended network of social relations, within an imagined new community of people whose relationship with me and my family transcended biology and reached to a universal kinship of commitment. No other force in my life has been stronger than this sense of connection with family and friends here and in other parts of the world.

During my school years, I was curious about how people developed crushes, about marriage, and about divorce. Early on, I recognized something remarkable—that people didn't always get along. Sometimes their hatred for each other blotted out what it was that initially brought them together: the stronger the love, the greater the ambivalence, the more destructive the hate. I have remained interested in these phenomena throughout my career: falling in love, maturing in a relationship, and dealing with a relationship that ends either because it has turned sour and mean, or because one partner or the other has discovered a fulfillment outside of the relationship, or when illness and death bring the relationship to its termination in the outer world. I have wondered increasingly about how these social processes evolve, become internalized, and are coupled with, and have the capacity to enrich, present and future relationships or to spoil the possibility for such relationships. These are the basic forces that stimulated my interest in the mysterious ways in which human connections are made. My sense is that many of us have scientific concerns stimulated by similar dynamics, scientific curiosity and personal (even ethical) commitments. These phenomena are aroused, too, as we think about what brings us to an area of research and sustains our relationship to a scientific field, such as the study of autism.

Actually, we know relatively little about the internal experiences, fantasies, and qualities of relationships of individuals with autism. Especially as the spectrum of autism expands, we are becoming more aware that the social dysfunctions are not all-or-none phenomena. There are gradients in the qualities of relationships. Individuals with autism experience, in their own ways, the forming of attachments and relationships, particularly with parents and siblings, disappointments in relationships, and sadness and loss (a terrible problem when there is rapid turnover of staff), as well as pleasures, satisfaction, and comfort in the dependence on others. Indeed, individuals with autism experience painful envy of siblings and others who are able to enjoy and navigate social life while they recognize how hard it is for them even to carry on a simple conversation or make a friendship. Part of our "humanization" of individuals with intellectual disabilities (mental retardation) has been to appreciate their need and capacity for loving, personal relationships, even for romantic love; understanding such capacities and needs—however atypical—for individuals with autism remains a goal of clinical investigation.

For me, research on autism also fits into a deep and persistent interest in philosophy and in psychology. During my university years, I majored in both fields. In college and then philosophy graduate school, I concentrated on the new philosophy of mind of the English analytic tradition, especially the implications of Wittgenstein's thinking. This interest in theory of mind was augmented by a remarkable opportunity I had to be part of the relatively early histories of both clinical neuropsychopharmacology and of applied behavioral analysis.

One summer, Dr. Spyridon Alivisatos, a gifted biochemist who had done his own postdoctoral work at Rockefeller University at a time when Wooley and Shaw developed the novel serotonin hypothesis for mental disorders, took me into his laboratory where he was studying serotonin. I had the chance to do research on histamine, which led to new methodologies for studying membrane transport and my first true experience of research. My interest was captured by central nervous system neurochemistry, so relevant at that time to the emerging work on the neurochemistry of psychiatric disorders and the role of LSD on the serotonin system. I became eager to see examples of the psychiatric patients I was reading about.

I thus went exploring, and had a moment of tremendous, unpredictable opportunity when Ogden Lindsley, who had earned his Ph.D. and did his post-doctoral research with B. F. Skinner at Harvard, was just beginning to develop the field of applied behavioral analysis in his Behavioral Research Laboratory at the Metropolitan State Hospital in Boston. Ogden was challenging the entire history of human psychology by creating the field of studies of human behavior using instrumental, Skinnerian approaches. In his basement laboratory, he applied operant conditioning paradigms extended from the pigeon lab at Harvard to study the structure of behavior of psychotic individuals and the impact of psychopharmacological agents on the systematic behavior generated by schedules of reinforcement. He offered me the chance to join the lab and to pursue his work on the operant conditioning of social behavior. This led to a passion for the research paradigms of applied behavioral analysis and to my first developmental paper, "Justin and His Peers: An Experimental Analysis of a Child's Social World" (1962). This paper was accepted by *Child Development* without any revisions (Cohen, 1962), one of those experiences that can create a false set of expectations for the future; the paper generated interest and was later anthologized, also very positive reinforcement. The operant research helped me to see the power of rigorous, theoretically based scientific studies of complex systems, such as social salience and facilitation, which underlay normal and atypical behavior.

Several years of work in the Behavior Research Laboratory also allowed me to spend a great deal of time with patients on the chronic psychiatric wards of a state hospital. Here I could observe a living textbook of serious psychopathology. I also experienced the dehumanizing and pathogenic environment that one found in a large, old-fashioned mental hospital. Among the patients were a few teenagers and older individuals who were called schizophrenic, but whom I learned to appreciate as suffering from autistic disorders. Just at this time, the world of autism was also shaken by the publication of Bernard Rimland's brilliantly written and revolutionary book on autism in which he gave a strong and convincing argument that this enigmatic disorder had a biological basis (Rimland, 1964).

These ideas and experiences stimulated in me a forty-year-long commitment to bringing together biological theories, behavioral analysis, psychology, and philosophy. My interests crystallized at these interfaces and coalesced in an abiding fascination with the vicissitudes of human relationships that you have so kindly recognized with your award. I entered Yale Medical School in 1962, one year after my mentor there, Daniel X. Freedman, discovered the most widely replicated biological finding in autism—peripheral hyperserotonemia. Dr. Freedman took me under his care and shaped my education as a child psychiatric researcher in many ways. He arranged for me to spend summers with Professor Peter Wolff at Harvard to learn about early development, provided a laboratory at Yale to study the regulation of arousal, and educated me about the new field of psychopharmacology and serotonin. For the next decades, he served as my scientific and personal mentor to whom I turned at points of important decisions. As a professor and editor of *Archives of General Psychiatry,* Dr. Freedman had an uncanny sense of what are important areas to study and the best new methods. He taught me that authentic clinical research changes a field and does not simply replicate, and about the value of pursuing one's own ideas deeply, however unpopular. Danny loved his students and wished for only one thing in return—our commitment to his values for pursuing scientific research on serious problems to the best of our abilities.

After medical school, I trained in pediatrics, general psychiatry, and child psychiatry at Harvard. Among a group of outstanding individuals in training, I had the possibility for immersion in clinical medicine and psychiatry. I saw many children with severe afflictions and could study them from varied clinical and scientific perspectives. It has been my belief that research on a particular disorder—such as autism—is enriched by a broad education including varied emotional, developmental, and neuropsychiatric disorders. Academics whose work too early and too exclusively focuses on autism—from graduate school through their postdoctoral research—or on only one methodology or perspective are at risk of not seeing the broadest context for exploring developmental psychopathology. Much is gained by early specialization on a disorder or method, but the possible drawbacks need to be considered as well.

During the years of pediatric internship, clinical research in pediatrics, and then my child psychiatry residency at the Children's Hospital, I had the chance to observe at the bedside several members of that remarkable generation of academic pediatricians who created new fields of scientific medicine—pediatric cardiology, hematology, immunology, etc.—after the Second World War. These clinician investigators showed how rigorous clinical research and concern for the whole child were synergistic. At that time, I had the fantasy of someday returning to the Children's Hospital and joining individuals such as these in creating a field of child psychiatry based on similar paradigms of authentic clinical care combined with open minded, broadly based clinical investigation. Why shouldn't early onset, developmental neuropsychiatric disorders be among the conditions deserving this type of special, scientific inquiry and care in a children's hospital? It has been my good fortune to help create such a setting in the Child Study Center, but, even today, there are precious few medical settings of this type.

Because of the current state of child psychiatry, I would like especially to emphasize the difference between this model of clinical investigation and what currently often is described as "biological child psychiatry." Nothing could be further apart in my own mind than the serious, meticulous understanding of an individual child, in all of his or her physiological and developmental complexity, on one hand, and the reductionistic use of categorical diagnosis followed by the rapid prescription of medication, on the other. I am convinced, too, that the paradigm of two-way translation from bedside to laboratory, and the recruitment of clinical scholars to this pursuit, serves as a counterbalance against the use of treatments that are not based on clear theory and empirical testing (and that all too often proliferate in relationship to autism).

After my internship and residency, I became a fellow in the intramural research program at the National Institute of Mental Health in 1970. NIMH was the base of the earliest studies on behavior genetics of psychiatric disorders; I had the privilege of learning about this thrilling new field in the Laboratory for Twin and Sibling Studies directed by Dr. William Pollin. A whole new epistemology of gene-environment interactions was emerging at just this time, and this perspective became a foundational influence on all of my future work.

In Washington, I was also detailed by the Public Health Service to the new Office of Child Development where I participated in helping shape national policy concerning children and families, as Professor Edward Zigler's special assistant. This opened the opportunity to participate with the advocacy group committed to children with autism, the National Society for Autistic Children. NSAC's first generation of leaders, including Bernard Rimland, Ruth Sullivan, and Amy Lettick, were remarkable individuals, parents of autistic children who were beginning to become empowered to create programs designed specifically to meet the needs of their children. NSAC made a strong appearance at the Office of Child Development in relationship to the follow-up of the 1970 White House Conference on Children, and I was given the chance to help lead this process. As a young Public Health Service officer, this follow-up activity involved planning several events and publications, including two monographs on day care that I wrote (Cohen, 1972, 1974b). I was also able to direct small amounts of funding for appropriate organizations, and in this way I was able to help NSAC at a critical juncture. Even more, I learned about autism and about legislation. One particular piece of legislation, the Developmental Disabilities Act, was targeted at children with mental retardation or cerebral palsy. The language of the act included "other disorders as found by the Secretary": before the lobbying efforts by the advocates for the named groups, the Secretary of Health had not included any other disorder within the coverage of the act.

As I learned how policy was shaped, I was able to work closely with NSAC in a lobbying effort. NSAC wrote to the Secretary and others about the importance of autism and its inclusion in the Developmental Disabilities legislation. At the same time, I was given permission to respond to this advocacy group, since I knew more about autism than others involved. And thus I responded quite frequently to the requests for consideration on behalf of the federal administration. This process led to the first amendment to the act and its inclusion of autism; my role was nicely recognized by NSAC. Here, again, an "accidental" opportunity strengthened my interest in autism and the families of children with autism—families whom I admired tremendously for their courage and for taking action.

The federal administration and legislators did not really know who should "own" autism—the agencies concerned with retardation, education, psychiatry, neurology, or child health. Most of the administrators tended to treat autism as a disorder that belonged elsewhere. In a way, policy issues have continued to arise in relationship to autism, perhaps as a reflection of the basic fact that pervasive developmental and autistic disorders involve alterations in the unfolding of many basic competencies across varied domains. Autism is a challenge to the epistemology or administrative structures that try to subdivide whole people by functions (social, emotional, cognitive), disciplines (psychology, neurology, education, child psychiatry, etc.), or ontology (mind versus body). One of the pleasures of research on autism is the potential for engaging our interests across the whole front of developmental sciences and philosophy.

The complicated, checkered history of autism care and research at the federal level underscores the historic policy achievements of the past several years, in large part because of the efforts of the new, effective advocacy groups and the unique support and vision of the National Institute of Child Health and Human Development (NICHD) directed by Dr. Duane Alexander; under his leadership, NICHD has emerged as the federal focal point, and Dr. Marie Bristol become the guardian angel of autism research. Also, the National Institute of Mental Health Research Units on Pediatric Psychopharmacology Autism Network, led with intelligence and perseverance by Dr. Benedetto Vitiello, is providing a firm foundation of model studies in a truly critical area of treatment. These agencies, groups, and networks are providing precisely the types of research resources that were dreamt about in the early 1970s—the base for sustained, rigorous research teams devoted to our field.

In 1972, as a "fully trained" child and adolescent psychiatrist, I was recruited to the Yale Child Study Center by Professors Albert Solnit and Edward Zigler to establish a research program in child psychiatry. I decided to study autism as the most serious, early onset psychiatric disorder, important in its own right because of the clinical needs of individuals and of value for understanding basic developmental phenomena. I had the remarkable good fortune of arriving at Yale the very same week as Dr. Bennett Shaywitz, the new chief of pediatric neurology. We shared an enthusiasm for neurobiological research on developmental disorders, and Bennett brought tremendous intelligence and expertise to the field. For the next decade, we worked closely on a range of studies, often developing new methods and applying approaches for the first time to studies of autism and other complex, developmental and neuropsychiatric disorders.

Along with systematic clinical research, my own research career, and a formative influence on the program at the Child Study Center, my close collaborations with programs for individuals with autism have always been of central importance. Even before arriving at Yale in 1972, I had met Amy Lettick, one of the dynamic younger leaders of the new parents' movement. She established a small program in New Haven for her severely autistic son, Ben, and three similar individuals. Benhaven's program was based on methods from special education, behavioral and educational curricula, and conditioning approaches, with a heavy influence of vocational training. Within a few years, Benhaven became a national model for children with severe autism and a site for development of new methods for education. During the course of those years, I had the chance to be part of Benhaven and its programs on a daily basis, and to become close to its children and families. This relationship continues within the Child Study Center to the present time, under the leadership of Dr. Fred Volkmar, who brilliantly directs the Child Study Center's research and clinical programs on autism and developmental disorders. Shortly after arriving at Yale, I was also fortunate to inherit several patients from the autism program that was initiated in the center in 1955 by Dr. Sally Provence, one of the world's great leaders in early child development. Thus, by 1972, there were opportunities for participating in the lives of autistic children in many ways. Some of those earliest family and child relationships that were established by Sally Provence, and then by me, continue today to be fostered and maintained by Fred Volkmar and Ami Klin and our current leaders in the field of autism.

In the early 1970s, there were only several researchers and no large research groups, other than UCLA, that had sustained, rigorous research programs on autism. A model for me was Dr. Edward Ritvo; a wonderful facilitator of young people entering the field, his kindness was a great support to me at the start of my own career. For Bennett Shaywitz and myself there seemed to be virtually an unlimited field of research options. Each new study held the promise of revealing an aspect of brain-behavior relationships and development, sometimes of relevance to autism, but always of considerable interest in charting the course of brain function and development and showing the role of various biological systems. The context of such research was quite different from the excellent scientific infrastructures in which we now can work. We were the first individuals to use many new biological and behavioral methods at Yale and virtually throughout the country. Our child patients were carefully characterized behaviorally, neuropsychologically, psychiatrically, and in relationship to their social and communicative competence. They were engaged in systematic clinical research over the course of long periods of time. We used many approaches for studying brain chemistry. In our very first studies, we focused on cerebrospinal fluid monoamine metabolites. Together with Dr. Malcolm Bowers, we established the role of methods such as the use of probenecid for clarifying rates of monoamine turnover in the brain; these became standards in the broader field of biological psychiatry. These methods were augmented by a range of studies on other bodily fluids, as well as studies that included other types of biological and behavioral measures. Our papers were always received with interest by colleagues, and we felt that we were able to help launch a field of biological child psychiatry, which was still very much in its infancy.

Soon, other young investigators joined in the work. The first new member was Dr. Jerry Young, who brought new methods and perspectives and established the first biological laboratory in the Child Study Center. We then recruited Dr. George Anderson, who has become the world expert in the neurochemistry of child psychiatric disorders; he helped enlarge the new Laboratory for Developmental Neurochemistry and further neurochemical research in child psychiatry. Progressively, we felt the work of a couple of individuals was being expanded into a research program. This research program, from its very initiation, was deeply based on forming clinical relationships with children and families, fostering familial and scientific collaborations, and helping to deliver the best type of education and clinical care to children who were volunteering for the research programs. This established a particular tone, for example sharing with families all of the records, having meetings with families in which the discussion was precisely the same that we would have among ourselves, and developing a language and an approach that was respectful of families and yet also scientifically accurate. This type of relationship building has become the model for the research program in the Child Study Center. Today, we take informed consent as mandated for human investigation; then, we felt it was mandated by our overarching principles of physician care as well as the ethics of scientific investigation. We also saw that it was pragmatic—that such a respectful approach brought families from throughout the nation to our research program, where they received from us all that we could provide and provided us openly their own experiences and research participation.

A review of papers from the 1970s and 1980s, will reveal a number of negative findings. In spite of our earnest efforts, we were surprised by the absence of marked differences, using the biological measures then available, between autistic children, with their developmental early onset disorders, and typical children. Indeed, this remains a remarkable phenomenon in the field of autism. How is it possible that our various biological measures, including our imaging studies, reveal, if anything, relatively subtle differences, and yet the behavior and development of children we are concerned about are grossly atypical from the very beginnings of life? I recall vividly our first attempt at computerized axial tomography of the brain. Beth was a teenager with moderate retardation, extraordinary anxiety, and severe impairment in her social relations. As a child, she had been diagnosed by Leo Kanner as autistic. When her family consulted us, more in support of furthering clinical research than in the hopes of obtaining some new form of treatment, they were recruited as active partners in a range of studies. Our first CAT scan was a major performance, attended by several faculty members from neurology and child psychiatry, the professor of radiology, an anesthesiologist, and our whole research team. It was our chance to see the brain of an individual with autism; we hoped, and perhaps even believed, that the "basic lesion" would now be apparent. While this hope was dashed, we were amazed to see that first CAT scan of a child with autism, and continued a series of studies that led to some interesting suggestions about reversals and small differences in some children with autism. Anyone working in our field must therefore be prepared for disappointment, yet open to the mysteries of the brain's development.

We accepted as axiomatic that autism reflected disturbances in the unfolding of basic neurobiological capacities, especially those involving social relationships and language. On the behavioral level, these atypicalities were apparent from the beginning of life; much of our research was aimed at finding correlates, for example between levels of homovanillic acid or 5-hydroxy-indole-acetic acid as reflections of dopaminergic and serotonergic functioning. From the perspective of behavioral research, an overarching concern was language and communication development, and the relations and differences between individuals with more relatively circumscribed language disorders and those with autism and autistic-spectrum disorders. In this broad area of work, our research program emphasized the centrality of the social dysfunctions over and above the language and intellectual difficulties. We proposed the importance of neurobiological mechanisms that related cortical with subcortical brain regions involved in the modulation of arousal and affects and their representation and transformation by symbolic systems in which language serves the primary role. These theories were elaborated in a series of papers in the 1980s and have remained relevant to current research on modularity and interconnections among brain regions.

Each new method provided us with confidence that autism, like any other serious psychiatric illness, could be and should be the focus of the most advanced methodologies. Because Yale was fortunate to have a Children's Clinical Research Center funded by the National Institutes of Health, always headed by a pediatrician and codirected by a child psychiatrist (for a decade I was codirector, a role now fulfilled by my close colleague and collaborator, Dr. James Leckman), we had the resources to use rigorous biomedical methods. In our Children's Clinical Research Center and the Child Study Center, autism became one more among other major medical disorders, such as leukemia and diabetes. This is a statement of the ideology that I formulated as a personal fantasy years earlier and I believe remains an important goal. Today, more than ever, we need to place autism not in a unique, isolated area as a boutique disorder, but in the context of other major developmental and pediatric conditions, which require and deserve to be studied by the most advanced methodologies.

In a sense, the research in autism during the 1980s went into somewhat of a lull. While programs and treatment approaches blossomed, often without firm scientific basis, basic research lacked a coherent focus. The development by Dr. Edward Ritvo of a diagnostic scheme provided a framework for describing the range of symptomatology in autism but did not find utility in the research at that time. I should add that Edward Ritvo played an important role in many of the major areas that still remain central in autism research, including studies of perception, serotonin metabolism, and, most dramatically, his recognition of the genetic contributions to autism. In many ways, he is the unheralded visionary of contemporary research in the field of autism and child and adolescent psychiatry.

Concurrent with Edward Ritvo's descriptions of the diagnostic criteria for autism, Professor Michael Rutter's contribution provided the radical simplification of criteria that gave a sense of clarity to the diagnosis of the disorder. As with Edward Ritvo, Michael Rutter too established groundbreaking new methodologies, particularly approaches that brought epidemiology and associated techniques into the study of child psychiatry, including autism, and the use of rigorous psychological methods. He demonstrated the value and possibility of rigorous neuropsychological and psychological studies, as well as the critical importance of international collaboration in studies of genetics and other domains of relevance in autism.

During the past few years, the new advances in developmental behavioral neuroscience, the recruitment into the field of outstandingly talented investigators from many different backgrounds, and the resurgence of support and interest from parents' organizations as well as the federal government have led to a change in the amount, the interest in, and the commitment of scientific talent to the field of autism. The field is more rigorous and more broad-gauged than ever before in its history. It reflects the most advanced approaches to behavioral and developmental neuroscience and applications to each of the major facets of autism, from its very earliest manifestations throughout the life course, from individuals with the most profound disabilities to those whose functioning in many ways approaches normal. This methodological, developmental, and conceptual expansion of the field of autism has led to a growing body of rigorous findings, as well as to scientific disagreements that are amenable to investigation and clarification.

A good example of cross-fertilization from other fields has been the emergence of an interest in cognitive processes as reflected, particularly, in research on theory of mind and the broader field of social cognition in autism. Here, we can see the extensions of methodologies and theories from the study of normal development, of processes such as shared attention, intersubjectivity, and social cognition, into developmental psychopathology; this both enriches the understanding of normal development and provides guiding ideas for understanding the underlying dysfunctions in serious psychopathology. Personally, I have been very fortunate to have been able to learn about this field from two superb investigators and colleagues—Simon Baron-Cohen and Helen Tager-Flusberg —with whom I have had the pleasure of producing two books on *Understanding Other Minds* (1993, 2000). Also, to be able to participate over these past several years in the newest phase of work on social cognition through the enthusiastic engagement of Dr. Ami Klin has been a high point of my learning about autism. New methodologies allow us to investigate the underlying cognitive and perceptual schemas, utilized by typical and atypical individuals, to organize their experiential world. We can "look" through the eyes of an individual with autism and see what she finds of interest and what she fails to grasp about social communication, intentionality, and affect.

Researchers in autism also have been at the forefront of developing methodologies involving functional and structural neuroimaging. What a huge leap between the "model T" CAT scan, which intrigued me and my colleagues two decades ago, and the high-performance imaging techniques that are rapidly transforming our field today. Indeed, these new methods offer promise for looking at a deep, theoretically driven set of questions that relate to the fundamental architecture of the brain—the structure and the connections between brain areas that underlie particular facets of the autistic spectrum of disorders. We take for granted today the notions that amygdala, fusiform gyrus, prefrontal areas, and other brain regions may each in their own way and in their interconnections make children vulnerable to difficulties that are expressed in the autistic syndromes. These brain regions and hypotheses are increasingly accessible to direct study, with each new investigation providing further confirmation of the kinds of ideas that were only speculations in the 1980s. My guide in the field of neuroimaging and neuropsychology, Dr. Robert Schultz, has literally depicted a new world for the field and for me.

There is an intimate relationship between studies of normal development and studies of autism. Autism continues to serve as a model experiment of nature. It provides an opportunity for enriching the investigation of the basis and unfolding of typical social relations with clinical observations on developmental psychopathology, on one hand, and also for using the findings from studies of normal development as a powerful scientific framework for understanding the core features, natural history, and specific abnormal biological and behavioral findings of autism. As a powerful example of this reciprocity, the discovery of genes and brain circuitry that regulate and participate in the formation of the earliest, most enduring social relations—the attachment between parents and offspring—provides a rich developmental framework for placing autistic social disorders. The new, powerful evolutionary models being elaborated by James F. Leckman complement recent studies (pursued by Flora Vaccarino and her colleagues) on pre- and post-natal environmental influences on brain plasticity. Taken together, these complementary perspectives on genetic and environmental contributions to the unfolding of bio-behavioral systems begin to provide rigorous models for exploring the most interesting questions in gene-environment interaction and social relations, from gestation through the course of development, in health and disease. This has been a guiding theme of my own interests and the program within the Child Study Center for decades; what seemed like science fiction two decades ago is now becoming a leading edge of empirical, child psychiatric research.

One of the messages from the field of autism is how to balance between the enthusiasm of the moment and our recognition that we are still in the very earliest phases of charting the complex oceans and new continents of neurobiology of social development. Each of us is motivated by the hope that this particular assay or that particular method will finally reveal the "secret" of human relationships and their derailment in disorders such as autism. Without such hope and optimism, it is hard to start a new study. Yet, those of us who have been part of the field for a while have grown aware that the tasks in front of us are unlikely to be solved in one fell swoop or with one coherent "Big Idea."

While being suitably skeptical, we also need to maintain a sense of hopeful engagement that will allow us to persevere in our exploration and discovery. There are good reasons for this optimism. We have increasingly sophisticated understanding of the underlying dimensions of social, communicative, emotional, cognitive, and arousal processes in normal development as well as in developmental psychopathology; methods allow investigators to examine specific genetic, neurochemical, neurofunctional, and social cognitive hypotheses concerning autism; we can integrate data more effectively from different perspectives; research teams are now collaborating, sharing information and concepts, while also pursuing areas of their own special interest at the cutting edges of knowledge; there are promising genetic leads; and there are new medications that have proven efficacy. I like to believe that some of these conceptual, methodological, and scientific advances (such as the increased understanding of the regulation of serotonin, advances in nosology and diagnostic criteria, emphasis on social and emotional development, new approaches to neuroimaging, the study of arousal, etc.) show the influence of the decades of work in the Child Study Center. In particular, I would like to take pride—which such an occasion elicits and I hope sanctions—in the Child Study Center providing a model of interdisciplinary, sustained, rigorous investigation on autism that is truly based on integrating advanced developmental science, optimal clinical care, and partnerships with families and individuals with autism.

Remarkably, after decades, I remain fascinated by the same phenomena that captured my imagination and enthusiasm from as early as I can remember myself. My first memories are vivid experiences that occurred at age 3 years, and no doubt were elaborated by layers of fantasy since then. In these memories, I am with my family in our country cottage in South Haven, Michigan. During the same summer, two things happened. One day my father arrived for the weekend with the other working men from the city ready to relax in the cool breeze of the countryside. I recall in my mind and in my body the exciting thrill of rushing across the grass to greet him. This is my very first memory—a vivid memory of rapprochement with a father who had been absent. My second memory from the same time is a visit from an uncle who was leaving for the Second World War. Handsome and heroic in his uniform, he was surrounded by a proud, anxious family knowing that he was about to be exposed to grave dangers. Here, at the same period, in my life, I experienced coming together and separating as central phenomena in life.

Today, I look out the window from my office, overlooking the playground of our Yale childcare program. What a thrill it is to see normal 3- and 4-year-olds playing together, enjoying their experiences, and turning to the childcare workers for support and care. For me, to watch preschool children interacting with one another is an endless source of fascination. We see the pure pleasure of early social relationships and the blossoming of the new capacities of imagination and thinking that emerge, as if by magic, during this phase of life. For children with typical endowment nothing is more engaging than the social world—especially the care, comforting, attention, and stimulation that they receive from their parents and closest caregivers. This is most evident at those intimate moments of life when children are alert and engaged, needy and tearful, or frightened and concerned.

What a stark contrast it is to see children with autism at the same age being evaluated by Fred and Ami. By age 3, often the most difficult moment for parents, the full burden of the inborn, neurobiological dysfunctions that strike at the core of human socialization have become apparent. The young autistic child stands apart from his peers at the playground, just as their parents often feel separated from parents of typical children who can delight in each new developmental phase while they feel increasingly isolated and dispirited. Handicapped by their inborn vulnerabilities and disruptions in laying down the templates for social engagement and pleasure in the very first months and years of life, individuals with autism remain forever off track in fully understanding their own inner life and the minds of others.

Children and adults with autism are the clinical exemplars of the most profound inborn dysfunctions—they become captive to their incapacity for finding the social and emotional world a source of endless curiosity, interest, and pleasure. While they may learn a great deal about the conventions of social life, they remain uncomfortable in trying to navigate the ever-changing seas of the actual social world. While typical children find their parents the most salient and critical aspects of the experiential world, and take them in and make their behaviors and feelings part of their own, children with autism, for reasons we are all dedicated to understanding, are unable to fully metabolize these experiences. To one degree or another, they are unable to make use of what their devoted and committed parents offer to them.

The emerging field of social-cognitive neuroscience places children with the most severe disorders of social, communicative, and emotional competence within a framework of advancing scientific theory and methodology. This field also overcomes the dichotomies we have accepted as traditional—between mind and body, biology and psychology. Instead, we have increasing opportunity to study children as whole people—mind and body and growing within families—and to use our emerging methods to understand the God-given capacities that allow for full humanization, as well as the tragedies of nature that block children from full participation in the human community. In many ways, autism challenges us, then, to understand and appreciate social relations of all types, and also to find ways of appreciating the strengths that emerge in the face of adversity—the strengths of individuals with serious disorders who struggle to find alternative adaptations and the strengths of families who, in spite of every hardship, persevere in loving and respecting their children. Also, we as a community of scholars and clinicians can join in a sense of pride for persevering in the care and study of individuals with autism, in spite of disappointments and difficulties. Our belief in the possibility of scientific investigation to be of help is also an example of one of the highest values of society.

In a special way autism, which strikes at the core of relationships, has become the glue for investigators, students and teachers, and truly an international community, which shares ideas, methods, data, and commitments to improving the lives of individuals with severe developmental disorders. The community of clinical researchers and basic researchers is an example of the ways in which we all can join together to enrich each other's science and lives by sharing and collaborating. To have individuals pick up your ideas, challenge them, and move them forward is the greatest compliment to a clinical researcher and represents the only true immortality that we know. It is a special pleasure to acknowledge all of the investigators in our field for what you have done and the promise that you hold for understanding the phenomena of autism and the broader field of human relations.

ACKNOWLEDGEMENTS

For thirty years, I have had the good fortune of supportive mentors and the collaboration with many outstanding clinicians and scholars. I would like to note especially the following individuals: Fred Volkmar (whose internationally recognized scientific talent, leadership, and commitment to individuals with autism and their families suffuse all aspects of the research and clinical programs on autism and associated disorders in the Child Study Center) and, in alphabetical order, George Anderson, Simon Baron-Cohen, Ami Klin, Nathaniel Laor, James Leckman, Paul Lombroso, Andrés Martin, Linda Mayes, Ruud Minderaa, Sharon Ort, David Pauls, Rhea Pauls, Larry Scahill, Robert Schultz, Matt State, Helen Tager-Flusberg, Sylvie Tordjman, Flora Vaccarino, and Jerry Young. To those who are not specifically noted, let me express the thought that they are also very much a part of the research program and of my memories.

Professors Albert Solnit and Edward Zigler recruited me to the Child Study Center and then provided an environment and resources that have shaped my career and life. The unique atmosphere of the Child Study Center—with its multidisciplinary faculty and historic ties with pediatrics—has been an academic haven for clinical scholarship and for me, personally. We have received long-term support from the National Institute of Child Health and Human Development (NICHD) and the National Institute of Mental Health (NIMH), starting at a point when our work was in a fledgling state. I am delighted that these agencies can now see some of the fruits of their engagement. The Korczak Foundation has provided support for research and international collaboration. Other foundations and individuals have been gracious and enthusiastic donors. I would like to acknowledge the unique support of Mr. Irving Harris and his family and the other Associates of the Child Study Center. These individuals have provided the ongoing, critical support that has allowed us to initiate new areas of research in the field of autism and also to provide clinical care and other services for all children, regardless of their means. And last but not least, I am grateful to my own family; all of us know what our spouses and children sacrifice for our work. These agencies, foundations, and individuals have made a lifetime of research on autism possible and a true source of joy for me and all who have participated in the research programs in the Child Study Center over three decades.

Part Two **Understanding Other Minds:**

Autism

Chapter 3 Desire and Fantasy:

A Psychoanalytic Perspective

on Theory of Mind and Autism

(1993)

Linda C. Mayes, Donald J. Cohen, and Ami Klin

The set of propositions defined by "theory of mind" address a question which is at the core of very young children's developing ability to be engaged in the social world: how, and when, does a child understand, and act on, the knowledge that its parents have beliefs, emotions, and desires (i.e. mental states) which guide their actions towards their children and others? From the standpoint of child psychoanalytic theory, a young child's ability to be differentially related to others begins to develop in the first months of life, and reflects the workings of two interrelated processes, the construction of self (for example self-other differentiation), and two interrelated mental states, knowledge about and desire for the other. The theory of mind literature addresses one of these processes, the construction of the mind of another. The contribution of child psychoanalysis to this debate is to suggest that the *desire to be with others* is a necessary precursor to knowing about the mind of the other.

First appeared in *Understanding Other Minds: Perspectives from Autism,* eds. S. Baron-Cohen, H. Tager-Flusberg, D. J. Cohen (London: Oxford University Press, 1993), 450–465. By permission of Oxford University Press.

A central difference between the psychoanalytic and cognitive theories of mind concerns the roots and functions of imagination as a capacity and a process. Stated quite simply, psychoanalytic theory directs our attention to children's inner world of desires and wishes, which underlies their understanding of the behaviors of others in the external world. Through the workings of fantasy and imagination, children create an inner world filled with mental representations of others. In this inner world, children play with different views of how others' beliefs and feelings influence their actions towards them (for example how a mother's caring actions reflect her thoughts and love). The child's desire for others motivates the workings of imagination and the creation of an inner world. This in turn influences how a child (or adult) views and responds to others' behaviors in the external world.

Desire for others gives life to fantasies about others, which in turn bring a depth and cohesiveness to the cognitive capacity to attribute meaning to human interactions. The child's knowledge of and desire for another are mutually dependent and complementary. Impairments in either could lead to distortions in social relatedness.

In the present chapter, we address the interface between psychoanalytic views of desire and fantasy and the "theory of mind" hypotheses. We shall consider several important issues: how the capacity to experience desire vis-à-vis another arises in the first years of life; why it varies so from individual to individual and within one individual across the life-span; and how basic impairments in the capacity to attribute meaning to others may reflect earlier impairments in the desire to be engaged and in the capacity to create an inner world. We have examined these questions through our studies both of the nature of the autistic individual's interpersonal world and of self-other differentiation in the first eighteen months.

THE INTERPERSONAL WORLD OF AUTISTIC
INDIVIDUALS: A LONGITUDINAL VIEW

For many years, we and others have asked how and why autistic individuals often fail in the social world. We have investigated several different areas of social functioning in autism, including affective regulation, communicative functioning, social adaptability, and the capacities to perceive and understand others (Cohen, 1980b; Volkmar and Cohen, 1988). Our observations and those of others reveal interrelationships in autism among selective attention, emotional responsivity, routines of shared activity in the first months of life, and social cognition and language (for example Caparulo and Cohen, 1983; Paul et al., 1983; Tager-Flusberg, 1989). There is marked individual variation in the degree of impairments autistic children show in these different functional areas (Volkmar, 1987). Such a finding speaks not only to the multivariate nature of the autistic syndrome, but also to the apparent lack of a single, underlying dysfunction. That is, autism may represent the final behavioral outcome for disturbances of functioning in a number of capacities that are involved in socialization and human relationships. No single disturbance of function in any one area accounts for all autistic individuals.

On the other hand, autistic children do show impairments in two interrelated, complementary processes—that of attributing and understanding meaning in the behaviors and feelings of others, as proposed by the theory of mind hypothesis, and that of creating their own inner lives, as proposed by psychoanalytic views of internalization and fantasy construction (Cohen, 1991a). These two processes form the biological and psychological underpinnings of what it means to be a social human being. By studying autism from this viewpoint, we may come to understand individual variations in the development and differentiation of self and other and in the process of fully engaging with the social world (Cohen et al., 1976). Furthermore, these two processes are constantly interacting in so far as children's efforts to understand others bring coherence to their own experiences of desire and love for their parents. In turn, having access to a coherent, organized inner world of representations and fantasies about others gives life to our actions to engage others and attribute meaning to their actions and affects.

Impairments either in the creation of an inner life or in the capacity to attribute meaning to others will lead to disturbances in social relatedness. Some individuals with these disturbances may meet the diagnostic criteria for autism. For all individuals, the maturation of these two processes reflects complicated interactions between constitutionally determined capacities and environmental experiences. These interactions may lead to the range of apparent behavioral, functional impairments in autism, that is, to the range of variation in the "autistic phenotype."

Understanding how these two processes fail to develop fully or even partially in autistic individuals is aided by the long-term study of a cohort of autistic children who were diagnosed in the 1950s and have now reached middle age. Some of these individuals have reached a sufficiently high level of function to be able to describe their own experiences vis-à-vis the social world (Volkmar and Cohen, 1985), while others have remained isolated by their seeming lack of awareness of others and their lack of verbal language. Through these long-term studies we have begun to understand the vicissitudes of the autistic individual's relationships and thoughts about others, and how desire, an inner psychic state, and the capacity to attribute meaning, interact. Two case histories help us to clarify these ideas.

CASE HISTORIES

Herbert's parents became worried about his lack of social responsiveness when he was just six months old (Cohen, 1991a, Volkmar 1985). Herbert did not make eye contact, and did not smile responsively. A diagnosis of "possible autism" was made at a relatively early age, thirteen months, because his parents persisted in seeking help with their concerns. By this time, Herbert babbled little, showed almost no response to speech, and did not point with his hand or finger to draw his parents' attention or indicate his needs. He looked at his mother only in rapid sideways glances, did not imitate her gestures, and was unable to hug or kiss.

For the next several years, Herbert and his family were involved in a number of early childhood intervention and treatment programs. As he grew older, Herbert became impossible to manage. If left unattended even for brief moments, he would climb on furniture, break windows, and unscrew any detachable object. By the age of three he had no expressive language, and looked through or past people. He responded to his mother, who was with him all day, with hardly more recognition than that usually shown a stranger. Only when he was upset would he seem to run to her intentionally. Efforts to make psychotherapeutic contact with Herbert by verbally labeling his actions or putting words to his presumed anxiety expressed as panic and wild behavior were apparently unsuccessful. Herbert seemed generally bewildered by the reactions of others, and was unable to use others' actions to direct or modify his own behavior. When he was placed in a nursery school for normal children, Herbert was unable to understand that the other children were frightened by his uncontrollable running and screeching. In turn, he was driven to states of confused excitement when his peers were engaged in active games.

By the age of seven Herbert was clearly a very retarded child, who drifted from place to place and activity to activity with little planning. He used others, including his siblings and parents, only to satisfy his basic needs, and would involve them by taking their hands or shoving them to what he wanted. When alone, he flicked his fingers or shook his hands before his eyes, rocked, and made guttural sounds or grimaced. When he was engaged in simple, repetitive tasks, his stereotypies decreased, and he seemed calmer. But by the time he entered puberty his face had become set into a mask-like dullness from years without normal affective responsivity.

By late adolescence Herbert could no longer be cared for at home, and his parents prepared for the time when he would move into a residential placement. They could not imagine what he would do without them. For eighteen years they had been constantly present for him—to protect him from running into the street, to try to comfort him when he was frightened by loud noises, to be always aware of where he was and to interpret for him what he needed. On the day they took him to the residential home, they were not prepared for his simply walking away, not looking back, not noticing their absence, not reflecting the meaning they presumed and hoped they had in his inner world. Herbert did not seem anxious without his parents, nor did he ever seem to miss them.

At the age of thirty, Herbert's life is one of quiet and orderly routines. He has no spontaneous play and no friendships, and lives a life of apparently calm structure without important others. Herbert's life history underscores not only his long-standing inability to respond to other persons, but just as poignantly his apparent lack of desire for interaction with others and his lack of longing in their absence. Herbert's frantic activity, his ease of excitability in the presence of others, and his bewildered responses to the affective behaviors of others suggest how confusing and disorganizing the social world was and is for him.

In contrast, Tony, who was able to tell his own story, gives us a closer view of the terrors of a social world he too could not interpret, but at the same time longed for (Volkmar and Cohen, 1985). At twenty-two years of age, Tony returned to the Yale Child Study Center to find the records of an evaluation done when he was twenty-six months old. As he reconstructed his own story, he wrote down his account of the experience of autism.

When he was referred for an evaluation at twenty-six months, Tony's parents were most concerned about his lack of speech and his poor social relatedness. From the first weeks of life, Tony had avoided human contact, was difficult to hold, had never smiled responsively, and was preoccupied with spinning objects and with looking at his own hands. With intensive education and psychotherapy, Tony made significant gains developmentally and socially, and by three years of age he was beginning to communicate meaningfully. As an adolescent and young adult Tony was very aware of being different from other people, and felt socially isolated and unable to understand or empathize with others. In his own (unedited) account, he states:

"I was living in a world of daydreaming and Fear revolving about my self I had no care about Human feelings or other people. I was afraid of everything!" (p. 49). And later, after entering school, "[I] was and still [am] very insecure! I was very cold Harted too. I[t] was impossible for me to Give or Receive love from anybody. I often repulse it by turning people off. That is still a problem today and related to other people. I liked things over people and dint care about People at all . . . And was very Nervous about everything. And Feared People and Social Activity Greatly" (p. 50).

That Tony was aware of "this hellish disease" (p. 51) and how his difficulties set him apart and kept him isolated raises a number of questions about how autistic individuals create an inner world for themselves out of the bewildering, often terrifying, complexity they encounter in the object world. Though Tony wrote clearly of his preference for "things" over people, he was nevertheless aware of his difficulties both in understanding and in desiring others. Through a variety of adaptive compromises, he found his way to a kind of responsiveness to others inasmuch as he was able to maintain a job and occasionally attempted again to be with people. He continued to find the social world bewildering, even hellish, but experienced a painful disappointment that his difficulties kept him isolated from it. We might reasonably ask was Tony in his own way, apparently unlike Herbert, able to experience longing for a social world, but, like Herbert, unable to be in it because he too could not make sense of it? The interplay between longing, desire, and the capacity to understand others is, in the most general sense, the contribution of psychoanalysis to the study of autism.

THE EMERGENCE OF DESIRE: FALLING IN LOVE

Initiating any social relationship requires the capacities to perceive, interpret, and act on the beliefs, feelings, and intentions of another. Yet enduring relationships also require the love of one for another and the understanding that such love is reciprocated. By love, we mean both the capacity and the desire to be deeply interested in the actions and feelings of another—for infants, in the actions and feelings of their parents. At some point in the first eighteen months of life, interest becomes too objective a word to describe infants' attraction to every detail of their parents' being and life. How parents look, smell, and sound, when they come and when they leave, how they can be brought near, and how sad it feels to have them far away consume infants' attention and motivate most, if not all, of their activities. Even those infant activities we label "purely" cognitive or information-processing fall under the sway of infants' relationships with their parents, for without the motivating influence of an effectively nurturing relationship, infants do not develop and learn in the expected ways. Importantly, the act of loving and the process of forming attachments to others are not synonymous. Attachment indicates those behaviors which are manifestly observable that mark differentiated and special relationships between individuals. The act of loving involves the inner affective state underlying those attachments.

That love occurs is clear, but how remains a mystery. The central tasks of adaptation for the species are social attachment, engagement, and communication. These tasks set the stage for love. There are also species-specific and individually variable perceptual and neuroregulatory capacities that single out social stimuli as the most salient and attractive to the human infant. These set the lights on for love. But the actual drama that unfolds is not described entirely by phylogenetic heritage or constitutional endowments. Evolution and biology become individualized and personified through the effects of early caring relationships on the psychic life of the infant. Love matures out of these early relationships. In other words, species-specific adaptive needs, neuroregulatory and perceptual capacities, and desire are the necessary ingredients of the infant's love relationships and eventual full membership in the social world. Impairments at any one of these levels of function lead to disorders of socialization and communication, some of which will meet the diagnostic criteria for autism.

Desire is a complex phenomenon, which may seem more secure in literary discourse than in research. From the psychoanalytic point of view, desire involves more than intentionality or the attribution of motivation or intentionality to another. To say that someone seeks to obtain a toy because he or she wants it is a statement attributing a motivational state to an observable action, that is, that a person acted intentionally because of a motivating wish (or desire) for that toy. The psychoanalytic view of desire suggests first that the manifest action does not necessarily reflect an internal state of desire for something or someone. What we do in observable action is the end-stage of a number of interdependent intrapsychic processes or conditions, only one of which may be a wish to possess something or someone. A manifest action may be enacted as much in the service of denying an intrapsychic wish as of fulfilling it. The context of the action does not unerringly show us the direction of the wish, and, more commonly than not, our actions represent complex compromises between one or multiple wishes and our conflicts over those wishes.

Secondly, not only is an inner state of desire not necessarily revealed or reflected in an individual's actions, but even more importantly, one need not engage in observable action to be acting on one's desire. Such are the nature and benefits of a fantasy life. We give our desires expression, if only to ourselves, and find ways to fulfill such desires through the inner psychic world of fantasy. Desire for others gains depth and complexity through the workings of fantasy, and the capacity to experience and express desire reflects a cohesive and active inner fantasy life. In our inner psychic lives we are able to create more variations on a theme, more scenarios to a story than would ever be possible if we depended on direct experiences with others and the memories of those experiences. Any active expression we give to our desires has been through many accounts and revisions in our inner psychic lives. In fantasy we take on the role of the other, and we experiment with the feelings of gratification, of frustration, of revenge, of immediate or delayed action. We write, produce, direct, and act in the screenplay of our choosing. And we learn about a person's desire most fully by learning about his or her inner fantasy life.

Thirdly, the psychoanalytic notion of desire for another is based on the cumulative effects of the individual's earliest experiences with others, that is, with parents. Desire is not an innate, constitutionally determined motivational state. It arises from the interaction between the infant's neurophysiological capacities for engaging others and the experiences that occur when the infant and others interact. The "hardwiring" underlying desire involves the various constitutionally given perceptual and neuroregulatory functions that promote the salience and inherent attraction of social stimuli or even the perceptual attributes of social stimuli (Mayes and Cohen, 1995).

For example, the earliest evidence of the capacities for social relationships is found in the newborn's preference for the human voice, and for a higher pitched voice, over other sounds (DeCasper and Fifer, 1980). Similarly, very young infants show a preference for curved lines over straight ones, for irregular patterns, for patterns with a high contour-density, and for symmetry (Olson and Sherman, 1983)—each features of faces and of the various facial expressions. Normal newborns are also endowed with the capacity for eliciting parental attention—for example, to respond with change in states to optimal care-giving—and for perceptually and motorically orienting themselves toward their parents—to remain physically close to, reach toward, and grasp on to their mothers. Without such capacities or with specific impairments, infants would have greater difficulty engaging their parents—for example, congenitally blind infants demonstrate autistic-like impairments in their social relatedness (Rapin, 1979). These capacities permit infants to be deeply engaged in trying to understand the world of their mothers' behavior—where is she, how can

I get her to me, why does she go, is this she or someone else, when does she come?

Without the desire to be engaged, these questions remain only cognitive puzzles. They become affective, deeply experienced dilemmas when the infant begins to experience desire for another. Then "where is she" is more than an idle wondering; it is a question of marked affective intensity. In other words, these constitutional capacities alone are not sufficient for conditions of loving and intense involvement with others. How does desire emerge out of these early engagements between infant and parent, how do the emergence of desire and the differentiation of self relate to each other, and how do we recognize the workings of a state of desire, or, more to the issue, how do we know when a social dysfunction reflects a lack of desire?

THE DEVELOPMENT OF DESIRE FOR THE OTHER

To consider how desire emerges intrapsychically out of these early engagements between parent and infant, we need to consider the nature of the earliest interactions between parent and infant. What follows is a psychoanalytic conceptualization or metaphor of the mind of the infant that emphasizes the continuity of experience in a mind that is rapidly maturing and differentiating. In many ways, this metaphor is similar to the notions of interpersonal intersubjectivity discussed by Hobson and others in their considerations of the affective structure of the child's developing "theory of mind" (Hobson, 1989).

At the beginning of psychological life, there is not an infant, but a mother-infant matrix (Winnicott, 1945b). In the earliest period of the infant-mother matrix, psychic activity occurs as a fused event of the matrix, as one "fleeting and very perishable mental entity" (Loewald, 1977, p. 215), which is neither ego nor object. From the infant's point of view, the outside world consists mainly of mother, or perhaps of mother not as person but as the source of food and warmth. At this stage, "mother" represents the world that acts contingently on the infant's needs; but she exists intrapsychically only inasmuch as the infant needs. She is neither a whole nor a differentiated object. The object, or interpersonal, world still lacks clear boundaries in the infant's psychic world. In the first weeks of life, needs are satisfied and social stimuli arouse pleasurable experiences without being attributed to the whole object "mother."

Such a stage cannot exist for long, since the infant soon experiences the frustration engendered by the mother's inevitable absences and delays. Desire for another is differentiated not through the pleasure of ever-present gratification but out of the frustration of unmet needs. Frustration and the ensuing discomfort represent a first break in the sensation of immediate gratification, and the first experience of the infant of the separateness between states of physical need and the satisfaction of such needs. Through such inevitably repeated experiences and the beginning feelings of separateness, desire for another takes shape—for it is that other who can alleviate discomfort. Because of frustration, the infant seeks out the mother and brings her closer by using those innate capacities for engagement. The contingency of a mother's nurturing acts on the infant's discomforts, and the association between her absence and the infant's sense of frustration establishes referencing links between the mother's behavior and the affective experience for the infant. The infant's experience of mother oscillates between pleasure and discomfort, satisfaction and frustration, i.e. between a state of being united and a state of loss. It is out of this "very polarity between separateness and union" (Fromm, 1955, p. 32) that desire is born and reborn.

It is centrally important to understand that, paradoxically, desire for another is not based solely on gratifying experiences. Instead, the onset of desire reflects the experiences of disappointment, and of painful discomfort. Anger and frustration are as necessary a precondition for desire as blissful satisfaction. Desire and separation, whether physically or through delayed responsiveness, go hand in hand. The emergence of separation-distress and of stranger-anxiety represent the ways infants learn about the importance of others to their own security and comfort. Infants' dysphoric changes in state (crying or angry protests) on anticipated separation and excited pleasure on reunion are evidence that, at least in a rudimentary way, infants recognize their own feelings in relation to their parents' actions.

Such recognition is evident behaviorally not only in stranger- or separation-anxiety, but very early on in infants' reactions to their mothers' assuming a still or neutral face. In such situations, infants as young as three months protest or increase their positive engaging behaviors in reaction to their mothers' unanticipated change in responsivity (Mayes and Carter, 1990; Tronick et al., 1978). Behaviors like these suggest that infants have a nascent "theory" of mind about their own states and feelings vis-à-vis the behaviors of another. In particular, infants' increased use of positive engaging behaviors, even more than distressed responses, underscores their expectation that social engagement with mother is a condition to be desired. Longing for another is mapped on to these very early "theories" of how others influence one's own affective states.

The recognition of the importance of the other to one's own comfort is also a powerful factor in the emergence of self (see Samet, 1993, for a philosophical discussion of the place of the self). From the psychoanalytic point of view, self begins to be defined through the effects of cumulative experiences with mother in the first days, weeks, and months. While even very young infants have the perceptual capacities to discriminate the external boundaries of another and to discriminate, for example, their own movements or those of another, the internal sense of self is bound up in the memorial layering of schema and the creation of representations from multiple experiences with another. Through the repeated experiences in the presence of another, memories laden with affective traces are created, and the other of the inner world gradually takes shape. In a sense, the child's earliest experiences with another person are organized around affects or, as Hobson has proposed, an "affective relatedness" (Hobson, 1989; Hobson, 1990b). Thus, the differentiation of desire and of self are parallel, interdependent processes. The desire that evolves into love relationships begins to emerge when self begins to be distinct from other (Loewald, 1977). When mother comes to represent the source of gratification that is not symbiotically available, she is becoming a separate and whole object, the object of love, a *desired* object. Similarly, when the infant experiences him or herself as an active agent in engaging the mother's interest and care, the process of individuation has begun (Mahler and Furer, 1968; Mahler et al., 1975).

Individuation, and hence the onset of desire for a differentiated object, also marks the workings of *internalization* and the beginnings of an inner life. Through repeated interactions with mother around basic biological needs, endogenous events such as hunger and exogenous experiences such as mother's warmth are incorporated into the infant's psychic life as memorial traces (Loewald, 1977). Gradually, good and bad memories and their associated affective currents are joined in the infant's inner world to define mother as a whole object toward whom one experiences a host of both angry and loving feelings (Klein, 1957). Thus, when infants experience their own dysphoria and elation in response to another, not only is self distinct from other beginning to emerge, but also developing is the capacity to call on memories of past interactions to help with current affective states.

Others increasingly populate the infant's internal world. He or she not only imagines different scenes, but uses these fantasies to organize his own sense of self and responses to others. The infant is able to represent a remembered story such as "I feel sad and angry to see her go but she will return and when she does, we will sit together, she will understand my anger and I will feel comforted as before." In the remembering and rewriting of the story, the infant is capable not only of a higher order of mental activity, but also of using such activity for his or her own affective regulation. The anger and distress are not necessarily disorganizing. Fantasy has begun to assume an active role in caring for self and in deepening love for others.

Through these love relationships as they are represented in the psychic world and through the parallel, ongoing processes of desire and self-differentiation, the child (and adult) becomes more self-aware. We learn about ourselves in large part vis-à-vis our love relationships to others, and the vicissitudes of those relationships. Processes of internalization continue throughout the life span. With every new love relationship, the process of making the other a part of one's inner world and the parallel process of increased self-awareness that comes with love occurs. It is not just the early separations that set the process of desire and self-other differentiation going. The sadness and the aggressive, hateful, destructive feelings mobilized by an actual or threatened loss of a loved one continue to be mutative processes for infants, children, and adults. Within limits, the experiences of threatened or actual loss deepen feelings of love for another and strengthen the sense that one's self persists even in the physical absence of others, that is, the others continue to exist in one's internal psychic world. Being able to grieve and mourn are the counterparts of being able to love. One does not occur without the other. Let us now turn to the relevance of this for autism.

THE ABSENCE OF DESIRE FOR THE OTHER IN AUTISM

It is our contention that autistic individuals neither fall in love readily, nor grieve or mourn the absence of presumably important others. When separated from parents or long-term caregivers, they may seem briefly unhappy, and conversely pleased if the person returns; but, generally, their responses to losses are as muted and brief as their displays of affection. It is as if their capacity to experience desire for another, to experience the full depth of love in their inner psychic lives is either absent or distorted. As one young autistic man said, responding to a picture of a young woman resting her head on a man's shoulder, "This is a husband and a wife embracing each other—typical of one's so-called human need for companionship" (Bemporad, 1979, p. 189).

To this point, however, it is important to emphasize as before the diversity of responses within the diagnostic category, and the fact that the social dysfunction in autism is not an all-or-nothing impairment. With maturation, many autistic individuals are not entirely oblivious to others—they often make many attempts to engage in the social world, and show both pleasure and longing to be with others. They may be acutely aware of a sense of loneliness and estrangement, and feel sad about how such impairments keep them apart from others. They are able to understand that relationships are important to other people, that there are such things as feelings, and that there are certain customary ways to interact with others.

For those autistic individuals who do become more socially engaged, it is as if they find compensatory mechanisms or structures for achieving some semblance of relatedness vis-à-vis others, and are able to experience in some way longing for others. They may, for example, learn social conventions, for example, that "How are you?" is generally followed by "I am fine, and how are you?" They may attend social functions, and appear interested in various activities such as dating or games (Bemporad, 1979). Yet, more often than not, even the brighter, more self-aware autistic individuals are puzzled by the depth of human relationships; they seem unable to "get it," and their social relations rarely have the multi-dimensional quality of love, even early childhood love. Their relations with others lack the spontaneity, the affective variation, the empathic quality that characterizes relatedness learned early. Whatever the nature of the inborn disorder that interferes with the autistic child's development of the earliest patterns for affective relatedness, the early difficulties persist in the autistic adult's personality structure, and set limits on the building of an inner fantasy life. The latter in turn limits the depth of involvement in any loving relationships.

These limits are most apparent when autistic individuals have sufficient communicative capacities to allow a glimpse into their inner lives. More often than not, whether or not the individual experiences some longing for the social world, the inner psychic view of others is monochromatic, puzzling, even at times frightening to them, and they find comfort in the more predictable, stable, and concrete non-object world. The powerful range of feeling, including anger and hate as well as caring, which are set into play by loving relationships may prove overwhelming for the autistic individual.

THE INTERFACE BETWEEN PSYCHOANALYSIS
AND THEORY OF MIND

The psychoanalytic view of mind draws our attention to the inner world of psychic representations and psychic action that is constantly behind the world of observable behaviors and capacities. Because what is observable in the external world may have multiple meanings in the psychic world, the psychoanalytic theory of mind complements the more cognitively oriented theory of mind conceptualized by several others.

For example, Baron-Cohen's descriptions (1993) abstract the cognitive prerequisites underlying social understanding, communicative skills, and pretend-play. They present a *competence model* of the ability to conceive of mental states in others and in oneself. The psychoanalytic view complements this model by adding the infant's *intrapsychic experiences* or inner world, and the affective and motivational *context* in which the infant's socio-cognitive development takes place. In other words, from the psychoanalytic frame of reference, the most central mental state to impute to others is the understanding that others reciprocate one's desire for them. Young children understand that their mothers appreciate and return their desire and love for them.

The psychoanalytic perspective also complements the developmental account of the origins of a cognitive theory of mind in several other respects. First, by encompassing the various intersubjective experiences evidenced in the infant-mother dyad before the advent of mental representations, it provides the continuity between innate social adaptive mechanisms and the momentous cognitive accomplishments described in the cognitive model. Second, by taking on board the multiple and individualized representations of the self and the other, it provides for the richness of individual inner lives and the variety of outcomes. Third, by contextualizing the competence model, it personalizes mental states, giving them the individual significance that is at the heart of human social experiences, and allows for the individual variation among autistic individuals' capacities to take the perspective of another.

There is, however, a broader issue highlighted by the differences between these two "theories of mind." In part, the categorical definition of autism defines what a theory of mind needs to explain. Metaphorically, a theory needing to account for a monochromatic visual world needs to explain far less complex phenomena than a theory accounting for the full range of the color spectrum. Similarly, if autism is defined by all-or-nothing categories of social relatedness, the theory to explain such categories does not need to account for the diversity within the diagnostic grouping and the changes over maturation. But the individual variation in the social development of autistic individuals is strikingly apparent in the many longitudinal accounts now available. Even on the measures of the autistic child's capacity to understand the mental states of believing, knowing, or desiring, there is a range of impairment. Some autistic individuals are quite able to appreciate the beliefs of others, and to take their perspective, correctly (Baron-Cohen, 1993).

What these observations of individual variation suggest is the need to understand the multiple ways infants and young children develop a theory of others and of mind. How do some children reach their third and fourth years of life apparently unable to understand the mental states of others? What are the multiple sources of variation in how children develop an inner sense of self and of the other and in how they come to desire and love others? Minimally, as we have outlined, the developmental emergence of an understanding of others involves the interaction in the first eighteen months between constitutionally given neuroperceptual and organizational capacities and the "metabolism" and integration of social information received from the environment. Impairments are possible at several different levels, not all of which result in the social dysfunction seen in autism. For instance, children who are blind may show a number of social impairments early in life; but they most often develop over time alternative pathways to socialization that allow them affectively rich and integrated lives (Rapin, 1979). How do we understand the "physiology" of apparently normal relatedness, and what are the sources of these alternate pathways?

By its focus on the development of inner psychic lives, the psychoanalytic view of social development offers one window on how a theory of mind about others comes into being. Considering the earliest roots of social experiences in the first eighteen months focuses investigative attention on the very early and generalized social deficits exhibited by autistic children (Klin et al., 1992), which otherwise would lie outside the scope of the cognitive model. Understanding the various biological mechanisms of adaptations and the complexities of the infant-mother matrix permits us to investigate the heterogeneity of the autistic phenotype. The longitudinal view gained from seeing children in the first years and following their development also informs our appreciation of the social adaptations many autistic individuals are able to obtain despite their impairments. And, conversely, through appreciating the inner lives of many higher-functioning autistic individuals, we may understand how, despite a cognitive ability to conceive of other people's minds, they remain estranged from the social world because they cannot share their feelings (Bemporad, 1979; Cohen, 1980b; Volkmar and Cohen, 1985).

Traditionally, psychoanalysis has viewed mental functioning and adaptation along a developmental continuum, and has considered mental impairments along a spectrum instead of as a categorical grouping. Adopting such a view changes our frame of reference about the social development of autistic individuals, and emphasizes that autism represents a range of social impairments and adaptations. By taking the intrapsychic perspective of the growing infant,

the psychoanalytic approach attempts to bridge the gap between modeled capacities and inner realities, between cognitive computations and affect-laden
fantasies, and between the depersonified social environment and the infant-
mother emerging love affair. The psychoanalytic view provides a new set of
questions and empirical dilemmas about how all individuals learn about themselves and others and come to experience deep and enduring feelings of desire
for another.

ACKNOWLEDGMENTS

We gratefully acknowledge our collaboration with our colleague Dr. Fred Volkmar, whose work with autistic individuals has greatly influenced the thoughts
presented in this chapter.

Chapter 4 Experiencing Self and Others: Contributions from Studies of Autism to the Psychoanalytic Theory of Social Development (1993)

Linda C. Mayes and Donald J. Cohen

Both the capacity and the desire to participate in deep, enduring relationships with others emerge in the first two years of life, and each requires an integrated sense of self and other. Standing at the core of the psychoanalytic view of self-object differentiation is the very young infant's maturing capacity to experience himself as a separate, active agent in interactions with parents and the concurrent elaboration of his own inner world of fantasy. To this end, child analysts have long been interested in developmental disorders such as autism, in which children apparently fail to develop an integrated sense of themselves and, as a result, have profound difficulties in experiencing differentiated feelings toward others or in developing a coherent inner world of internalized objects (Hobson, 1990a; Mahler, 1958; Mahler and Furer, 1968; Putnam et al., 1948; Rank and MacNaughton, 1950; Ritvo and Provence, 1953; Shapiro and Hertzig, 1991; Tustin, 1983; Weiland and Rudnick, 1961).

First appeared in *Journal of the American Psychoanalytic Association* 42: 191–219 (1993). Republished with permission of the American Psychoanalytic Association; permission conveyed through Copyright Clearance Center, Inc.

In this paper, we explore how our psychoanalytic understanding of the process of the emergence and maintenance of self and of inner world may be informed by recent findings from developmental psychology about how normal and autistic children develop the capacity to attribute meaning and mental states to others, a capacity that is both a requirement for and a reflection of the differentiation of self and other. Understanding that people behave toward each other in ways that are interpretable on the basis of mental states such as desires, feelings, and beliefs is a fundamental part of social relatedness. At some point in early development, before age six, children acquire a so-called theory of mind or a theory of others' language, actions, and behaviors toward them[1] that takes into account the mental states of the other, separate person (Astington et al., 1988; Hobson, 1990a; Wellman, 1988). The child understands that we act because we want something, love someone, believe a condition is true, or think that another person feels toward us in a certain way.

Achieving a theory to explain others' actions and words that draws on mental states is a significant developmental transition. It frees the child from the limitations of a sensory/perceptual world in which cause and effect seem related to concrete, observable, material events. With an understanding of mental states and the underlying mental life of desires and feelings, the child can understand that others separate from him nevertheless act toward him because of their feelings for him. A capacity to call on mental phenomena to interpret and give meaning to the actions of oneself and others expands the child's world to include events and states he cannot observe, but must infer. It makes it possible for him to have an inner world of fantasy, or more specifically, an inner world populated by others whom he imbues with the feelings and beliefs he imagines them to have (Mayes and Cohen, 1992).

Because autistic individuals frequently fail to develop an understanding of the relation between feelings or beliefs and the behaviors of themselves or others (Baron-Cohen, 1989a; Baron-Cohen, 1989b; Baron-Cohen, 1991a; Baron-Cohen et al., 1985), studies of autism provide a clinical model for how these neurocognitively based functions related to acquiring a theory of mind are also involved in the elaboration of an inner world and in the ongoing definition of self. At the very least, the concept of achieving a theory of the mind of the other offers analysts a way of thinking about the constitutional or neurodevelopmental components that are a part of the process of defining a separate self. Further, understanding how both autistic and normal children develop, or fail to develop, the capacity to attribute meaning to others' actions, beliefs, and feelings speaks to psychoanalytic notions of internalization, identification, and introjection and provides a neurocognitive frame for how representations of self and others are created in the inner world. Conversely, the psychoanalytic view that the infant's emerging sense of self is also shaped by the infant's desire for mother underscores that affective precursors are absolutely necessary for a theory of mind to emerge. Stated simply, *desire for the other* is a necessary precursor to knowing about the mind of the other; and it is at this level that children with pervasive developmental disorders such as autism exhibit their earliest difficulties—in their capacities to seek out and respond to another and to experience longing for the other's presence (Mayes et al., 1993).

THE INTERPERSONAL WORLD OF AUTISTIC INDIVIDUALS

The psychological phenomena of autism reveal interrelations among impairments in selective attention, emotional responsivity, routines of shared activity in the first months of life, and in social cognition and language (Caparulo and Cohen, 1983; Cohen, 1980b; Paul et al., 1983; Shapiro and Hertzig, 1991; Tager-Flusberg, 1989; Volkmar and Cohen, 1988). No single disturbance of function in any one area accounts for all autistic individuals. The autistic child's failure in the social world is a symptom of his inability to make sense of that world and of the people in it, but not necessarily of his capacity to perceive correctly or understand the stimulus conditions (Caparulo and Cohen, 1983). Similarly, his difficulty in using language to convey what he feels reflects the deeper difficulty in understanding the social/affective nature of language and of the social world as a condition to be desired.

Several psychoanalysts have considered the difficulties autistic children have in responding to and making sense of social information as fundamental to the apparent deficit in concepts of self in the first two years (Ekstein and Wallerstein, 1954; Hobson, 1990a; Klein, 1930; Klein, 1957; Mahler, 1958; Mahler and Furer, 1968; Putnam et al., 1948; Rank and MacNaughton, 1950; Ritvo and Provence, 1953; Shapiro and Hertzig, 1991; Tustin, 1983; Weil, 1953; Weiland and Rudnick, 1961). Before Kanner's (1943) description, Klein (1930) spoke of the presumably biologically based inability of autistic individuals to integrate their sensory experiences into whole forms such as persons, or to construct internalized representations of the social world. Similarly, Mahler and Furer (1968) suggested that autistic children lacked the biologically based capacities to react to others' behavioral responses, affective appearances, and efforts toward social engagement. In other words, the perceptual information that surrounds and defines a social context is not meaningful to autistic individuals at an integrative level. It is as if the basic building blocks are there, correctly perceived, but the capacity for constructing such blocks into meaningful, affect-laden, representations fails. Although autistic individuals may identify specific affective states or correctly perceive separate social cues, such as a smile, they are unable to understand or respond to the social meanings associated with such affects or communicative behaviors. For example, autistic individuals show the same ability to match, recognize, and label affects as mental-age matched controls, but have considerably more difficulty on tasks involving the imitation or expression of emotions, that is, tasks requiring an understanding of the social communicative intent of emotional expressions (Braverman et al., 1989; Hertzig et al., 1989; Hobson, 1986).

Mahler and Furer (1968), among others, also believed these impairments in integrating social communications into meaningful events meant the autistic child was unable to use "the auxiliary executive ego functions of the (symbiotic) partner, the mother, to orient himself in the outer or inner world" (p. 67). Autistic children fail to recognize other people as animate beings available for interaction and, consequently, often use other persons as tools or mechanical extensions (e.g., moving a person's hand to a desired object). Because they are unable to respond to mother as person or to use the efforts of any adult to help with affective regulation (e.g., soothing), they are also unable to respond to the affects of others, and increasingly withdraw from others and isolate themselves.

Several psychoanalytically informed investigators have considered some of the manifest behavioral impairments in autism (e.g., echolalia, increasing social withdrawal) as defensive maneuvers in response to the difficulties caused by the more primary functional incomprehension of self and other (Mahler and Furer, 1968; Weil, 1953). For example, the child's primary impairments in being able to use the mother's responses for comfort and organization lead to further difficulties in coping with the complexities of various social demands. The child, in turn, withdraws further and tries "to shut out, to hallucinate away, the potential sources of sensory perception, particularly the infinitely variable ones of the living world, which demand emotional social responses" (Mahler and Furer, 1968, p. 69).

Similarly, the various impairments in communication, such as echolalia, may serve in part a secondary defensive or organizing function in response to the more basic failure to integrate the perceived bits and pieces of the social world into a whole representation defining self. As Caparulo and Cohen (1977) and Shapiro (1977) suggest, precisely because the social world is so perplexing, because the autistic child tries but simply cannot make sense of that world, he develops a variety of strategies to contain the floods of anxiety he experiences in the face of his bewilderment. Echolalia is one such strategy that may reflect an inner feeling of "I know you're talking and that I should respond in some way, but I don't know what to say, so I'll just say what you did, and hope you'll stop asking so much of me" (Caparulo and Cohen, 1977, p. 641). Conversely, echolalia may also reflect the child's attempt, albeit distorted and aberrant, to make some contact with others through rudimentary imitation, a behavior reflecting some form of internalization of the other (Ekstein and Caruth, 1969). In any case, these various strategies and behavioral responses reflect an early and primary failure to integrate the myriad complex perceptual events in the social world into an integrated sense of self. These ongoing, layered deficits continue to deprive the child of the capacity to understand both the shared and different meanings a situation may have for self and for other (Hobson, 1989).

Clinically, children with early disorders of social relatedness seem unable to "metabolize" the affective and caring input of others. The effects of such primary functional deficits are expressed in myriad changing ways throughout development. There is a profound failure in the use of fantasy for anxiety regulation and for developing relationships with others, and their inner worlds appear impoverished and fragmented by a pervasive sense of tension. Rarely are they able to engage in fantasy play or pretend (Sherman et al., 1983). While the thought content, which those autistic individuals with the capacity for language describe, may have some of the characteristics of a fantasy creation, the products of their imagination are frequently terrifying, fragmented, and sometimes impoverished. For example, they may wonder whether their dreams had actually taken place, or imagine violent stories of bodily harm they suddenly fear have really occurred (Cohen et al., 1995). It is not only the blurring of the distinction between pretend and real, but also the failure to imagine others' feelings, beliefs, and wishes that mark these disorders as examples of the failure to develop an autonomous self that supports ongoing social differentiation. Ordinary social moments are perplexing because these children do not understand what they are feeling or how their own behaviors make others feel. They are puzzled by the object world and may recognize their isolation from it, but at the same time do not understand it as a condition to be desired.

Making sense of the social world and self-other differentiation involves two interrelated, complementary processes—that of attributing and understanding meaning in the behaviors and feelings of others, and that of creating one's own inner life (Cohen, 1991a). Autistic individuals show impairment in both processes. These very activities—understanding others, caring about what they feel, and longing for their presence—form the biological and psychological underpinnings of what it means to be a separate self intrapsychically. These two processes are constantly interactive inasmuch as children's efforts to understand others bring a coherence to their own internal states and experiences of desire and love for their parents. In turn, having access to a coherent, organized inner world of representations and fantasies about others gives life to a child's efforts to engage others and attribute meaning to their actions and affects. Psychoanalytic theory of self-differentiation draws our attention to the creation of a fantasy life, while studies of a developing theory of mind focus on the child's emerging capacity to understand feelings and beliefs and to attribute meaning to the actions of others.

INTERACTION BETWEEN CREATING AN
INTERNAL SENSE OF SELF AND ATTRIBUTING
MEANING TO OTHERS

In the first three years of life, for normally developing children, several perceptual, neurological, and cognitive functions mature in such a way as to allow the child increasing separateness and differentiation from the parent. The coming together of these various early perceptual and neurocognitive functions into a capacity to remember the other in his or her absence (and later to imagine the other in whatever ways the child wishes) fosters the child's increasing independence and moves toward separation and allows him to tolerate the frustration, fear, and sadness engendered by such separation.

At the beginning of psychological life, mother represents the world that acts contingently on the infant's needs, but she exists intrapsychically only insofar as the infant needs her physically (Loewald, 1977; Mahler and McDevitt, 1982). Such a stage does not exist for long since the infant soon experiences the frustration engendered by the mother's inevitable absences and delays (Loewald, 1977). Frustration and the ensuing discomfort represent a first break in the sensation of immediate gratification and the first experience of the infant with the separateness between states of physical need and satisfaction of such needs. Through such inevitably repeated experiences and the beginning feelings of separateness, desire for and thoughts about another take shape, for it is that other who can alleviate discomfort.

The contingency of a mother's nurturing acts on the infant's discomforts and the association between her absence and the infant's sense of frustration establish referencing links between the mother's behavior and the affective outcome for the infant. These links in turn contribute to the beginning of a representational world. Through these repeated experiences, both frustrating and gratifying, in the presence of another, memories laden with affective traces are created, and the other of the inner, representational world gradually takes shape (Loewald, 1977; Mahler et al., 1975). In the psychoanalytic frame of reference, we say the infant has begun to internalize a sense of the other through the collective memories, now beginning representations, of repeatedly satisfying (or frustrating) experiences. In the neurocognitive frame of reference, we say the infant has developed a set of schemas based on previous experiences with another person, and such schemas are the basis of his expectations that the other will reappear and behave toward him in certain predictable ways (Lewis and Goldberg, 1969). With time, the infant is able to draw on these beginning representations in moments of discomfort or frustration and evoke memories of previously gratifying moments with mother (Loewald, 1977). Consider, for example, how the crying, hungry infant is temporarily soothed by the sound of his mother's voice calling out from another room. Theories of attachment and the creation of internal working models (Bowlby, 1969–1982; Bretherton, 1985) provide another frame of reference for conceptualizing these early events. Through repeated transactions with the object world, infants construct increasingly complex internal working models of important persons and of their expectable responses. These internal working models guide the infant's appraisal of and responses to new situations and persons. For example, infants who are accustomed to their mother's presence when they are distressed develop an internalized working model of her comforting-responses that with time they come to rely upon in her absence.

Whatever the theoretical frame of reference we use to conceptualize the effects of early experiences, beginning to create a sense of the other as separate from self with the attendant emergence of a representational world requires the integration of a number of basic perceptual and neuroregulatory functions. In the first six months, these include the capacities to quiet oneself and to maintain a sustained alert state, to attend to selected elements of the environment, and to make the auditory, visual, and tactile discriminations that are critical for interactions in the animate world (Mayes and Cohen, 1995). For example, within the first three months, infants are able to discriminate visual patterns of increasing complexity and contour density (Banks and Salapatek, 1983) and to discriminate changes in the pitch of a speech sequence (Kessen et al., 1979). Capacities such as these make it possible for the infant to take the input from the social world and to begin to form early representations of social experiences. In the terms of precursors for a theory of mind, these neurophysiological functions, such as perceptual discrimination or sustained attention, form the biological substrate for the emerging capacity to attribute meaning to others. For example, the infant must first be able to discriminate changes in another's affective states before attributing meaning to these affective shifts.

Defects in the metabolism of social information probably lead to defects in how such experiences are stored memorially and how they are available, if at all, for recall. These may be the earliest roots of autistic individuals' describing social experiences as perceptually fragmented and terrifying and in their partial or complete failure to develop a theory of others' minds. It is not that the individual elements of a social exchange are incorrectly perceived or ignored, but rather that these elements cannot be integrated into an affect-laden memory and into a nascent sense of other as someone with feelings toward the infant, that is, into a nascent theory of mind. The basic organizational, integrative deficits also lead to unpredictable shifts in arousal and floods of anxiety, which make even rudimentary social integration difficult. The child withdraws from a terrifying, overwhelming social world. The representational experiences of that world, if formed in any integrated sense, are connected to unpleasant, frightening sensations and do not foster an increasingly integrated sense of self. Similarly, such basic integrative deficits impair the infant's ability to conceive of the other as differentially related to the infant. These are the beginnings, or failures thereof, in the infant's capacities to attribute meanings to others.

In the latter half of the first year and beginning of the second, infants respond with greater specificity and directedness to their social world, a circumstance that speaks to the increasing fidelity of their mental representations of others and a developing sense of self as agent. The infant becomes the active initiator of more and more communicative exchanges, which also become more specific and differentiated (Bullowa, 1979b). The infant draws his mother's attention to a situation—e.g., "joint attention" (Bruner, 1975)—and she in turn provides the contextual meaning for the situation and for the infant's actions. Through their joint efforts, the infant learns to use his feelings and actions to engage others (Shotter and Gregory, 1976) not just for comfort and care, but now for play and shared communications. During this time, infants delightedly respond to and sometimes seek out disappearing games such as peek-a-boo that enact with shared pretense the brief comings and goings of the other. The ability to tolerate such games and even to seek them out with pleasure precedes (and is a necessary precondition for) the capacity to create similar situations in thought, that is, to imagine the comings and goings of another. Also, the infant's pleasure with such games contrasted to his distress with actual separations during this period suggests that there is a rudimentary sense of pretense, that he "knows" mother is really there and both parties "know" the external reality. Being able to engage another in a playful context, or more accurately, to pretend to alter the external conditions, is a precondition for being able to imagine or attribute beliefs and feelings different from one's own to others.

The increasingly differentiated meaning of the parent to the child is also seen during this period by the child's reaction to both a parent's absence and a stranger's presence. The child's crying or angry protests on anticipated separation and excited pleasure on reunion are evidence that the child is beginning to make at least rudimentary connections between his own feelings in relation to his parents and their actions and to understand that others are available to appreciate and care about his distress. Situations such as the response to separation and the child's social referencing in response to novelty or uncertainty are paradigmatic for the increasing differentiation of self as agent. Not only is the child able to draw on the stored representations of early experiences with the other, but he now encounters himself as an active agent in engaging the other. At this point, wishes, desires, and expectations for the other are not only possible, but also the beginning understanding that one possesses an inner subjective world. The self-object world has begun to fill out and move beyond the bounds of pleasurable or unpleasurable experiences or of simply regulating tension states. It has acquired the dimensions of causality and intentionality, of agency, and the infant's appreciation that other people have differentiated feelings is more evident. From the psychoanalytic point of view, these shifts or maturation in the definition of self are manifest in an increasingly elaborate inner world of differentiated wishes toward another. Others increasingly populate the child's internal world, and he draws on them, remembers them, and experiences differentiated feelings in response to his memories.

In contrast, during the second year, autistic children often seem increasingly inattentive, socially distant, and nearly inaccessible (Cohen, 1980b). The mind, beliefs, and intentions of others toward them are not their central concerns. They are rarely upset by the comings and goings of important others. Instead, they may become preoccupied with one toy and spend hours looking at their fingers or rocking quietly. Their increasing sensitivity to changes in routine or physical environment, such as changes in feeding schedule, speaks both to their anxiety and near panic with unfamiliar conditions and to an inability to use others for comfort and for guidance about new people, situations, and settings.

Because autistic infants are unable to access or to use the object-related world and are unable to engage others in the self-defining actions of joint attention, their inner worlds are necessarily constrained. Disorganizing affects of fear or anxiety are best contained and prevented by avoiding unfamiliar settings and by remaining socially aloof, since even familiar people afford little meaning and comfort.

These developments in the first year and a half of life in both normal and autistic children are the underlying substrate for a capacity to attribute meaning to the actions of others. Subsequently, between twenty-four and forty-eight months of age, maturing neurocognitive capacities allow the child to grasp the difference between the physical and the mental worlds and to understand that thinking about something or someone is an action of mind different from being physically with that person or possessing the toy. These capacities make it possible for the normally developing child to create a world in which people behave toward him because of certain feelings he imagines them to have. In short, he not only looks to others for their affective reactions as he did in the first two years, but he now attributes beliefs and feelings to the others of his inner world. He imbues them with mental states that guide their actions toward him and ultimately his actions toward them.

Consider the following often repeated scene for a normally developing four-year-old boy, the content of which would not be available for an autistic child. The boy's parents have gone out for the evening and left him with a familiar and favorite sitter. He and his sitter play quietly together, and soon he involves her in setting up a scene with several figures getting into cars and going away on long trips, always leaving one or another figure behind. As the storyteller, he explains to his sitter and to the lonely character in the play that the others will return because they have gone off together to do something very special for him since he has been left behind. They know the boy left behind is lonely and they are worried about him. They had to leave on their trip, but they feel very guilty and upset. Transparently, behind the play and the boy's story, is his own wondering where his parents have gone, what are they doing together, and his thought that when they return, his mother will put him to bed as she always does, read him a story, sing to him, and his disappointment from early in the evening will be eased by the specialness of the time he will have later. He plays in comforted and comfortable anticipation for his parents' return.

Several features of the story reflect aspects of the integration of neurocognitive and psychic processes that emerge between twenty-four and forty-eight months, or in the case of autism, fail to emerge, and are a part of the ongoing differentiation of self and of a subjective, inner world. The boy moves freely between pretense and reality, and he comfortably involves his sitter in his play, with the implied message that she and he understand he is telling a story that carries both an imagined, enacted narrative and a statement of his own feelings. Like the infant uses evocative memory activity at moments of frustration, the boy is able to use his imagination in the service of easing his loneliness and disappointment. But unlike the infant, he is now able to add to the story, to attribute beliefs and feelings to his parents and the characters in his play. He imagines that the characters in his story and his parents, particularly his mother, want to return to have a special time with him. The desire and concern each of the adults has for the lonely boy will bring them back to him. He attributes to the adults the mental states of loving and desire, which motivate their actions toward the character in the play or the boy himself. And the boy imagines that the adults want to be with each other also, that his mother and father have feelings and wishes for each other as well as for him. He understands and represents in his play his separateness from his parents, but fills in that separateness through an act of mind.

UNDERSTANDING THE CONCEPTS OF THE
MENTAL WORLD AND MENTAL STATES

Understanding the relation between action and mental states is the neurocognitive underpinning necessary for the creation of a full inner fantasy life that further supports self-definition, and for the child's entry into full and complex loving relationships with others. For young children, appreciating that they and others have a mental life that guides talk and action requires the minimal understanding that there is a difference between the subjective mental world and the externally perceivable world, or more fundamentally, that things and people exist in memory and thought even when they are not directly perceivable. Equally essential is the understanding that the mental world is made up of feelings and beliefs, and that these are expressed in various ways—dreams and daydreams, memories, wishes, feelings, thoughts—each of which, though not directly perceivable, is nevertheless real.

In contrast to earlier theories that presumed children did not understand mental states until at least age six or seven years (Piaget, 1929), it now seems clear that as early as three years of age, children are able to distinguish the mental and physical worlds (Estes et al., 1989; Flavell et al., 1990; Wellman and Estes, 1986). As they become more autonomous and active in their interactions with others by late in the second year, they begin to be able to rely on their mental activities to modulate that autonomy. They understand that there is a distinction between mental entities and the corresponding real objects, and do not attribute observable sensory properties to mental phenomena (Wellman and Estes, 1986). Young children between the ages of three and four are also able to distinguish between a real state (e.g., a boy who has a new bicycle) and a mental state (e.g., a boy who is thinking about a new bicycle). In the first case, the bicycle, whether actually physically present or not, is a physical entity in the boy's possession, whereas in the second, it is in the boy's "imagination"—remembered or fantasied (Estes et al., 1989; Wellman and Estes, 1986). And three-to-four-year-old children understand that while one may be able to visualize one's own thoughts, others cannot (Estes et al., 1989; Flavell et al., 1990). Mental states do exist apart from the external world, and from the beginning of toddlerhood onward, normal children are aware of different mental states such as desires, thoughts, promises, and beliefs (Harris, 1988).

After appreciating the nature of the mental world, the child needs to make the link between mental states and behavior, that is, that for the most part, we act because of the content (conscious or unconscious) of our mental world. The understanding that people act on their desires and wishes is apparent even before the understanding of what particular beliefs or presumed knowledge may have guided the action. For example, in explaining actions, three-year-olds consistently cite the individual's wish (e.g., He wants the apple) even if they are unable to understand the belief behind the person's action to fulfill that wish (e.g., He thinks the apple is in the red basket; thus, he looked there first) (Moses and Flavell, 1990). Even two-year-olds understand that because people desire or want something, they try to get it and react differentially when their desires are not met (Wellman, 1990; Wellman and Woolley, 1990). They are either happy because of their success or disappointed and sad with their failure. Subsequently, children appreciate that beliefs as well as desires guide actions, that people do things because they hold to a particular belief or they think a given condition is true. For example, in the terms of an inner fantasy life, a four-year-old child acts toward his parents in a certain way because he holds to certain beliefs (as well as desires) about how his parents will behave toward him. Conversely, he "understands," or at least feels that he understands, that his parents' actions toward him give him information about the beliefs they hold to be true, especially those beliefs that pertain to him. He uses his appreciation of the link between actions and mental states to measure the depth of his parents' love or disapproval, their pride or disappointment.

Finally, and perhaps most important, is the understanding that the mental world not only exists separately from the sensory world, but that it can be in direct contradiction to it, that is, we may hold to beliefs that are false in the context of external situations, but nevertheless act on such beliefs, however false they may be. Examples range from the simplest situation of looking for something where we last saw it, and thus believe it to be even if the external conditions are now different, to believing that others return our love, act toward us just as we expect or want them to do, or that another is able to fulfill all that we wish and desire. Such is the stuff of imagination, fantasy, and transference. Further, the ability to hold to a belief even in the face of contradictory reality makes it possible for us to tolerate separations, to complete mourning, and to be alone.

Complex social interactions demand not only that the child be able to understand the relation between mental states and behaviors, but also that he be able to judge the "correctness" of such states relative to the world as he both perceives it and believes it to be. Through understanding the relation between beliefs and behaviors, one individual indicates his or her capacity to take the perspective of the other or to understand the other's mental state even if it contradicts his or her own. Several (e.g., Wellman, 1988; Wimmer and Perner, 1983) have argued that an individual's understanding of the notion of false belief and action is the most stringent test of the existence of a capacity for a theory of mind. In the case of a false belief, children must distinguish between their own (or true) belief and their awareness of another's different (false) belief, and demonstrate the understanding that the other person is acting based on his false belief. Procedures have been developed to test for such a capacity; each involves either displacement of an object or change in a directly perceivable situation.

For example, in a standard task, a child being tested watches a toy first being placed in a basket and then moved to a second basket after the toy's owner leaves the room. When the owner returns, he or she does not know of the displacement and must believe the toy is still in its original location. The question for the child being tested is where does the owner look for her toy, the implication being where does she believe the toy is? Between four and six years of age, normal children begin to demonstrate the capacity to understand that the owner will incorrectly look for the toy in the first basket because that is where he or she believes, or thinks, it to be (Bartsch and Wellman, 1989; Moses and Flavell, 1990; Wimmer and Perner, 1983). The observing child takes the perspective of the child who went out of the room, and understands that since that child did not see the displacement of the toy, he or she still holds to the belief that the toy is in its original position. Failure to take the perspective of the other would result in the observing child's insistence that the owner will look in the second box where the toy really is since that is the true, directly perceivable situation.

Autistic children show impairments at each of these levels necessary to develop a notion of mind, but they have particular difficulty on tasks that require them to take the perspective of another. Children with autism often fail on false-belief tasks and seem to have difficulty understanding the mental state of belief (Baron-Cohen, 1991a; Baron-Cohen et al., 1985). Such a finding has been consistent across several replications using a number of variations of the false-belief task just described (Perner et al., 1989). In addition, autistic children frequently fail to develop a sense of the other as a person having feelings, beliefs, thoughts, and fantasies (Baron-Cohen, 1989a; Baron-Cohen, 1989b; Baron-Cohen, 1991a; Baron-Cohen, 1991b; Baron-Cohen et al., 1985), and they seem to have considerable problems understanding the associations between mental states such as between beliefs and feelings (Baron-Cohen, 1991a).

INTERFACE BETWEEN PSYCHOANALYTIC
MODELS OF SELF-OTHER DIFFERENTIATION
AND THEORIES OF MIND

From the psychoanalytic point of view, the process of self-other differentiation and the emergence of desire that occurs in the first 18 months form the substrate to take another's perspective and to attribute knowledge, beliefs, and desires to others. The psychoanalytic view of the infant's experiences outlines a mind in which affect and inner representations—fantasy life—play an important role in the emergence of the capacities for relatedness. It also provides an account of how essential neuroperceptual skills and capacities are intricately interwoven with the child's feelings and representations. These early neuroperceptual capacities are quickly contextualized by experience with another. An infant turns to sound or looks at a face not just because of an ability, but because in the context of previous experiences, the actions of such capacities carry affective meaning. Gradually, multiple affect-laden memories schematized as representations provide the infant with the ability to conceive self and other in multiple ways.

Conversely, the notion of a maturing capacity to attribute meanings to others, to take their perspective, and understand that others have mental states calls our attention as analysts to a fundamental process that must occur in order for other psychic processes to be possible. As the experiences of many autistic individuals illustrate, with a distorted or absent capacity to attribute meanings to others, even rudimentary experiences of longing do not bring the individual to enduring relationships or a cohesive inner world. While we have yet to understand the specific neurobiological concomitants of the capacity to attribute meanings to others, such a capacity is basic to being able to develop an enduring sense of self and other. Further, these constitutional, "hardwired" capacities to perceive the other as separate, to engage the other, and finally to attribute meaning to others' actions and feelings form a backdrop for the multiple variations in an individual's adaptation to the social world.

In summary, with the achievement of an understanding of mental states, of the relation between mind and action, the child has opened to him a vastly enlarged world not only for fantasy, but also for deepened relationships with others. Integrating these models for the development of a theory of mental states and the mind of the other with more traditional psychoanalytic views of the emergence of an inner life and the process of internalization provides us with a new set of empirical questions about the sources of individual differences in the development of an awareness of mental life.

Part Three The Thin, Translucent Veil:

Tourette's Syndrome

In this work, we will join with Harry and his family in wondering what he can and cannot control, what is his Tourette's and what is Harry. In testing the limits of his capacity to bring greater coherence to his self and actions, we will be learning more about the thin, translucent veil between psychological and biological processes in childhood. (Cohen, 2001b)

Chapter 5 The Self Under Siege (1999)

Donald J. Cohen and James F. Leckman

The human body is the best picture of the human soul.
—Ludwig Wittgenstein (1958)

When Georges Gilles de la Tourette and Sigmund Freud were young, clinical scholars in Charcot's clinic in the Salpetriere at the end of the nineteenth century, they were introduced to patients with complex tic syndromes. Gilles de la Tourette became acquainted with the case of a fascinating princess with many years of motor and very colorful vocal tics. Although she was never treated directly by him, this individual and a small handful of other patients became the basis for his clinical description in 1885 of the syndrome that carries his name. This work launched a line of neurological investigations on the organization and nature of tics, obsessions, and compulsions that continues until today.

In Paris, Freud was also introduced to Charcot's methods, his find-

First appeared as the Introduction to *Tourette's Syndrome—Tics, Obsessions, Compulsions: Developmental Psychopathology and Clinical Care,* eds. J. F. Leckman and D. J. Cohen (New York: Wiley, 1999): 1–22. Copyright © 1999, John Wiley & Sons. Reprinted with permission of John Wiley & Sons, Inc.

ings on hysteria, and the studies on tics. Back in Vienna, he continued to investigate the origin and symptoms of patients with the vast array of symptoms that constituted turn-of-the-century "hysteria." These clinical disorders illuminated the permeable boundaries between voluntary and involuntary, conscious and unconscious, and meaningful and meaningless mental disorders. In 1893, Freud included a detailed report of his treatment of Frau Emmy von N whose complex emotional disorder included dramatic tic symptoms (Freud, 1953). As with Gilles de la Tourette, Freud's work also launched a new field and a continuing line of psychoanalytic investigation of the psychology of the inner world.

In Freud's theory, there was an intrinsic relationship between neurological and constitutional factors, on one hand, and the dynamic processes of the unconscious mental life. Both normal development and neurosis expressed both types of forces and, he believed, eventually science would be able to create more accurate maps of the brain and behavior that would be complementary perspectives on human mental life and behavior (Mayes and Cohen, 1995).

Throughout this century, these two traditions—the neurological view of Gilles de la Tourette and the psychological one of Freud—occasionally came into contact, in the work of particular clinicians and theorists. Yet, they were mainly divergent and hard to integrate. Tourette's syndrome hovered between the two domains of study, sometimes located more in the territory of the brain and sometimes that of the mind.

TOURETTE'S SYNDROME AND THE
INTEGRATION OF BIOLOGY AND PSYCHOLOGY

In the 1970s, biological and psychological perspectives began to converge and form a vigorous new hybrid—the investigation of brain-behavior relations in neuropsychiatric disorders. Freud's vision of complementarity had appeared to become a more likely prospect. In this rapprochement, the strange clinical syndromes of mind and body that fascinated Freud and Gilles de la Tourette have served as a valuable nodal point.

Throughout most of the century, Tourette's syndrome was considered a rare and exotic condition, seen by a clinician only a few times in a career. However, the availability of a new medication, haloperidol, and the pioneering work of Drs. Arthur and Elaine Shapiro suddenly focused attention on Tourette's syndrome as an easily diagnosed and not so rare condition (Shapiro and Shapiro, 1968; Shapiro et al., 1978). Soon, the Tourette Syndrome Association (TSA) succeeded in generating a far greater awareness of the diagnosis among physicians and the public, and patients recognized themselves in the clinical accounts and came for treatment. The century-long tradition of two points of view continued, as they do today: Tourette's syndrome was conceptualized as a neurological disorder with psychological consequences when seen by neurologists, or a psychiatric disorder with a biological basis when seen by psychiatrists.

In the early 1970s, a good deal of biologically oriented, psychiatric research focused on brain neurochemistry because of the increasing understanding of the synthesis, release, and metabolism of neurotransmitters and the effects of medication on these systems. Clinical researchers searched for biological correlates of rigorously defined conditions. Our research program on Tourette's syndrome and associated disorders originated in this intellectual milieu. The studies from this program are leading exemplars of a new paradigm: the field of research and care that integrates the neurology of Gilles de la Tourette, the phenomenology of Freud, and the advances in the developmental biological and behavioral sciences.

Through listening to, caring for, and studying patients, a new perspective on Tourette's syndrome began to arise. This view of Tourette's syndrome was within the clinical framework of developmental psychopathology and was based on the cross-fertilization of developmental neuroscience, developmental psychology, and child psychiatry (Cicchetti and Cohen, 1995b). Tourette's syndrome became the model neuropsychiatric disorder for studying the interacting contributions of genetic vulnerability and varied experiences, from gestation through the course of the first years of life, in the shaping of the lines of personal development of the individual and the nature and severity of a psychiatric disorder (Mayes and Cohen, 1996b). In a sense, Tourette's syndrome became our hysteria—the model disorder for exploring mind-brain relationships in health and disease.

In the middle 1970s, the patients with the most severe forms of Tourette's syndrome were just beginning to be seen and treated by a very few physicians, particularly those who worked initially with Dr. Arthur Shapiro. Initially, huge doses of haloperidol (up to 200 mg/day) were used along with other compounds, but clinicians soon settled down on a general standard of evaluation and care. Along with the expansion of clinical engagement with families with Tourette's syndrome, investigators in the United States and abroad soon started to systematically study the symptoms, treatment, and, to a limited extent, biological correlates of the disorders. In addition to Arthur Shapiro, some of the early leaders in this field were Ruth D. Bruun, Gerald S. Golden, C. D.

Marsden, Gerald Erenberg, Arnold J. Friedhoff, Masaya Segawa, Harold H. Klawans, Yishiko Nomura, Roger Freeman, and Harvey S. Singer, among others. Over a few years, Tourette's syndrome emerged as an often undiagnosed, or wrongly diagnosed, but rather common condition.

The research program within the Yale Child Study Center on childhood neuropsychiatric disorders started in 1972, with a focus on children and adolescents with autism, pervasive developmental disorders, developmental language disorders, attentional disorders, and other complex conditions (Cohen, 1974). Our founding, small research group included child and adolescent psychiatrists, a pediatric neurologist, and an adult psychiatrist. Soon, specialists in developmental neurochemistry and then a range of other fields joined in, including human genetics, nursing, psychology, neuroradiology, pharmacology, and education. We were especially interested in disorders that seemed to reflect disturbance in the unfolding of biological endowment and that, like Tourette's syndrome, hovered between developmental neurology and child psychiatry, between body and mind. Tourette's syndrome became the model system for testing new methods in the investigation of biological endowment and for charting the unfolding of developmental competence and dysfunctions in maturational processes.

The program in the Yale Child Study Center was especially influenced by the Center's commitment to doing research within the context of providing clinical care. In an important way, this tradition opened special opportunities for intensive observation and engagement with families over long periods of time.

In medical research, clinicians have a particular, privileged epistemological position. Because of their primary responsibility for providing care, they are allowed access to patients in privacy, to hear about all aspects of their lives, and to be with and observe patients at their most vulnerable and intimate moments. Clinicians may intervene with guidance and specific treatments, even when knowledge is limited; and the systematic observation of the impact of interventions offers further data about the underlying processes. A clinician's data are as rich as the lived experience of the patients and the physician's own ability to sustain the relationship, be curious and remain observant. In this process, the clinician-investigator can and should include all aspects of human biology and psychology as potentially relevant to understanding the patient and providing suitable treatment.

This breadth of the clinical epistemology contrasts with the needs of a laboratory scientist to concentrate on a small domain to test specific hypotheses with a sharply defined methodology. The clinical perspective that has provided the tone for our research program on Tourette's syndrome has encouraged multiple disciplines and perspectives to pool knowledge and methods while, at the same time, keeping the patient and family at the center of attention. Just as the clinician has the task of integrating history, current findings, and laboratory tests into a coherent, narrative, clinical formulation, in our research program the varied and always changing methodologies of clinical and basic research have been integrated by the clinician's concern for the whole patient, living in a family and society.

The first patients with Tourette's syndrome that we saw, in the middle of the 1970s, were referred most often as clinical enigmas. They were among the most seriously impaired patients we have ever seen. They suffered from painful, extreme forms of the disorder that we now recognize in far milder variants. Arthur Shapiro referred to some of these patients as "polymorphous" because of their range of symptoms; active clinicians shared a small number of such patients as they made the rounds among the "experts" and taught many of us a good deal—including humility. We were keenly aware of how much there was to be learned. In the Child Study Center, we learned a great deal from these patients about the onset and progression of symptoms, the range and fluctuation of tics, the emergence of obsessions and compulsions, their inner experiences and the traumas they experienced with parents, teachers, and society, and from within themselves.

Much of the early work within the Center was descriptive of these remarkable phenomena. Even today, after having cared for thousands of patients and families, we remain intrigued by the clinical phenomenology—the clinical surface of signs and symptoms, as well as the patient's experiences and the underlying processes. In teaching medical students, residents, and fellows, we have an opportunity to return to the lived phenomena again and to see them through fresh eyes. Are the tics voluntary or involuntary, physical or mental? Why do they come and go? If patients don't have them when they are in the office, why do tics appear as soon as they walk down the hall to the elevator? What accounts for the specific symptoms, the virtuosity with which they are chosen and executed? What makes the patient feel better when the tic is finally emitted? Are tics, then, like sneezes or masturbation? Like an itch or a scratch? Why do patients curse? How do they learn curse words? Why are mothers so often the target of aggressive attacks—attacking words, pinching, yelling, and controlling? When a child is doing something his parents and he hate, can he control it? How do you know what is intentional and what is beyond control? Is Tourette's syndrome organic or functional?

THE PSYCHOBIOLOGY OF TOURETTE'S
SYNDROME: CLINICAL FEATURES,
NEUROBIOLOGY, AND GENETICS

The organizing biological hypothesis in the 1970's was the concept of dopaminergic over-reactivity or hypersensitivity of dopamine receptors. The remarkable therapeutic benefits of haloperidol and other neuroleptics—and our recognition of the exacerbation of tics by stimulants—seemed to clearly support the role of dopamine excess at some point in the pathophysiology, if not as the cause. At Yale, the methods were being developed for studying central catecholamine and serotoninergic functioning through sampling of cerebrospinal fluid (CSF) for the major metabolites, homovanillic acid (HVA) and 5-hydroxyindoleacetic acid (5-HIAA), respectively (Cohen et al., 1980b). At that time, loading with probenecid was used to prevent their egress from the CSF and increase their concentration; 5ml of CSF fluid or more was needed for the assays that can now be performed on a drop.

The findings of these studies on cerebrospinal fluid metabolite, at Yale and elsewhere, supported the dopaminergic hypothesis and propelled the field forward (Cohen et al., 1978; Cohen et al., 1979a). We are all thrilled with these first studies—not only with the results but also with the ability to study something in the CSF that appeared to be related to profound psychological processes. Whether the findings have stood the test of time (Leckman et al., 1995) is less important than the impetus they provided for using current methods of biological psychiatry in the study of developmental, child psychiatric disorders.

We did not just study neurochemical systems, such as CSF metabolites in bodily fluids. The clinical needs of the children, families, and the breadth of their difficulties as well as their capacity for personal engagement captivated us. These sensitive, intelligent, and tormented children and their distressed families are remarkably evocative of our clinical empathy and intellectual interest. In Tourette's syndrome, we found a disorder that had an immediate demand on our clinical conceptualization of the mysterious leap between mind and body. Patients described the origin of their tics from within, from an urge that could not be resisted and to which they eventually capitulated; they thought that in some way the tic was voluntary; and yet it was not at all wished for, and was the result, in some inscrutable way, of forces in the brain-mind that were below the surface of consciousness, just as the forces described one century earlier by Freud in his research on hysteria (Bliss, 1980).

During the next several years, we felt like the explorers in a new world in which neurobiology and depth psychology were being joined. Very intensive, clinical discussions with parents and patients suggested that tics, obsessions, and compulsions were not isolated to the patient but seemed to occur among other family members. The classic literature reported that there were rare situations in which a father and son both had Tourette's syndrome, but the common wisdom was that Tourette's syndrome had no specific genetics. Yet, in case after case, we would sit with parents and hear a different family saga. Sometimes, a father would deny having had any tic symptoms only to have them recalled, often quite gently, by his wife, or to "remember" a period in childhood when he, too, had eyeblinking and sniffing, or more. As we became more adept, the histories became richer and the multigenerational nature of tic symptoms became clear. Also, another theme emerged. In clinical cases, it was already recognized that some patients had not only motor and vocal tics, but also more complex behaviors, complex tics, and mental symptoms that could be considered mental tics or obsessions. Deeper study of individual patients made clear that they had all the symptoms and signs of obsessive-compulsive disorder as well as tic symptoms. For generations, there had been a debate about whether Tourette's syndrome could be seen as a motor form of obsessive-compulsive disorder or whether obsessive-compulsive disorder was a mental form of Tourette's syndrome. Our careful clinical studies of individual patients and their families revealed that the epistemological issues could be addressed differently by appreciating that these were two perspectives on the same set of phenomena.

The clinical observations became scientific hypotheses that were amenable to rigorous testing (Kidd et al., 1980; Pauls et al., 1981). This translation of clinical observations to formal scientific scrutiny is precisely the reason for having research clinics that bring physician/clinicians into close contact with basic researchers from various disciplines.

Advances in the field of Tourette's syndrome exemplify this back-and-forth movement from clinic to laboratory to clinic. Soon, with the great boost of the TSA, rigorous genetic research using formal methods of assessment and analysis confirmed the clinical impressions of the familiality of Tourette's syndrome and its association with obsessive-compulsive disorder. The first, quick-and-dirty genetic studies were strongly supportive of a familial and genetic nature of Tourette's syndrome and very quickly led to great interest in genetic factors in Tourette's syndrome among other research groups and in relation to other disorders. The first pedigrees so much resembled classic depictions of dominant genetic transmission that we were surprised the genetics of Tourette's syndrome had for so long gone unappreciated. Now, decades later, the genetic story continues to unfold its complexities.

Another example of clinical and basic research converging came from the studies of the neuropharmacology of neuronal activity. In the late 1970s and early 1980s, basic neurobiological researchers at Yale were engrossed in the studies of the locus ceruleus (LC), a small neuronal center deep in the brain that serves as switching station for many neurotransmitter systems and regulates the noradrenergic system outflow. Basic investigators studied the regulation of the firing rate of the LC in exquisite recordings. Clonidine, an anti-hypertension medication that stimulates the inhibitory, presynaptic, adrenergic receptors, sharply reduced the rate of LC firing and the functioning of the noradrenergic system, the neuronal pathways intimately involved in arousal and anxiety.

Within a very short time, the basic laboratory studies of noradrenergic regulation were translated into clinical practice. The earliest clinical translations were in the treatment of individuals who were suffering from the terrible withdrawal symptoms from narcotics. Dramatically, clonidine blunted their automatic over-responsivity and the pains of withdrawal. Shortly after that, we wondered if some aspect of Tourette's syndrome might also reflect the over-activity of the noradrenergic system. For the first trial, we selected one of the most profoundly impaired youngsters, a boy who engaged in nonstop yelling, a myriad of tic movements and aggressive outbursts. We estimated the dose and then gathered around his bedside. Forty minutes after the first dose, he fell asleep. When he awoke in one hour, he was already calmer. Over the next days, his symptoms abated, and he became more easily engaged socially and in treatment. The clinical benefits of clonidine in the treatment of the disorder seemed apparent in other patients, as well (Cohen et al., 1980a; Cohen et al., 1979b). Later, more rigorous, systematic trials continued to demonstrate a clinical effectiveness for clonidine, although, as in much else in life, further knowledge complicated the story (Leckman et al., 1991).

Decades later, it still appears that clonidine has a clinical role, perhaps through its inhibition of the LC and reduction of stress responsivity and hyperarousal, or by acting on other brain regions. Yet, the specific value of clonidine was perhaps less critical than the fact that it opened up a new approach to studying a well-defined brain system related to anxiety and arousal in a child psychiatric disorder. We used clonidine as a provocative agent to study the degree of reduction of the major metabolite of norepinephrine, 3-methoxy, 4-hydroxyphenylene glycol (MHPG); degree of lowering blood pressure; and extent of increase in a hormonal system (growth hormone) regulated in part by norepinephrine (NE) (Leckman et al., 1984; Young and Penney, 1984).

In these early studies of Tourette's syndrome, biological systems could be monitored along with clinical changes in tic frequency and severity, and improvements in a child's attention and overall functioning (Harcherik et al., 1984; Leckman et al., 1989). The new field of biological child psychiatry envisioned the possibility of integrating biological systems and behavioral change (Leckman et al., 1986). These studies suggested that this promissory note could be fulfilled, suggested new studies, and shaped strategies of rigorous psychobiological research. The significance of this impact can be estimated by comparing the research that was now possible with the state of investigation in child psychiatry one decade earlier. Even in the 1970s, broad-based, psychobiologically oriented research on child psychiatric disorders was limited to only a few sites that were, like us, helping to shape a field of research and the methodologies for studying and understanding child psychiatric disorders in general. Each new methodology—from studying cerebrospinal fluid and metabolites in urine and plasma, to investigation of hormonal response, enzymes, developmental changes in measures of behavior and biology—had to be approved for use with children, studied in normal and contrast groups, and refined as an instrument while, at the same time, being used to explore the disorders.

During the 1980s, research on Tourette's syndrome became increasingly robust and popular throughout the world. A new cadre of investigators from around the world began to make their voices heard, including Christopher C. Goetz, David E. Comings, Joseph Jankovic, Thomas N. Chase, Anthony E. Lang, Mary M. Robertson, Roger Kurlan, Ben J. M. van de Wetering, Paul R. Sanberg, Ari Rothenberger, Alan Apter, and Amos D. Korczyn. By 1982, there was sufficient research underway for the TSA to organize the first international scientific congress (Friedhoff and Chase, 1982). Many of the papers were quite preliminary. Our paper conveyed the flavor of the research program: "Interaction of biological and psychological factors in the natural history of Tourette's syndrome: a paradigm for childhood neuropsychiatric disorders" (Cohen et al., 1982). At this time, we began to describe Tourette's syndrome as a model neuropsychiatric disorder. This status also justified the degree of research and clinical attention that this remarkable condition was receiving. We felt that the methods and findings of research on Tourette's syndrome would have implications for many other conditions. One decade after the first international congress, a second international symposium brought together the burgeoning field of systematic research on Tourette's syndrome (Chase et al., 1992).

The Tourette's syndrome research portfolio in the Child Study Center was richly expanded during the 1980s. The advent of brain imaging—computerized tomography—offered the chance to study brain structure and search for possible major alterations that could underlie the diathesis to Tourette's syndrome and other neuropsychiatric disorders. The first computerized axial tomograms (CAT) scans were done in a state of great awe; a group of clinicians and neuroradiologists gathered around the machine and waited expectantly for the images to be developed (Caparulo et al., 1981; Harcherik et al., 1984). Each new technological advance in imaging—including the most recent functional magnetic resonance imaging (MRI) methodologies—has generated the same breath-holding expectation as we wait to see if the lesion will finally be revealed (Peterson et al., 1993; Peterson et al., 1998).

Twin studies at this time supported the role of genetic factors, and also gave some room to think about non-genetic, environmental sources of variance (Price et al., 1985). The importance of nongenetic, environmental factors (Leckman et al., 1990) was consistent with the general models of developmental psychopathology, which guided our understanding not only of Tourette's syndrome but the broad range of childhood disorders (Cicchetti and Cohen, 1995a; Cicchetti and Cohen, 1995b; Leckman et al., 1997; Peterson et al., 1995).

The Child Study Center research program on the genetics of Tourette's syndrome discovered that the clinical impressions about the close relation between tics and obsessive-compulsive disorder actually could be documented in rigorous clinical studies (Pauls et al., 1986). The family genetic methodology and genetic modeling quickly moved to the center of research interest worldwide (Pauls and Leckman, 1986). During the last few years, an international genetics collaboration has worked energetically to obtain DNA from well characterized patients and families, and many laboratories in the United States and Europe are collaborating in the search for the genetic locus or loci. So far, no genetic linkage or strong genetic candidate gene has emerged, but both are only a matter of time. Perhaps it is naïve to predict—especially since we made the same prediction five years ago—that within a few years, there will be important discoveries of a gene or small set of genes that convey vulnerability to Tourette's syndrome. Yet, we will make the prediction and feel quite certain that we are not being misled by false optimism.

As more children were being seen clinically and in research projects, the severity of patients' symptoms, as a group, seemed to decrease; patients were receiving the diagnosis of Tourette's syndrome who were not markedly impaired.

This trend has continued until today, and we are no longer quite sure where to draw the line between the quite frequent, rather innocent appearing tics of young schoolchildren exhibited at some point by perhaps 10% of all children in the first grades of elementary school and a "true" case of a tic syndrome or even Tourette's syndrome. If every child with a few tics is diagnosed as having Tourette's syndrome, then it is among the most common of conditions and might drift into expected normalcy (just like a few freckles are part of the normal variations in biology). Yet, there are children who clearly do not seem to be just on the normal distribution but for whom the frequency and vigor of the tics leads to real disruption of functioning. However valuable for the purposes of defining a case and need for treatment, any demarcation may seem arbitrary (e.g., that the tics must persist for more than a year or that there is some degree of real clinical impairment, or both). Diagnostic issues are not just scholastic exercises, as they enter importantly into rigorous research studies of genetics, neurochemistry, and treatment, as well as practical decisions about reimbursement for care. Diagnostic issues also are central to epidemiology, which requires clear specification of what will constitute a case (Apter et al., 1992).

In the middle 1980s, clinicians caring for children with Tourette's syndrome were delighted with the availability of a new agent that could be used in the treatment of obsessive-compulsive disorder. Alongside haloperidol and pimozide for tics, clinicians could try a medication that operated on a problem that was often even more disabling. When clomipramine became available in the United States, we could see for ourselves that it actually could liberate some children who were frozen with obsessions and compulsions. The rapid introduction of the serotonin reuptake inhibitors (SRIs) a few years later greatly expanded the possibilities for pediatric psychopharmacology of Tourette's syndrome and obsessive-compulsive disorder. The availability of new medications was coupled with the commitment within the Center and in other academic departments of child psychiatry to systematic, rigorous psychopharmacological research on short- and long-term efficacy, effectiveness, and side effects of medication. Today, with available medications, most patients who require pharmacological intervention for tics, obsessions, compulsions, attentional problems, and aggressiveness can be offered some degree of relief. Yet, no medication is ideal, nor are the clinical improvements often complete. There is thus continuing hope that genetic and developmental neuroscience research will reveal new targets for molecular intervention, just as the basic work on the LC was a critical step on the road to trying clonidine in patients.

CLINICAL UNDERSTANDING AND CARE

Every year there are patients who come for care who open up new ideas for research and treatment. One decade ago, we reviewed our understanding of clinical care (Cohen et al., 1988). Since then, our understanding has continued to be deepened by clinical immersion, especially with those patients with Tourette's syndrome whom we have followed closely for many years and who stand as our own, internal representational images of the mechanisms and processes expressed in the clinical disorder.

Each clinician in the Tourette's syndrome program in the Child Study Center has had a small group of patients with whom we have shared our lives; we have learned more than usual from these patients because of our closeness and concern, and the frequency of our meetings, especially during crises. They have served as the basis for our theorizing about the integration of biology and psychology over the course of development (Cohen, 1991a). Abe has been one such patient:

Case Example

At age 17, Abe's parents brought him for evaluation tied to a chair to prevent his horrible, self-injurious behavior. He lurched forward, hanged his head, threw whatever came to reach, yelled, and cursed. At his worst, he was tied to a bed or allowed to simply thrash about for hours. His mind and body were trapped by rituals of touching one part of the body and then another, repeating, jerking, calling out. His eyes would be magnetically attracted to particular patterns, especially intersecting lines and squares, from which he could not disengage. For an hour or two, he would sit in frozen concentration, moving his eyes from one corner to another of the pattern, unable to detach. He would become drenched with sweat and finally would be able to pull himself back by a force of great will when he felt, for some reason, that he had done the pattern "just right" and "correctly." He had "crazy" ideas that he had to hold himself back from. Between paroxysms of tics and compulsions, he begged for help.

For more than 18 years, Abe has been in our office two to four times a week for discussion and treatment. During these almost two decades, we have jointly gone through very long and difficult periods. When things were at their worst, Abe was in nonstop movement. He had tics of every part of the body, gyrations of the trunk, head- and body-banging, and dystonic tensing of his upper torso. He would get stuck in postures, and yell so loudly at the top of his lungs that his face would puff up and be beet red and he would seem about to burst. He was frightening and frightened, and when he really banged at his face, to the point of breaking his nose, he looked like a prizefighter who had just lost a major match.

Abe was a good describer of his inner world. Inside his mind, there were two bulls that attacked each other—pulling and pushing in opposite directions—and he was caught in between. He could not clear his mind of crazy ideas, and the only way to soothe the crescendos of tension was to do something strong, powerful, and abrupt like yelling or banging. His mind became glued to a particular thought, and he had to think the thought or do the actions that were incessantly on his mind. For years, he had to search his body for each and every pubic hair that had then to be pulled; during many months, he felt compelled to stick his finger up his nose until blood gushed; he could not shower without spending hours in washing rituals. He became obsessed with the number three. He had to count: 1, 2, 3, and then be sure that he did not stop on 3, and so return to: "1, 2,3853,4,5, 6. No: not 3, back to 1." In any internal conflict, the victory of one force left the other force defeated, and Abe was on both sides of the battle and thus always a loser.

From Abe, we learned about the nonstop, every-minute burden of feeling overwhelmed from within by attacking forces that were within one's self and, at the same time, outside of it.

Over months and then years, Abe became increasingly the winner against the internal demons that possessed his mind. His courage was stunning in this many-year war. He had tremendous pride in his achievements and maintained the sense that he would, eventually, move ahead in his life to fulfill his ambitions in sports and business. His warm heartedness, humor, and concern for others—including a genuine and deeply touching concern for his clinicians and their families—brought him a circle of friends and enduring relations. Although as a young adult, he has not achieved the goals he set for himself, he does not stop trying or hoping. Dressed in a handsome suit, he is a good looking, strong young man whose physical and emotional scars are badges of his heroic combat.

One of us (DJC) read the above account to Abe (not his real name) to obtain consent for publication. Abe appreciated hearing the description: "I want others to know what I have gone through and what I have achieved. Especially younger children." He discussed his feeling that although he is now about to be engaged to a very caring woman, he would not want to have children after they were married. "I wouldn't want my son to have to go through what I have." And then daydreamed about what it would be like to have a son to teach football, to take to places, to make into a man as strong as he. He then retold the story of the bulls that were locked in combat inside of his mind: "One of the bulls is the mind and the other bull is the body. They are charging each other with their horns, inside my mind. I can see them banging against each other, and I am both of them. They keep attacking until they get caught in each other, their horns are locked. And then I can stop." With this, Abe, a bull of a man whose avocation is weight-lifting, embraced his scholastic clinician and lifted him from the floor. "You are just like my father." The embrace represented a respite—the mind-body coming together, for both of them.

We have seen literally hundreds of schoolage boys and girls who offer poignant accounts of their internal experiences of tics and obsessions. They draw their tics for us (sometimes, with spidery legs just like forest ticks) and provide their own accounts of the "abnormal pathways in their brains" that have been explained to them by their doctors and the pamphlets they have read. They blame that "dopamine stuff" that poisons them inside and that can be stopped by medications. One sweet child offered a theory that his tic started as a mucus in his throat and then went into his brain, where the tics really came from. We have heard teenagers describe that they know that they are thinking too much about something—a girl who is perfect in every way, a fearful thought that they will hurt someone, a dread that they might have to come into contact with AIDS by sitting near someone on the bus—but who, in spite of knowing their thoughts are not rational, are not able to use their reason to subjugate the worries. They know and do not know.

Often, the children with Tourette's syndrome become expert observers of their own experiences. Indeed, we have often felt that they become too good at this and spend too much time engaged in focusing attention on the self and inner experiences. They think about their minds in the same way that a child with a chronic physical condition, such as diabetes, may become too good a biologist and too preoccupied with how his body works. Children should take their bodies and minds more for granted. While increasing meta-representation is a developmental achievement that allows for self-reflection, too much reflection on the self is a heavy burden and can lead to a narcissistic over-investment in the self. This introspection and reflection may also be an aspect of the diathesis itself, as if inner attunement and outward sensitivity to details are both a gift and a curse. When other schoolage children use their energy and channel their aggression into learning, sports, and figuring out the outer world, these children are caught up prematurely in focusing on how their minds work and what to do about their impulses. This preoccupation with their own feelings and responses may lead them to premature thoughtfulness and a remarkable ability and openness to portray the flow of their thoughts, feelings, and fantasies. This skill in free association and description is acquired by more constricted adults only after years of psychoanalytic therapy, if then.

We have also learned the many ways that Tourette's is a family affair. When we say that tics, obsessions, and compulsions run in families, this may seem blandly true. But the full implications of familiality are profound. Imagine the pain of a father who himself has tics when he sees that his beloved son is beginning to clear his throat one morning at breakfast, and then cannot stop the noise. Another father described that he saw his daughter get up from bed, go to the closet and straighten her shoes. At that moment, he knew that she, too, had Tourette's syndrome, and that her life, and the life of the family, would never be quite the same.

The parents of children with Tourette's syndrome, who themselves have had similar symptoms or saw them in their own families, are often doubly burdened. Like all parents, a child's illness or troubles are a great distress for the parent, especially when the difficulties are persistent, impairing, and socially painful. But when there is a hereditary factor, the parent's unhappiness may be compounded by personal guilt as well as the anger that may come from the partner—and the partner's family—who may feel free of the pathogenic taint. Converting the parental knowledge of his or her own experiences with tics and parental guilt into helpful concern is part of the therapeutic process. Indeed, most children who are afflicted with tics and associated problems are reassured that even with such difficulties, one may grow up to be like a beloved parent. And parents, too, can use their own coping and overcoming as reassurance for their child and themselves.

One of the pleasures of a long involvement with children with Tourette's syndrome has been to see that this optimistic attitude is quite often empirically valid. Indeed, most children with Tourette's syndrome, even those with the most severe difficulties in the school age years, develop into functioning and competent adults. Often, they are free of tics, or virtually free of them, unless under stress. Their tics become less noticeable as they are no longer under the microscopic scrutiny of parents and other adults who often see a child's imperfections under a high degree of magnification. Even those with persistent obsessions, compulsions, and tics, generally are able to cope and move ahead in their lives—to finish school, go on to college or a job, to marry, and then to have their own families. It is when they are about to marry or are just married, that many of these children now return, with fiancé or spouse, to discuss the implications of their disorder for the next generation. Then a special opportunity is provided to help the patient reflect on and integrate childhood experiences and to share them with his or her chosen life partner. Current genetic information can be conveyed that can be supportive of the young family in their considerations about their own children's fate. While there is no genetic marker that allows for prenatal diagnosis, most families can be told that available knowledge suggests that only a small percentage of the children of individuals with Tourette's syndrome are likely to have any clinically significant symptoms or any symptoms at all. Hopefully, when tics do emerge in a family that we have been caring for, and this has happened often enough, the young parents can work with us to reduce the likelihood of a devastating outcome by keeping the focus on the child, not the tics.

This can serve as the mantra for our approach to clinical care. For any illness that cannot be cured—and even for those that can but where the treatment is painful or prolonged—a major responsibility of the clinician is to help maintain the child's development on course. This means keeping the clinical eye on the child, not the symptoms. Children with many tics may do quite well at home, with friends, and in school, and feel good and effective. In such a situation, allowing nature to run its course is probably a reasonable option. In any case, all treatment needs to be assessed by its impact on social, emotional, and cognitive development, and the adequacy of a child in meeting the various tasks of development. Over the long haul, we have seen very good therapeutic results, even for those children who still have troubling symptoms, with education of the family, support, guidance, psychotherapy, cognitive behavioral therapy, and judicious use of medication, in various combinations.

Yet, all too often, we have seen development become derailed not only because of the severity of symptoms and the repercussions in family and community of tics and obsessive-compulsive disorder, but because of the pursuit of "cure" through many treatments, including zealous use of medication. In the 1970s, we saw children and adolescents who had not received timely, sufficient, or appropriately targeted therapy; their Tourette's syndrome was not diagnosed or managed. Today, we see children who have had many medications started, raised, and lowered in rapid succession, without careful monitoring, and who are receiving four, five, or six medications concurrently. They become confused about their bodily states, what and why they feel the way they do, and what is under their control. Their sense of autonomy becomes eroded. Helping a child remain a person through the process of being a patient is an important part of clinical care.

Clinicians can learn a great deal about neurobiology and about the broad principles of clinical care by being part of the lives of children and families dealing with Tourette's syndrome and its treatment. With the involvement of many professionals in the care of a patient—teachers, therapists, pediatrician, psychiatrist—the clinician also can hold the parts together for the child and help the child in his attempts to integrate all of the experiences into an understanding of what is being done to and for him.

THE DEVELOPMENT AND MAINTENANCE OF THE SELF

Our theoretical understanding of the experience of Tourette's syndrome, and thus our guide to treatment, derives from developmental, behavioral, and neurosciences, as well as psychoanalysis. In our theories, we attempt to understand the patient's inner experiences in a manner that will also help the patient and family understand what they are living through. A major part of mental life is devoted to understanding life as it is being lived and has been experienced. This task of understanding is a central developmental process for all children. In normal development, children from the first months of life start to build up a sense of coherence. They feel the security that comes from being cared for by loving parents, who have continuity in space and time, and are there for them when they are expected. They relate this moment to what just happened, and they learn to anticipate the next steps in a sequence. They experience that their various sensations—touch, taste, sight, sound—are related to each other, and are different aspects of their perceptions of a person or thing in the outside world. They trust in the veracity of their senses and mental constructions, and feel that they can count on their perceptions and ideas to guide them safely. Even in the first year of life, children learn about their own intentionality. They anticipate the future and act as agents to achieve immediate and then increasingly distant goals. They have internal representations and plans. They know they need others to achieve their goals, at times, but also that they can get things on their own. They can wish for something, act on the wish, and reach a target. They know their desire may differ from their parents' desires for them, and they can assert their right to pursue their goal, even when this means recognizing and dealing with conflict. They develop a sense of independence and of autonomy, of being a separate person. They progressively develop a folk psychology, a "natural" psychological theory that explains behavior on the basis of desires and intentions. They thus evolve a theory of how their own mind and the minds of others work. As they do, they grow to recognize that they may be of two minds; when they have to choose between one option and another, they learn to deal with internal as well as external conflicts.

In all these ways, children develop a conscious sense of who they are as individuals and an unconscious, not fully represented sense of self—of an internal locus of integration of desires, abilities, values, and intentions that is suffused with feelings of pride and competence. At times of great stress or illness, or when falling asleep, children will fall apart, and the coherent sense of self as stable over time and within itself may break down. When children do not develop a sense of the psychological functioning of others or an understanding of their own minds, when they break down acutely or persistently, they lose their grasp on the coherence of the outer and inner worlds, which become unpredictable and frightening (Baron-Cohen et al., 1993; Mayes and Cohen, 1996a).

These natural, developmental processes occur so effortlessly and smoothly for most children that the complexities of building a stable sense of self are not visible on the surface. Children just seem to become more and more like little people—they know and act like themselves. How this comes about, biologically and psychologically, is a fascinating story that is only beginning to be approached empirically. In this epic, prominent roles are played by neurobiological mechanisms for the operation of each of the perceptual and cognitive modules and the integration into wholes of the various subsystems of perception, attention, emotion, and cognition and their shaping into patterns of intention and memory. Some of these activities are performed by specific cortical areas and by the parallel neuronal systems that connect the cortex and midbrain structures, the corticostriatal-thalamo-cortical pathways (CSTC).

The overlapping CSTC pathways subserve subsystems such as the regulation of attention, perception, motor control, and the coordination of emotion with the internal and external situation. The systems are brought together into a harmoniously orchestrated whole by brain centers, which serve integrative roles, including cortical thalamic, amygdala, and other regions (Leckman et al., 1997). The functioning of these integrated neuronal systems, in normal children and adults and in those with various types of disorders, can now be studied using neuroimaging techniques (such as functional MRI, Peterson et al., 1998).

The unfolding of a coherent sense of self—based on an integrated functioning CNS—occurs when a child has the normal, developmental preconditions; the normal genetic endowment that shapes brain maturation during gestation and postnatally; an appropriate or good-enough environment, particularly the necessary continuity of loving care; protection from adversity; good health; and luck (Cicchetti and Cohen, 1995a).

THE SELF UNDER SIEGE

The normal processes that lead to integrated, coherent, historical experience and stable self-representation provide a theoretical and emotional foundation for understanding the self (Cohen, 1980b; Cohen, 1991b). Developmental psychopathology utilizes these concepts as a framework for understanding and treating disorders (Peterson and Cohen, 1998). For children with Tourette's syndrome, disturbances in the regulation of attention and behavior may appear during the first years of life, before tics, as a harbinger of early dysfunctions in CNS maturation and integration. In these children, the tics may emerge gradually, as if restless overactivity and fidgeting were prodromal to the full disorder. For other children, the onset of tics at ages 6, 7, or 8 years may occur as if a genetic switch were thrown. A parent described looking out the window one morning and to her horror, she thought her perfectly well child was starting to have a seizure. His paroxysmal movements were the first signs of a tic disorder, which persisted for many years.

The unfolding of tics, obsessions, and compulsions can heuristically be related to the elaboration and recruitment of various CSTC connections. Metaphorically, the symptoms appear to reflect patterns of breakdown in the normal grammar or intrinsic rules that govern the relations of experience and behavior. When the normal grammar of integrated CNS and self-functioning break down, the individual experiences and emits fragments of normal behavior patterns, disjoined from their normal syntax and thus out of context and apparently meaningless. Or recursive cycles of behavior become activated (Peterson and Leckman, 1998), as if a feedback system starts to function and cannot be terminated at reaching its normal end, a satisfactorily completed action; the child never feels fully satisfied, the behavior does not fully match the internal template that initiated the behavior (Leckman et al., 1993; Leckman et al., 1994). The child thus stops only with exhaustion or the activation of a competitive response. The "electrical shorts" between CSTC mechanisms (Peterson et al., 1998), the recruitment of inappropriate pathways, as in cardiac arrhythmias, lead the child to feel bewildered by what he is feeling, thinking, and needing to do.

Models such as these suggest the nature of the psychological challenge to a child and adolescent who must try to make sense of an experiential world that is not governed by the usual rules, a world in which his thoughts and actions are both his and also alien to him. His self is under siege from forces within and yet out of his own sphere of autonomy. There are eruptions into consciousness and behavior of feelings, thoughts, and acts that are deeply encoded and yet normally are below the perceptual threshold or that might signal a need for action but that now lead to funny feelings in different parts of the body, relieved only by the sudden movement that is a tic (Leckman et al., 1993).

THE THERAPEUTIC PROCESS AND THE COHERENCE OF THE SELF

The therapeutic process for children with these breakdowns in internal integration, who feel they are possessed and going crazy, is aimed at reconstitution of coherence and meaningfulness. Thus, at the very start, explanations, education, and guidance are meant to reduce anxiety and the feeling of isolation. In the relationship with a family, the clinician creates an external, prosthetic integration—a holding of the patient and parents and a containment of their anxiety. As the child and family come to identify with the therapist's goals and attitudes, including his lack of anxiety or need to immediately do something, they can regain their own composure. The process of listening to the child and family's stories, in depth and over time, is an important aspect not only of obtaining their histories, but also helping to shape their current adaptation. Often, these stories are already quite distorted by the period of uncertainty before the diagnosis, which now is becoming shorter; ill-advised interventions, including overuse or misuse of medications; and the familial tensions and peer difficulties that often accompany the disorders.

More specific therapeutic interventions then can occur in the clinical context of the relationship, with fully shared concern and knowledge. These include a range of options—cognitive and behavioral approaches, psychotherapy, school interventions, and, of course, medication. Taken together, available interventions are effective for the majority of individuals. Even those patients whose tics, obsessions, and compulsions persist can be offered support and optimism to cope with their troubles, including the consolation that childhood is usually harder than adulthood. We know that adult adaptation—vocation, intimacy, marriage, and life satisfactions—is far more a function of personal coping and development than of the severity of tics, as such (Towbin et al., 1988).

The self, once formed, needs a great deal to maintain its vigorous functioning as the locus of integration of desires, abilities, and values and as an experiential core of coherence in time and space. While the self of a child grows out of his biological endowment and intimate experiences, it is reinforced by the achievements at each phase of development, including mastering the basic tasks of development (learning, peer relations, and pleasure in activities).

In subtle ways, a touch of the Tourette's syndrome/obsessive-compulsive diathesis may help provide a particular flavor to self-development, one marked by increased awareness of one's own feelings and of the feelings of others. This diathesis may also have some adaptive functioning in relation to conscientiousness, attentiveness to vital details and changes, orderliness, regularity, cleanliness, amid other useful traits (Leckman and Mayes, 1998a, 1998b). CSTC pathways and specific brain centers that subserve neurobiological integration may also help to structure the self in these domains of functioning. However, when the Tourette's syndrome diathesis becomes a full-blown disorder, the underpinnings of the self are attacked. Therapeutic goals must then be aimed at helping the individual to regain a sense of his or her autonomous and coherent self and to resume normal development.

During the past 20 years, we have accompanied hundreds of children, adolescents, and adults through this therapeutic process. As is true generally of children with Tourette's syndrome, the majority have done nicely as whole people (Leckman and Mayes, 1998a). Advances in genetics, neuroimaging, neuropharmacology, and behavioral research will, no doubt, enhance the therapeutic possibilities. And, who knows, developmental neuroscience and prenatal diagnosis may actually reduce the incidence of Tourette's syndrome and associated disorders or virtually eliminate the disorders all together. If so, there will be a reduction in the burden of illness experienced by many children and families. In a strange way, there may also be a loss to humanity, since the biological vulnerability may also have adaptive value. There are some redeeming features—energy, talents, humor, zest for life, as well as conscientiousness and orderliness—that seem to accompany and grow out of the vulnerability to Tourette's syndrome and in the ways that individuals with Tourette's syndrome learn to successfully cope with their adversity. It is the task of clinicians to help preserve these gifts in children and adults with Tourette's syndrome who come for their care.

Part Four **Hardworking Road Show: Play and**

Child Analysis

Chapter 6 Enduring Sadness:

Early Loss, Vulnerability, and

the Shaping of Character

(1990)

Donald J. Cohen

This paper describes the psychoanalyses of two individuals, a child (Andrew) and an adult (Quentin), who suffered from early disruptions in their families. Their fathers played prominent roles as caregivers during prolonged periods and buffered the traumatic loss of their mothers. Both Andrew and Quentin had family histories of depression and both developed depressive and characterological difficulties marked by disturbances in the regulation of aggression, with sadistic and masochistic features. Their early childhoods and experience of recurrent loss, longing, and anger were reconstructed during psychoanalysis. Psychoanalysis was therapeutically useful in relieving acute symptoms and in helping both patients move ahead in their development more securely and less burdened by diffuse, inner- and outer-directed rage. Andrew returned for psychotherapy twice, in early and late adolescence, and it was possible to follow the course of

First appeared in *The Psychoanalytic Study of the Child,* Volume 45, eds. Albert J. Solnit, Peter B. Neubauer, Samuel Abrams, and A. Scott Dowling (New Haven: Yale University Press, 1990). Copyright © 1990, Albert J. Solnit, Peter B. Neubauer, Samuel Abrams, and A. Scott Dowling. All rights reserved.

his character development during the transition from childhood into young adulthood. Using the clinical psychoanalyses as a base, the paper describes aspects of the development of character with a special emphasis on the roles of loss and the representation of aggression.

Throughout its history, the psychoanalytic theory of character has grappled with questions about what it is to be a person and to have the mind that is specifically my own. In approaching such concerns, the theory has bordered on philosophical inquiry. Analysts have wondered about the origin of the self, the emergence of the inner world and its demarcation from the outer world, the organization of feelings and fantasies that define experience, and the sense of continuity of the person over space and time. We have speculated about the processes that differentiate people, with shared biology and mental mechanisms, into unique individuals of definable types. Recently, there has been a convergence of knowledge from child observation, genetic research, and psychoanalytic theory about temperament, socialization, and stability of some characteristics, such as self-esteem. Observations within clinical psychoanalysis, however, continue to offer the deepest conviction. From clinical engagement, we learn most deeply about the intertwined forces at the start of psychological life that provide the matrix for all future experience, the background out of which our unique troubles and pleasures arise.

This presentation focuses on character within clinical psychoanalysis, using the analyses of two patients whose early grief suffused their characters with gloom and longing.

ANDREW

Andrew was the third child of a mother with psychotic depressions and a father who was subdued and serious; from both parents he inherited several generations of depression and emotional severity. His infancy was marked by marital crises and maternal hospitalizations for emotional illnesses. His mother felt she had cancer or other dreaded illnesses; she often took to bed, bringing Andrew into bed with her as a comforter. His parents separated when he was 3, and by 4 he was anxious and withdrawn. At age 7, he was immovably sad and failing in all spheres. He spoke little, lay on the floor sucking his thumb, ate with his hands, and at times crawled and barked like a puppy dog. From ages 7 through 10, he was engaged in psychoanalysis. During the analysis, he began to understand the nature of his anger and sadness and the roots of many of his symptoms. He discovered artistic talent that flowered, served its therapeutic purposes, and faded. He was able to move ahead in his school life and with a few pals, but he remained a quiet and very sober boy. During the course of his analysis, it was possible to reconstruct Andrew's experience of recurrent loss; this analytic work was done mainly through nonverbal modes of communication (Cohen, 1980a).

When we first met, Andrew's diagnostic sessions were characterized by imaginative play with small figures who went on airplane trips and had crash landings or who engaged in ritual games of cowboys and Indians. The capacity for play and elaboration of fantasies was reassuring in light of the ominous history of years of withdrawal, depression, and bizarre symptoms. When the analysis started, however, play disappeared. The first months were spent in virtual silence. It was with hesitancy that Andrew started to make use of play materials. Finally, his fancy was caught by a Polaroid camera, and he began to photograph the room and the construction of a building taking place outside of the office window. Around the creation of an album of photos the analysis took on a sense of direction: quiet talk, photographing, and archiving the building's progress. This album continued for years. It was followed by other projects, such as the building of a pioneer village with coffee stirrers and the creation of a frontier populated by pioneers and Indians resigned to rather bland friendship. In this American West, the frontier was at perpetual peace and aggression was avoided; my encouragement toward warfare was met with firm truce.

I vigorously interpreted Andrew's silences—his fear of being flooded with sadness and anger that he couldn't control; his fear that I couldn't understand how frightened and lonely he was or that I wouldn't care, as his mother hadn't cared; his rage at his father for not keeping his mother. Why would anyone care? Why bother to show feelings? Whom can you trust? If he wasn't so bad, why would he have been treated so badly?

In forming interpretations, I used whatever was presented by play; what could be inferred from my knowledge of Andrew's life and the sadness, reserve, and withdrawal that I observed; and, perhaps most powerfully, the feelings and fantasies that were stirred up in me during hours of quiet sitting and empathic engagement. From slight facial changes and bodily tensions and relaxations, I felt I could read, better and better, Andrew's inner life and his reactions to what I could offer.

The cumulative force of analytic inquiry and concern eventually seemed to penetrate the inhibition and withdrawal that characterized Andrew's relation to everyone, including me. One day he took the crayons and paper that were always near at hand but which previously were pushed aside with the statement,

"I can't draw." He did his first drawing of a cloud and raindrop, which then became a suburban scene. Andrew was obviously pleased by what had come from somewhere inside of himself. Each day he drew a new scene on the highway, and the pages were taped together to become a scroll depicting a journey through villages and the countryside, during summer and winter, in good spirits and bad. The drawings had a remarkable vividness—in color, shape, and content—and they led to associations and memories. Men in danger, cars in collision, funny scenes depicting counterphobic clowns and the like filled page after page. I interpreted the experience of being held and falling; of searching for someone and trusting and not trusting; of finding and not finding pleasure, fun, security, and inner calm.

The scroll ended at the shore where a large boat—bearing the name of his mother who had in reality left Andrew to go overseas and never returned—was about to sail. The boat did not or could not leave shore. Instead, a child on a raft drifted off into the ocean and was threatened by sharks and submarines from which he was, but perhaps was not, saved. The child was a victim of powers far beyond his own. The scroll was finished when it led to the object of Andrew's desire, his mother; he then no longer felt like drawing. The themes it opened and expressed, however, remained available for discussion, in the quiet, tentative, and short-phrased speech that was available to Andrew. There was one more large project in the analysis—the building of boats out of scrap—and several other activities such as cartooning. At the end of the analysis, during termination, Andrew built a large, free-form sculpture out of scraps of wood which he painted in bright colors. The sculpture juxtaposed interesting shapes with realistic models. Primary objects included a man with a cigar walking a pet dog and a fish swimming in manic lightness through the sky. Andrew called this sculpture "the thing." It was a monument to the possibility of the potential for play, especially within psychoanalysis, to represent existential absurdity—the experience, shared by all of us, of living a life in a world which is not rational and which we make our own by trying to understand.

The analytic work touched on many of the areas central to Andrew's earliest experiences of neglect and overstimulation. His vague somatic concerns and clumsiness were given a context of meaning in relation to the bodily care he missed and the bodily distress that plagued his mother. Yet, his primary identification with her was an integral part of his own personality, which was barely accessible for discussion and seemed immutable. His father's relationships with women triggered his curiosity and wishful longing, and these feelings, too, became available for discussion in relation to one particular woman whom Andrew courted with enthusiasm.

By the end of the analysis, Andrew's acute symptoms were no longer present. He was not obviously depressed; his clumsiness was replaced by dexterity; and his progress in school was acceptable, although not what it might have been. He had a few friends with whom he liked to pass time, and he spoke more easily with them. He generally did not trust adults and remained quiet. When asked a question, he responded in as few words as possible. He was a sober boy.

A child analysis such as this one raises multiple questions for clinical investigation in relation to the development of character, the emergence of an explicit infantile neurosis out of the vulnerabilities in character, and particular symptoms. Questions also are raised about the appropriate mode and possible goals of analytic treatment of developmental disturbances, as Anna Freud (Freud, 1965) called these earliest deviations. A helpful, supportive adult can be very useful for a child such as Andrew during an acute depression, especially if the depression is closely linked with a loss, which the adult can help to fill in. But often such an adult, as Andrew's father clearly was, is not sufficient. The child needs the process of therapy to make use of the people who are available for investment and reciprocity. Equally, a child analyst can be only of limited value during a depression if he is not able to be what the child needs to find in him. The analyst for such a child becomes an important person—a dependable, caring adult who listens and tries to understand (Abrams, 1988). Progress of the analysis depends on this relationship at least as much as on interpreting activities as such. Andrew's analysis reflected these interrelated phenomena—his appreciation of my engagement as well as the impact of the interpretations and clarifications. For Andrew, I represented a place of refuge and of dependability: I was a good friend who was pleased to see him, in his fantasies as well as in reality. I was also his mother and his idealized father, and therefore I was inevitably a source of disappointment. All of these feelings were commented on, as best as I could. Yet, Andrew's anger was never fully brought to life, in play or discussion or transference. Aggression was inhibited, perhaps. Or so diffusely present it could not achieve representation. It remained a pitfall.

A child such as Andrew evokes, in turn, a range of feelings and fantasies in the analyst. Days of boredom and annoyance evoke anger as well as desire to rescue or move beyond the bounds of analysis. At times, one feels like throwing a child like Andrew out; at other times, like taking him in wholly. There were sessions when we ate crackers and drank tea together: orality was represented and enacted. Slowly, the analysis took its shape, and there was a feeling of the kind of work that carries analytic conviction. At this time, there was no shortage of pride—for either of us. Phenomena of these types were among the best clues to the underlying fantasies; recognition of countertransference served a vital function.

Several years after the termination of the analysis, Andrew was arrested for stealing. The storeowner had observed his pacing back and forth in front of the cassette-tape counter for several days in a row. When Andrew finally stole a tape featuring a series of love songs by a popular female singer, he was easily spotted. During a course of therapy following this episode, we had the chance of reviewing his first years and the depressive experience of adolescence—feeling alone, anxious about sexual urges, fearful of being unacceptable to any girl or deserving of affection, worried about masturbation. He felt he needed to catch his pleasures on the sneak, to steal them, as it were, if need be. Therapy at age 14 was similar to that at age 7. Andrew was now a husky, solid youngster; his silence was magnified by his physical bulk and tension.

At age 17, Andrew again returned to treatment in the midst of crisis. A group of young men in the auto parts store where he worked were caught after having stolen some petty cash and merchandise. Andrew had taken nothing, or perhaps had taken a few things; he may have been a lookout. He was arrested and incriminated in the conspiracy. He was again the silent sufferer; he wanted to tell nothing of what he knew, neither to the police nor to me. We sat quietly together as he slowly, over months, put into words a reflection of his emptiness, feelings for which no words could be found, that related to those very first years of deprivation and rage.

Soon afterward, his mother drowned while swimming off a boat in a calm, South American lake. His fantasies of eventual reconciliation were shattered. He grieved deeply; he felt liberated as well. He was joined in his mourning by others who remembered her as the beautiful, ebullient person she had been decades before.

Not long thereafter, his father found a mature woman with whom a loving and sustained relationship evolved. Andrew was detached and wary; he offered little information about his activities and less about what he felt. Slowly, he tested the waters by occasionally making demands and seeing how Margaret and his father responded to the crises in his life. He was no longer the child who could be won over by his father's girlfriends, as he had been earlier. He tested Margaret's commitment to his father and to him. Would she too disappear after he fell in love? At this time, Andrew, his father, and Margaret met for weekly family discussions with me. We reviewed the ways in which Andrew needed to learn about his past, including what had happened actually and how he and his father remembered their past, and how he had responded to these traumas. We also discussed what Andrew was actively doing to himself and was passively not doing for himself, his hopelessness and anger, his defensive withdrawal and wariness. Margaret became integrated into the family. Concurrent with her more than passing the trials, Andrew became freer in his emotional expressivity, initially with friends and then, gradually, with his father and Margaret. He talked at length and with humor to a widening circle of friends, and was more genuinely present with the few adults whom he felt would always be there with him.

In his early 20s, Andrew is a broad-shouldered, decent, hardworking young man who is the co-manager of a small firm that crafts fine furniture; his family wonders if he has enough fun. He succeeds in a career that is lower down the social ladder than are his parents, but it is of his own making. He is quiet with adults—he keeps his guard up—but close to a few friends. In deep ways, he is the same boy he was 15 years ago, vulnerable to depression and despair, the victim of the double burdens of genetics and experience. Yet, he has benefited from several advantages—his stoic, courageous perseverance, even when everything seemed to be going wrong during childhood and adolescence; the intelligent and empathic involvement of his father; the entrance into his world of Margaret; and the process of self-understanding that was initiated during his analysis and which he continued for himself and then during his return to treatment. While continuities over the decades are apparent, he is no longer depressed. He has gradually become more self-sufficient, engaged, and proud. Maturation continues. One wonders, now, about what fate and his character hold in store, particularly whether he will have the good fortune of finding his own Margaret or will feel the need to repeat the relationship with a woman too much like his mother.

QUENTIN

Quentin entered analysis for help with depression and uncertainty about all major decisions. At age 31, he felt adrift and indecisive; he still didn't know where he was going, although he was well launched as a medievalist and had already published a monograph and several essays. He was a good-looking, light-haired man, with deep-set, soulful eyes; he had a studied, donnish quality of seriousness and preoccupation. He clenched his jaw as he spoke with much feeling about regrets, worries, and hopes. He entered analysis, which lasted five years, with a capacity for disarming honesty.

Early in the analysis he felt that time and again he made decisions that seemed right and well informed, only to realize painfully that the goals were not attainable or of real interest. Other preoccupying themes soon emerged—the impact of his mother's depressions when he was 2 and 3, the divorce at age 4, and recurrent troubles with women. Quentin's mother was from a titled French family whose fortune was long spent but whose style retained charm and eccentricity. Both sets of grandparents as well as his parents were divorced; there were a few suicides, including his grandmother's when he was an infant. His mother's Bohemian life did not blunt her unhappiness. His father started as a landscape painter of some promise but drifted into designing billboards and neon signs for a living.

Throughout his childhood Quentin moved from the home of one parent to the other. When he was with his mother, he battled with her and was highstrung; when he was with his father, he felt lonely and daydreamed. He was a diligent student, yet he procrastinated, and his work was not fully up to his potential; in books and masturbation he found distraction from brooding. During college, his long, serious papers about medieval literature brought him academic recognition; his teachers thought he had talent that needed to be liberated.

After his father died from injuries he sustained in an auto accident, Quentin was left in a state of stocktaking and anguish. His mother belittled his unhappiness. He was stuck in writing a book on which his career depended.

The first months of analysis were marked by profoundly moving, novelistic descriptions of early childhood with a depressed mother, her attacks on him, and his observations of her with Puerto Rican and Cuban men. In contrast, there were accounts of joyful times with his father who would clown at the breakfast table, recount his youthful adventures, and relate an endless bedtime tale of the history of the world. This father of early childhood was contrasted with a far more preoccupied father of later childhood. During Quentin's adolescence his father was burdened with financial and familial worries and struggled to find his own meaning in life. During this period Quentin felt relatively rejected by him, just as he felt rejected by so many others who were important to him.

Quentin was capable of acute, merciless self-observation; his nuanced narration, however, alternated with one-sided descriptions of battles with authorities. He was provoked into battling with individuals who he felt were above or in charge, including me; he was relatively unaware of his own contributions. In such confrontations, he would pay a high price to avoid seeming in need of another man, even if this price was failure. He longed for a great professor—or perhaps president of a large foundation—who would come along, see his brilliance, and crown him as successor; yet, positive gestures, in or out of analysis, were met with disdain.

Quentin was a wonderful dreamer and fantasizer. Early in the analysis, he dreamed of a tour with his mother to the rural Southwest:

> We make a lucky connection with people—some Spanish people. There is a woman there with whom I once had a sexual contact, an Asian. My mother has brought things to give to them—cosmetics, trinkets. I get the woman's name wrong and my mother corrects me. Her son tells me to take something from a bin in a store—some sausages and some beans. Next, I'm in a police station. A policeman starts to frisk me. I lie on the ground and this guy is really thorough. I'm afraid he'll get to the pocket where I've got this stuff I shouldn't have taken—the sausages. He says, "Aha, I got something here." I get panicked that he'll pull out the sausages . . . But when he reaches in, he just pulls out some innocent things—a string and a small piece of wood. He takes it to the property clerk who says they can't arrest me for having an innocent thing in my pocket. I start talking big. I use black jive talk: "If you arrest me, I'll sue ya' . . . take your house, your car, yea, I'll take your wife." I put on a big show for everyone.

Associations were to belittling experiences, humiliations, to feeling like a little boy; and then to a scene while sitting on the john in the bathroom at the Center for Medieval Studies in Paris. Graffiti was drawn on the door: a keyhole was made into a female sex organ, and the key would then be the male sex organ. It made him think it was exciting to stick his penis into a forbidden black hole. He became furious with his mother for being so patronizing. The sausage related to lunch and then to food in the Southwest. "You can't help thinking about a big black penis when you have a sausage sandwich like that." His mother had a black Cuban boyfriend—handsome, quiet, thoughtful—but "I hated to see him in the house. I would fly into a terror sometimes when he was on the couch . . . Or start crying. Nobody could figure it out." The dream sausage that was not discovered by the policeman was Quentin's big male phallus which was concealed, covered over with a little, innocent child's plaything. Masturbation was here, too, and then bravado in arguing with the internal prosecutor who failed in his attempt to catch him in his criminal act.

Seeing his mother with her boyfriends aroused not only jealousy but also excitement. Such memories led to the opening up of a paradigmatic masturbatory fantasy:

Almost always it's about a dark, Hispanic woman from Arizona I almost slept with but didn't . . . Or some other ethnic woman . . . The woman is very submissive . . . My part is aggressive. I'm not beating her up, but I'm forceful. It's a fantasy of power. She submits to my will.

Early in the analysis Quentin started a relationship with a sensitive and highly intelligent writer and literary critic. Anne was capable of productive and zestful work—her first volume of poetry had been very well reviewed—and she enjoyed a rich social life. Quentin was often detached and irritable; he was painfully aware of his discomfort in social groups, and he was competitive with Anne's friends. He was dissatisfied with himself and could not fully commit himself to Anne, as he had been unable to commit himself to other women earlier in life who were ready to meet him more than halfway and provide the mothering that he seemed so much to need.

Quentin felt humiliated with women. As a child he burned with rage at being sent from the house when his mother entertained a boyfriend, or when he would return to find her in her slip, and these feelings of being hurt by her and being shunted to the side were easily revived. The masturbatory fantasy became elaborated:

There's a group of Black boys standing around. They're jiving about something. I think they want to beat me up or something like that. I think that it's stupid to be worried, they're just having a good time . . . Then I think about the Chicano woman I've told you about. She starts to snuggle up to me, and I act tough and then force myself on her . . . I don't know what happens to the Black kids. I think they are sort of impressed or go away.

He was rivalrous with established scholars, with witty young men, with a great-uncle who made a mint at investment banking, with everyone who seemed confident, comfortable, or successful. A day wouldn't pass without an envy attack. He worried about losing control and yelling at a colleague; he could become rude during a conversation and persist even when he knew he was creating an awkward scene.

He felt like a phony. He longed for closeness with a powerful and charming man, whose graciousness would rub off on him. He dreamed:

I unzip my fly. The guy next to me unzips his fly and wants me to take out his penis . . . I don't want to. He shows me how he has a withered arm and can't get his out, but he finally manages to get his penis out on his own. I win the contest . . . I pee the farthest.

His mother criticized his scholarship as pedantic footnoting; she described his thoughtfulness as nervous and old ladyish. She couldn't understand why he couldn't be a tougher figure—a calm, confident, bourbon-drinking, real man who could go backpacking in Utah and also keep up with the New York intellectual elite. He couldn't resist her seductions into argument when he felt she was calling him a fag; he emerged more enraged and diminished. "She cuts me down and wonders why I am so uncertain . . . My whole life has been one utter condemnation of who I am." Although there were two sisters, he was his mother's only enduring relationship, the center of her life. They were deeply loyal to each other. They argued to avoid the frightening pull to be together.

Quentin had varied bodily worries—sniffles that stayed too long, body odors which were not controlled by showers, an occasional palpitation, tension in the scrotum that resisted diagnosis, shortness of breath, stomach spasms. Bodily sensitivities dated to childhood. "As a child," he remembered, "I always had a rash somewhere. I pulled my ears, picked my nose, sucked my thumb." Yet he was proud that he never succumbed to illnesses and that he had a perfect record of school attendance.

> I was a nervous kid, but I don't know if anyone really noticed anything except that I wet my bed for a long time. I remember one vivid dream when I wet my bed. I dreamed about a toy fort my father had just bought for me, a kind of military camp with soldiers and tanks surrounded by a fortress wall. I walked on top of the walls around the fort and then I felt the need to urinate. I dreamed that I walked down the stairs to a bathroom that was in the camp and I urinated there. I felt proud that I was a big boy and didn't urinate where I shouldn't. But then I wet the bed. I think about how odd that was—here I was trying to be grown up and walk to the bathroom and I do just the opposite; I act like a baby and wet the bed.

In this bedwetting dream, urinating is represented as a controlled and prideful achievement; it captures Quentin's conflict between acting like an independent, big boy and his wish that the adults would have enough time and concern to notice how much care he needed. Other bedwetting fantasies expressed anger, humiliation for loss of control, and exhibitionism. Through analysis of current physical symptoms the infantile neurosis was reconstructed, along with the move into the house of one of mother's boyfriends, which led to Quentin's moving out. From that time on there was a crystallization of the earlier, pre-Oedipal disturbance in self-esteem, distance from full engagement in lively experience, lowered mood, seething rage, and longing. Quentin experienced life from age 3 or 4 encased in the shell of a compliant false self, as an observer who stifled his responses for fear of exploding in tears, rage, or girlish dependence. He took pride in his control, in needing nobody, in not giving in.

> Boy, did I sulk. What else could a kid do? Go up to his mom and say how I felt with her walking around the house in a nightgown in front of me and some guy? I became inarticulate. Really, if you asked me then, I wouldn't have been able to say what was moving me. Not too different from now, when you think about it. I suppose you can say I had one prolonged sulk with my mother, lasting for decades.

Scenes of self-defeating social awkwardness were sometimes connected with sulking and crapping. One may serve as a set piece to display the intertwining of character themes:

> After my lecture at the symposium on medieval architecture and sculpture I felt the young Turks were crapping on me, not asking good questions but simply trying to show me that they thought I was not as brilliant as Professor Werholt. He reads texts in languages that I'll never even study. When he was discussing my paper, he made a pun in Church Latin . . . I was furious, sulking . . . I stopped at the bathroom in the conference center on the way to dinner. I needed to take a crap. A guy was shaving by a sink. I asked him, "Is this the co-ed bathroom?" He was an assistant professor from Stanford, a cocky guy I never spoke with before. I don't think he recognized me. He got really annoyed. Glowered at me. I sat down and took a crap. When I finished, the toilet wouldn't flush. I called out to the guy—he was showering—if the toilet worked. He said to turn the handle on the pipe to let in the water. Simple. I should have known. I did it and the toilet flushed. As I was walking out, I said to the guy, "I didn't know that this was a do-it-yourself bathroom." I was trying to thank him for helping with the toilet. By this time he was really mad, I mean really mad. He said, "Fuck you." Like I was telling him he should flush the toilet for me—or something else, maybe wipe my ass. Inside I felt deeply humiliated. I had wanted to seem friendly and to make a bantering joke. I produced the opposite result to what I had intended.

Quentin knew that he had put the man off from the very start, slurring the fellow's masculinity, which made defecating in his presence exciting and dangerous. Quentin's tone seemed disdainful. Inside, Quentin felt confused and hurt by the audience's response to his lecture and longed for the self-confidence he felt the young man possessed; he wanted to act poised and ended up feeling exposed.

Another short dream:

> It takes place in a bathroom. A black man is sodomizing a white man. Next: I am trying to escape over a fence.

He associated to walking toward a urinal in an office building a few days before. He unzipped his fly in anticipation. "A black kid came out of a stall and walked by. I thought it was funny to do it as I had . . . walk with my fly open." Then: "I am always comparing my work with everyone else's. When I read the journals I worry about who has achieved more than I and why I haven't published more. I'm working on a very difficult text now . . . it's never been edited." He felt hurt by the old-fart editor of the Proceedings of the Classics Society who asked him to revise a paper, by his father taking off and leaving him with his mother, by his mother leaving him for degraded men, and on and on. This led to a concluding association: "My dependence is so intense that people reject it . . . I've learned to become stony and independent." The next day he reported a new experience:

> While I was leaving the gym, another guy was walking up the stairs. He stopped to talk with a friend. He was wearing shorts. I had the urge to grab at his penis . . . No, not in a forceful way. "Grab" sounds too aggressive. Really, to take hold of his penis, to hold on.

If Quentin gave up the control he expressed in detachment and surliness, he would have all his desires exposed and his impulses unleashed. He needed an infusion of masculine self-worth. When a man did something thoughtful or complimented him, however, he felt that there must be something underlying the praise or friendship—either the man saw that Quentin needed support, which was dreadful, or the person himself was a wimp.

Quentin of course wondered what I could or would offer, with whom I studied, and what I cared about:

> One time, I was alone in a plaza in Madrid. I had an hour between buses. It was beautiful. A few young men were drinking beer at a cafe table. They looked like childhood friends. I thought how nice it would be to share the hour with someone. I was so lonely it hurt.
>
> [He then paused, and continued:] See, if I really could feel close to you, in a personal way, not just a professional way, I would ask if you had ever been to Madrid and seen the square. That would be the normal thing to ask, when you are talking about a place.

Quentin avoided the fear of closeness, of the shared and moving hour, by reminding me of the professional rules by which we both must abide. Interpretation led to a rivalrous put-down. This opened a line of fantasy about seeing me from up front, sitting at a table away from New Haven, and the abstinence of analysis. Away from here, we could talk like two childhood friends.

A dream appeared as an association to the day residue of this analytic discussion:

> I was looking up a hill. There were layerings of medieval houses. Suddenly I see an alley leading up to a church. I see it from the back, from behind. It might be a famous church. If I could see it from the front, I might identify it.

Quentin increasingly acknowledged his wishes for my care and to be like the child patients he thought I played with; he wondered if I ever sat them on my lap and read to them. He grew less disdainful. He was aware of the layerings of meanings surrounding homosexual longings—their early roots in wishes for the joy of being close again to a lively, enthusiastic father, their expression of need for a man's encouragement, their defensive functions in avoiding the tensions of oedipal conflict. Continuities were represented across the decades—from Quentin's first years of life through the early school years, and then onward through bookishness, withdrawal, blocked creativity, self-doubt, and eventual depression and emptiness.

During the terminal phase, the paradigmatic masturbatory fantasy was elaborated, including the variant aggressive themes and the cast of characters—Hispanic and other dark-skinned women, a girlfriend who enjoyed oral sex, Black boys who were onlookers, and others. Intrusive fantasies with masturbatory excitement that earlier had appeared "out of the blue" were placed in context:

> Someone tried to take the chain off a bike in front of the research institute. I thought it must have been the Black kids I saw around . . . I have fantasies of beating these kids up, really hurting them. Violent, sadistic fantasies. I think about hitting one of these kids over the head with a wrench. I seethe with aggression.

The fantasies were lucid expressions of passive and masochistic desires, wishes for the love not only of his mother but of the big men whose penises he saw through their underwear or perhaps more directly in his mother's home. In fantasies of forcing himself on women, he thought of these boys looking at him with the same awe he had felt, years before; he envied Puerto Rican and Black men their freedom and verve, their cockiness, and hoped to show them that he had what it took.

Termination was brooding and dark, as Quentin reviewed his father's brain trauma and seizures; the rejections by women and men; humiliations with colleagues; the infantile void that could never be filled. At the same time, he felt closer to the pleasures with his father that had provided his early childhood with whatever vitality it had and which led, in a circuitous route, to his own academic interests in medieval art. He felt I knew him better than anyone ever had, or would.

Yet, at the end he felt there was something—something that he could not put into words—that he hadn't gotten from me. He felt it as something that I could not give him. He knew that at least in part this lack of fulfillment was the reflection of what he could not give or show to me. In dreams and then more openly, he expressed the wish to be penetrated, to have me forcefully take him from behind, and for him to resist my penetration. There was little resistance to this interpretation. To feel fulfilled, to have the strength and security he desired, to have his infantile void filled was deeply desired but a profound threat to his being his own man (Loewald, 1970).

By termination, Quentin had found more than what he felt was his share of happiness with Anne, whose love for him had endured his years of preoccupation and which he was now far more able to reciprocate. They looked forward to marriage and children.

ANDREW AND QUENTIN

Andrew and Quentin shared a similar fate, to be born within families with a heritage of generations of depression, suicide, family warfare, and divorce. Their mothers were depressed and anxious and openly angry at their fathers; their first years were lived in families in the process of dissolution. Both found more security in their fathers than their mothers. From his father, Andrew derived a sense of containment and capacity for loyalty that later were expressed in young adulthood. From his father, Quentin acquired his gift for language and for telling stories about himself and the unfolding of life around him. By age 4, Andrew and Quentin were subdued and unhappy. The geography of their inner lives had already taken shape. The characters, thematic outlines, desires, and fantasies through which all future experience was to be filtered would undergo remodeling but were no longer fully plastic. By 6, both boys became neurotically symptomatic: Andrew lay on the floor, barked like the dog who accompanied his mother on her impulsive excursions from the family, moped and was miserable; Quentin was an irritable, picky, and critical boy with enuresis and inhibition in finding pleasure who felt he could not express his needs but had to act as grown up as possible.

In the course of his childhood analysis, Andrew explored his hurt and desires, but he could never give full voice to his rage, which was beyond words; he overcame his acute symptoms but remained serious, under the shadow, uncommunicative, and vulnerable.

In his analysis, Quentin overcame his depression and became more tolerant of his desires; he blamed himself and his parents less, and his need to punish or be punished diminished. Gentleness and humor emerged, and he enjoyed cooking for others and giving gifts, including himself. As he reviewed the benefits of psychoanalysis, he particularly felt that it had helped him to remain steady in his course and to avoid characteristic self-destructive acts and undoing of decisions: he was able to sustain relations with colleagues, even when he was indignant and rivalrous; with Anne, even when he was unhappy and unsatisfied; and with me, even when he was disappointed. Although he sometimes felt bitter, he did not get up and leave. Yet, he never forgot that life was difficult—"a bitch"; that he had been deprived, and that if he ever were so lucky as to have children, he hoped he would not repeat his family destiny of messing things up.

During analysis, both Quentin and Andrew moved ahead developmentally through understanding of their desires and recognition of their rightful anger and its self-destructive power. Through good fortune, both had opportunities for warmth with new women who provided tenderness and constancy that they had earlier missed with their mothers; both were able to continue a process of self-understanding, which they experienced during analysis.

Quentin's and Andrew's analyses opened the way to looking at genetics and early experience, the shaping of inner worlds around longings and fears, and the emergence of dominating themes of adolescence and adulthood, especially the search for and fear of intimacy. Damaged so early, neither Andrew nor Quentin was able to make full use of others to create or sustain their sense of personal value. The objects of their desire could never be achieved, and their mourning remained partial. Their characters were shaped under the constellation of rage. Rage shaped their childhood experiences; it operated in fantasy, action, and in silence; it suffused their inner lives and provided its distinctive, characterological resonance.

CHARACTER, AGGRESSION, AND FANTASY

These clinical psychoanalyses raise more issues than any concluding discussion of theory should hope to address; I will use them to illustrate several central concerns within our field.

The most fundamental concerns of psychoanalytic theory of character are the processes of mental functioning, which create what we mean by being a person, including continuity of experience, intentionality, and the growing sense of personal responsibility (Loewald, 1978a). Analytic theory has tried to describe the *origins* of the ego or self, the ways in which the child's conception that he is the locus of experience emerges from both the "child's gesture"—as Winnicott, (1960) called spontaneous activity—and the responsiveness of caregivers who provide the child's act with meaning and shape need into desire (Loewald, 1978b). Yet, there remains a mystery—I believe Freud would consider it a biological mystery—in the process by which I come to appreciate that I am an I, across different states of arousal, while calm and distressed, in my mother's arms and while alone. The self is not created inductively. From constitutionally given competencies and temperament, from the undifferentiated state and the mother-child matrix, the mind emerges and new functions and structures evolve; the mind as seen by psychoanalysis builds itself in response to its own experiences and discoveries about its urges, fears, and capacities. In this process of self-creation, narcissism and concern for others are delicately balanced; both have their origins soon after birth, are progressively expressed in fantasy and act, and mature in close interdependence.

Along with trying to understand the origins of those mental phenomena which are found in all people, except those with devastating disorders such as autism, psychoanalytic theory of character has also addressed the processes which lead to specific types of mental organization; it is these which differentiate individuals into groups or personality types. Here, analytic theory of character has emphasized the vicissitudes of instinctual life, particularly the role of aggression. The earliest and best worked-out paradigm—in early Freud (1909) and then Abraham (1921) and Reich (1900) and many others—related to anal sadism and obsessive personality development; the heuristic power of these paradigms of instinctual transformation has influenced all of future psychoanalytic thinking, grounding it in the body and its role in fantasy as well as its relation to others.

Much of our analytic clinical work focuses on the accidents of life, what we have done and have had done to us, particularly in matters of love. And these powerful experiences of childhood and adolescence are conveyed, not only in popular discussions, as formative of character. Yet, from its origins, psychoanalytic theory has emphasized the biological grounding or precursors of character—the biological basis of strength of the drives, individual differences in the ego, fluidity of libido, the constitutionally given rates of maturation of ego vs. id, and so on. We might now speak of the genetic contributions or vulnerability to depression as an exemplar of biological grounding, expressed in psychic life. But for decades, the more deeply they have analyzed, the more convinced analysts have been that character emerges from the body—from its needs and from the experiences of its satisfactions and deprivations. Since Freud, analysts have looked to biology to explain what the child is constitutionally born as, what he brings into his interactions at the start of the process of becoming the person he uniquely is. The categorization of bodies into male and female is, for psychoanalysis, a basic determinant of character, not just in the oedipal phase, as Freud at times suggested, but from the first months of life, as emphasized by Melanie Klein (1957). Also, biological factors of many different types play profound roles—the actual way in which the mouth sucks and the gastrointestinal tract works in satiation and defecation; the thresholds of sensitivity of the skin; the capacity for quieting down with feeding and the flow between sleep, wakefulness, and distress; the physical pain from illness or surgery; and the influences of chromosomal and endocrinological abnormalities on mind and brain—all of these influence the individuality of the person. If Andrew and Quentin had had different bodies, different genes, they might have emerged as very different individuals from the terrible adversities of their childhood. They might have been resilient or searched out adventure, they might have been more prone to inflict their suffering on others. As it was, given who they were born as and the families in which they were nurtured, they turned inward toward silent, hateful brooding.

The real body, with all its orifices and organs, as well as the fantasized body, have been central to analytic theory from its start, as it is in the development of the individual. Particularly in early life and at special, pregnant moments throughout life, the mind is in these orifices and organs, as much as in the head. Along with the presence or representation, one might say, of the mind in the body, there is the potent presence of the body in the mind's fantasies. The body being soothed or tortured, one's own body or one's lover's, is at the core of analytic theory of character, as was so clear in Quentin's fantasies. The psychoanalytic theory of character is a theory of psychosomatic integrity. Thus, within psychoanalysis, the split between body and mind is a fantasy that has defensive functions in need of analysis. (Specific fantasies might include details on how mind and body are connected by circuits or computer networks, how they both cohabit the head, how the body sends feelings to the mind and the mind transmits messages or commands to the body, how they are competing forces facing each other across a no-man's land, etc.)

As a counterweight to its biological footing, the analytic theory of character is also attuned to what we think of as character in ordinary language, the social functioning of individuals in their "highest" ethical activities—honesty, integrity, conscientiousness, and concern for others (Loewald, 1988). Thus, in analytic theory, the concept of character bridges between biology and maturation, on the one hand, and socialization and culture, on the other. In its early history, psychoanalysis shocked precisely because of this bridging; and perhaps we no longer are surprised enough by the discovery that scrupulosity or generosity, or cleanliness and morality, originate in the gratifications of instinctual life, in the prolongation of drives, sublimation, and reaction formation.

The operation and maturation of underlying forces in psychic life were of interest to Freud from the start to the end of his thinking about character. As is well known, his earlier views emphasized the sexual instincts and the fusion of sexuality and aggression; these forces were at root biological and then interactional; they matured on timetables given by brain and endocrine maturation (Freud, 1924). Traces of these conceptions remain visible, across decades of change, at the very end (Freud, 1937). Here, however, the forces are universal, and the human psyche is only one of the locations in which the forces of Life and Death are instantiated and represented here on earth. We should not dismiss too quickly these broodings of old Freud. In many ways, Freud's later theory reworks the earliest, instinctual theory in the light of decades of the data concerning the limits of change and the wisdom which comes with age and suffering. If it appears pessimistic, it also offers the benefit of avoiding disappointment.

Phenomenologically, also, it is not by accident that analytic theory of character emerged from the study of how the mind appreciates its own aggression, hurting and being hurt, and the gratifications of attacking and being attacked as conceptualized in the anal phase. Recurrently, as analysts, we are awestruck by repetition and masochism, as well as by clinical experience with the permutations of negativity in response to our therapeutic actions. For Andrew and Quentin, masochistic qualities of character could be followed to the bedrock of experience, to the distribution of aggression, the psychic ambassador of Thanatos, in the earliest phases of development (Winnicott, 1950). Within psychoanalysis, the development of character in general—and for any particular child—can be understood as how aggression becomes bound to libido or not, is projected outwardly, is organized in the superego, or remains unbound or unrepresented as an ethereal and yet powerful reservoir of gloom (see Hartmann and Loewenstein, 1962). In this history of character being forged in the furnace of aggression, we can see fantasy as an expression of those vital forces of

Life which represent the mind trying to understand and integrate itself. Perhaps this point can be put even more strongly—in a way which is reminiscent of Reich—if we think of character in terms of fantasy configurations fueled mostly by aggression and modulated by love.

Later contributions to the analytic theory of character have speculated on the process by which the distribution of aggression and its fantasized representations are influenced by experience. Loewald (1971, 1978b) has vividly conveyed the origins of the aggressive instincts in parallel to those of the libidinal; we now speak comfortably of how, from a psychological point of view, all instinctual life—destructiveness vs. affiliation, aggression vs. love, Thanatos vs. Eros—emerges from the context of social, and particularly mother-child, interaction. In this, he echoes Klein's (1957) concern for the early appearance of persistent patterns of experience of aggression in the oral phase and Jacobson's (1954) theories of pre-genital patterning. But Klein, in contrast with Loewald, diminishes the mother in the matrix to emphasize the child's contributions. For her, the characterological patterning of aggression owes more to the child's hunger—his fantasies of greed and his response to the recognition of responsibility—than to the caregiving environment in which it is experienced.

From whatever orientation, disturbances in the earliest modulation of aggression are seen within psychoanalysis today to have enduring impact on character. Such disturbances may arise from inborn or constitutional factors (including hereditary factors or congenital disturbances in the sensory system); from early and persistent pain or disruption of the pleasure-pain balance (e.g., from the trauma of physical illness or abuse); or from deviations in early caregiving, as with our patients who were doubly burdened with genetic predisposition (see Greenacre, 1967). The lives of individuals with impaired modulation of aggression are more or less forever shaped by the struggle to represent or make sense of aggression, and to find enough nurturance to enable the building up of internal structures of self-esteem regulation (such as the internalized, good-enough breast that becomes a function of the self) which can withstand fragmentation in the face of hurt and rage (Kohut, 1971; Kohut, 1977). Some aspects of the balance between the child's constitution and parental responsivity have been conveyed under the rubric of "attunement" and the mother's capacity for primary maternal preoccupation (Winnicott, 1956). Similar phenomena have been pointed to in relation to "mirroring" (Kohut, 1971).

For whatever reasons, when the modulation of aggression has been impaired, a person is vulnerable to a disorder of internalization of the types experienced by Andrew and Quentin. And where the child has not been able to create the template of the caregiving other as a constituent part of the self, the good-enough breast as self-object, there will be later failures of internalization during processes which are potentially therapeutic in the course of life, for example, in friendship and in analysis. Individuals with autism have inborn errors of metabolism: they cannot make use of others from the start; those with early failures of internalization have acquired errors of metabolism: they cannot make use of the nutrients of caregiving later for enrichment of self and development of higher levels of representation of aggression. Each opportunity for renovation also poses a threat for disappointment, and thus more enragement. Psychoanalysis is such an opportunity, and the threat of negative therapeutic reaction is the danger (Loewald, 1972a). For Andrew, aggression was not well enough represented to be open to interpretative mutation; for Quentin, it threatened therapy but ultimately was met in therapeutic combat (Freud, 1972a).

The psychoanalytic theory of character has a tendency to appear metaphysical since it deals with origins at the beginning of inner life and with endings, in the recognition that at the completion of analysis and of development, I can have no other body than this one and must remain wary of losing what I am and have. Psychoanalytic theory also approaches the field of ethics, the value of leading an authentic life true to one's values and respectful of the needs and rights of others. In this presentation, I have emphasized the pragmatism of the theory, its clinical application, and confrontation of the psychoanalyst's conceptions of therapy and its goals.

ACKNOWLEDGMENTS

Dr. Albert J. Solnit's teaching and encouragement are reflected throughout this paper, which is dedicated to him on the occasion of his 70th birthday.

Chapter 7 Playing and Therapeutic Action in Child Analysis (1993)

Linda C. Mayes and Donald J. Cohen

Child psychoanalysts are called upon to help with children whose development has often gone markedly off course. In the forty years since Anna Freud (Freud, 1957) began seeing children at the Hampstead clinic, psychoanalytic forms of treatment have been used with children exhibiting many types of impairments in their early development. These have included children with disorders of conduct and the regulation of aggression; those markedly inhibited by their anxious concerns about separation and object loss; and those for whom the social world remains essentially an enigma. While we are only beginning to address systematically what aspects of child analytic technique are beneficial for what types of developmental disturbance, the richness and depth of the experience accumulated by child analysts across the world has brought about a number of important shifts in technique and theory (Sandler et al., 1980).

Unlike analysis with adults, child analysis necessarily takes place in the face of rapidly occurring maturational shifts and tensions that

First appeared in *International Journal of Psychoanalysis* 74(6): 1235–1244 (1993).

bring issues of biology and endowment more immediately within the analytic frame of reference (Mayes and Cohen, 1995). Such developmental urgency often requires the analyst to be actively involved in the child's reality-based outer as well as imaginary inner worlds. At the very least, the child analyst serves not only as an observer and interpreter of the material the child presents within the hour, but often is called upon actually to participate in the child's play, to keep the child physically safe during moments of intense anger and frustration, and to interact directly with the child's family. The immediacy of action and impulses pushing for expression in children has required child analysts to consider in depth issues of permitted gratification or frustration of wishes, and to place these technical interventions in a developmental frame. Actually gratifying a 3-year-old's wish for physical closeness may be essential for the analytic process, while the same might not be true for a latency age child. Contributions from other fields similarly concerned with understanding the emergence of various psychic functions in early childhood have also aided in the gradual defining and remodeling of child analytic technique. For instance, how to structure and phrase interpretations at developmentally appropriate levels is informed by ongoing research in related fields about young children's capacities to understand affects, beliefs, and related notions of mental functions in themselves and others (e.g. Mayes and Cohen, 1992; Mayes and Cohen, 1994).

Indeed, the technical acts broadly encompassed by the term interpretation take on a different cast in work with pre-adolescent children precisely because of their varying capacities to express and understand verbally the wishes and conflicts of their own and others' inner worlds. Child analysts are by necessity quite cognizant of the multiple, nonverbal modalities that are readily available for conveying affects, thoughts, and fantasies. An essential, daily, child analytic task is to find (and understand) the substitutes for verbal communication that will adequately convey to both child and analyst the essential nature of the child's developmentally stagnating conflicts. The familiar modes of verbal clarification and interpretation fundamental to analytic work with adults are often of limited value for many youngsters entering analysis and may only gradually, and to a limited extent, become the central medium of the therapeutic work. For some children, playing carries much of the therapeutic work aimed at facilitating the child's return to developmentally appropriate and adaptive psychic functioning. The creation of the therapeutic space in which playing may unfold and the utilization of play in the service of treatment are tasks unique to the child analyst.

Several analysts have discussed the role of play as an aide to interpretation, for through play the child is able to externalize and displace apparently disruptive, confusing, conflict-laden wishes (e.g. Neubauer, 1987; Ritvo, 1978). The capacity for fantasy play draws upon a number of mental actions, including the ability to appreciate the subjective nature of the mental world; that is, to appreciate that "just pretending" provides a world where the child is able to try out relationships, identifications, and solutions. In the provision of a subjective space for trial action and thought, the medium of play facilitates the emergence of unconscious material. Using the content of the play, the analyst may, in turn, phrase interpretations that are at least one step removed from speaking directly to and about the child. For some children, interpreting in this manner within the play is less anxiety-provoking and threatening. However, there arise inevitable tensions between allowing play to emerge as a therapeutic process in its own right and the usual psychoanalytic emphasis on clarification, verbalization and, above all, interpretation within and about the transference. For example, Anna Freud and others have often cautioned that the child's fantasy play may serve equally well the roles of defense and resistance (Sandler et al., 1980), and that at some point the analyst must, in effect, step outside the play and bring the material back to the child's own self, wishes and conflicts.

The apparent tension between creating a space that facilitates the child's efforts to play and the overall analytic goal of verbal interpretation to make explicit unconscious wishes and conflicts raises at least two questions. Firstly, the issue of timing: how and when does the child analyst decide to make explicit the child's externalization of his own self in the story and action of the play? Constructing an interpretation that suggests to the child that he often feels or behaves like the characters represented in his fantasy play requests that he accept at another level of awareness the content of his play narrative. The second and related question concerns the therapeutic action of play itself; that is, that the very process of enactment through fantasy play in the space of the analysis is, in and of itself, developmentally restorative. In this context, the role of the analyst is to facilitate and support the child's efforts toward fantasy play; interpretations are, in effect, contained within and elaborate upon the story represented in the fantasy.

In the two case examples that follow, we describe two children for whom the process of enactment within the fantasy play itself was apparently therapeutic, as evidenced by their improved adaptive capacities outside the analysis and their increased ability within the analysis to move freely between their fantasy play and references to themselves and their own difficulties. Two caveats are in order before presenting the illustrative clinical material. Firstly, when speaking of play as a therapeutic process, we are referring to imaginary or fantasy play. Children use a number of different modes of playing within any therapeutic relationship, such as persistently and intently playing board games, demonstrating their physical, athletic abilities, or carefully arranging the play space in preparation for a sometimes only very brief imaginary scene. These modes of playing are also communicative to the analyst about the child and may have restorative functions, but are more often the child's prelude (or impediment) either to a more elaborate fantasy or a more direct expression of their conflicts and worries. The second caveat is that we do not wish to create an artificial dichotomy between interpreting within the child's fantasy or, as it were, from outside. As the clinical examples will illustrate, these are not two mutually exclusive therapeutic approaches, but rather they serve as both complementary and alternative techniques for any given hour with any particular child. The apparent dichotomy highlighted for the purposes of this discussion allows clarification of both a metapsychological issue and a point of technique. Metapsychologically, the question is: how can fantasy play be psychologically and developmentally restorative? The technical task is to decide for which child and at what moment is it more appropriate to rely upon the therapeutic impact of the fantasy action itself.

CLINICAL ILLUSTRATIONS

Clare

Clare was a verbally precocious, petite girl, who entered analysis at the age of 38 months because of a combination of withholding stools and constipation, and increasing difficulties at moments of separation from her parents. New persons or situations predictably sent Clare hiding behind her mother and clinging tightly to her mother's legs. If urged to join the group or try the new activity, she would adamantly scream "no," cover her face, and cling ever tighter, or else dissolve into tearful, panicked fright. She often woke her parents at night when she experienced abdominal cramping due to her constipation, but also seemed to need, beyond their physical care, the reassurance that they were quickly available and ever present. Her clinging need to hold on and stay close seemed to pervade nearly every aspect of her daily life, and she became more and more frequently and easily upset by changes in her routine. Though Clare was able to attend a nursery school program at least two of the four mornings a week, she would tearfully and anxiously protest her mother's leaving her behind. Clare's parents were perplexed and worried for they had always been with her. Clare's mother stayed at home and her father was often able to be with his daughter at different times during the day. They watched in distress as their verbal, bright daughter seemed increasingly tormented and sad.

In her pre-analytic, diagnostic sessions, Clare, though reticent and wary, quickly took verbal control and carried on a lengthy discourse about the various materials and toys in the room. She carefully rearranged and ordered the toys that were on a table and declared adamantly that she preferred to do puzzles and other similarly structured tasks. She did not want to pretend or play with toys and despite the analyst's attempts to interest her in drawings with stories, she insisted that the pictures were just pictures—there were no stories involved. However, during a later diagnostic session she volunteered that she thought her blanket, which she carried everywhere, was very sick and might need to see a doctor for a long time, "perhaps at least two or three weeks." She asked the analyst to tell her a story about a toy figure sitting on the table, whom she also thought might be quite sick. When the analyst said that the toy did seem to have quite a few worries and was at times very unhappy, Clare stared intently at the analyst and then soberly asked for more information about what the toy might be worried about and whether the doctor would be able to help with these worries.

Such clarification and work within an albeit highly-structured and ordered play characterized the first weeks to months of Clare's analysis. During this time, Clare did not allow the analyst to speak directly about her or to suggest that she too might have worries or that the "mad, angry" faces she often drew bore any relation to her own inner world. For weeks into the analysis she would begin her sessions by urgently announcing the "plan" for what she would do—the puzzles to be worked, the number of drawings of shapes to be completed, the types of duplo-block structures she would make—all without associated fantasy, but rather "just shapes." The analyst interpreted this as a need for predictability—for the safety of knowing exactly what would happen—just as she wanted to know just where her parents were, and worried about being left alone or about letting loose scary feelings, but Clare remained stolidly wedded to her strategic plans. Gradually, it became clearer that her determined planning also served to mediate how close she could, or would, allow herself to be with the analyst. While intently drawing yet another picture of various geometric shapes she said, "I love to draw because only I know what the drawing will do—you don't know, I do."

As the first weeks moved into months, Clare gradually relaxed her self-imposed restriction on her own symbolic and fantasy life. She increasingly used her structured activities as a safe haven when the implicit freedom to play imaginatively apparently became too stressful. Her first move into explicit symbolic expression occurred when she picked up a container of modeling clay and began almost absent-mindedly rolling round balls. Suddenly, she looked up, held up a ball of clay, and said "my poops" and proceeded to speak in detail about the somatic symptom that had in part brought her into analysis. In the middle of her discussion, she dropped the clay and ran to a toy phone to call her mother who was waiting just outside the playroom door. As her primary somatic symptom was slowly resolved in the weeks that followed, Clare began to play imaginatively and filled the hours with play about broken things that urgently needed fixing. She created settings in which characters held on to special secrets that they smilingly refused ever to let out. During this period, Clare again allowed the analyst to interpret only within the context of her created stories and to attribute wishes and conflicts to the characters in the play but never to her. Any violation of this critical distinction sent her urgently back to her familiar ordering and structure-building.

As Clare's fantasy play deepened, so for a time did her difficulties with separations. Every situation seemed to her laden with the possibility of loss—it was as if when she surrendered some of her need for sameness and structure, the worries she had about being close or being separate were ever upon her. She had difficulties beginning and ending sessions. Often, even as she was standing on one foot poised on the threshold of the playroom door, with a worried look she would throw her beloved blanket in first, both as an apparent trial separation and as a sacrifice to the dangers lurking in the playroom, as affects and wishes were freed. Toward the end of her first 15 months of analysis, Clare was earnestly playing with characters caught in the painfully inevitable dilemma of growing up and the agonies of renouncing babyish ways for the mixed blessings of being older, which carried with it so many unknowns. She joyfully created games about all-powerful, magical beings who were able to give people new bodies and to make the old young again. The limitlessness of the roles she created alternated with a sober maturity as she solemnly told some of the characters in her stories that hard as they might wish to be a baby again, it was not possible. Her characters never enthusiastically, or with any sense of adventure or achievement, left their familiar surroundings for long. They always returned; sometimes with a foreboding dread that there would he many changes in the people or places they had left behind. It seemed that, even as she became more freely playful at home and at school, for Clare, just beyond what she could not see or hear, there were always inner dragons, which she confronted directly through her emerging capacity for fantasy.

Through her fantasy play, Clare created for herself a stage on which she represented in only thinly disguised verse the issues that had stalled her development. The displacement on to the stage was apparently crucial for her. The work of the analysis was to interpret gradually what made it difficult or frightening for Clare to play and how, when she was scared of what might happen in her stories, she returned to the safety of controlled routines that at the same time made it difficult for her to move forward. Clare slowly developed a greater ease in shifting in and out of the pretend and the context of the play, and in then allowing the themes of her stories to be brought home to her. One day, as she listened to a book she was quite fond of that told a story about the ever-present changes in the seasons and a little girl's struggle to understand these changes, she agreed that the little girl was like her, but younger, because the girl couldn't yet swim. Gradually, with an explicitly expressed mixture of sadness and pride, Clare went on to longer days at school, surrendered her crib, left her blanket at home (except when she came to her analysis), and moved out into the world of her peers. Her teachers described her as a leader and as a cheerfully imaginative child, and her parents felt she was more and more relaxed and free. Transitions, an ever-present worry for Clare, became times when she was able more readily to use the world of fantasy in the service of mastery. But occasionally the transitional moment was too much, and she would return to the comfort and predictability of her routines.

Jep

Jep was the most active boy in his Montessori nursery school. His teacher notified his parents that in all her years she had never seen a boy who seemed so hyped up, so full of energy and ideas that he could not concentrate on the small tasks at hand. He would start a clever plan, but then would quickly lose interest and move on to something else. Of greatest interest to him was the activity of another child; he would start by helping but within minutes would create chaos. A physician had prescribed and tried a course of stimulant medications, which had made Jep irritable and unhappy. A therapist had attempted and terminated a course of therapy, which Jep had "resisted"; he simply would not listen to anything she said and he seemed set on showing her that nobody could be his boss.

Jep's father was a creative novelist and intellectual consultant, a winner of international prizes who made large sums of money on individual projects and then drank up the profits in months of intoxication. His mother was a beautiful, level-headed, and gifted actress who had worked her way up from a lower middle-class, janitor's family into social prominence. If you were entertaining the Shah of Iran, she would be the woman you would seat him next to at dinner, or, more likely, she would be asked to host the dinner and make the toast. Jep's younger brother was a sweet child who was interested in nature and drawing.

Jep entered analysis at the age of 5 as a beautiful, sparkling, whirling dervish. Within minutes, the office was covered with play materials as he engaged in non-stop organizing and disorganizing and discoursed on whatever popped into his mind. Over the course of months, the bouts of play became longer and the tension between activity and passivity became enacted in relation to the analyst. At times he would stand on top of the desk or the bookcase and threaten to jump. Occasionally, he would jump, hurt himself, sprawl on the floor, and then deny that he had felt any pain. At other times, he would seem depleted and dazed and would come close and sit on the analyst's lap or near his feet.

Dramatic themes were elaborated within the play and became routines into which Jep and the analyst could move quickly. These included a routine in which Jep was the editor and the analyst was a worker on a newspaper; one in which he was superman and the analyst was a friend who sometimes needed to be helped; and in another, both were hunters in the forest behind Jep's house and there were wild dogs. Much wild play had to do with small figures who were wrestling, examining each other's bodies, vomiting, and yelling. The small object play could quickly become transformed into Jep taking on one of the roles in the room and throwing, pretending to feel sick, or the like.

A good deal of the analytic work over the course of two years was involved in trying to slow down the rush of ideas and transitions through interpretation, within the play, of the worries that were being expressed about loss of control, fears of being hurt, bewilderment about the behavior of adults, and fear of strong sexual feelings, which poured out in play, masturbation and diffuse overactivity and arousal. With time, Jep was able to move outside the play and describe more of what he had seen during his father's drinking binges—the slapping, throwing of pots and pans, passing out. His father would hug him and say sweet things about his beauty and importance: "You are the most wonderful thing I have ever created." A few minutes later, his father might throw him out of the study for messing something up or just slump into his chair and fall asleep snoring, leaving Jep standing nearby. He would hear his mother scream at his father for what he was doing to the family, and then see his mother burst into tears, or leave the house threatening never to return. He was also able to describe fleetingly the excitement of undressing with an older boy and playing with each other.

How could a 6- or 7-year-old communicate and then attempt to understand the rapid shifts between being the child savior of the family and then being ignored, as the adults collapsed, battled or escaped? Except through his play, Jep could not find words to convey the sexual and aggressive excitement in which he lived, into which he was pulled, and out of which he created a thrilling mode of stimulating himself to the point of exhaustion. His own self-representation was not as a child, but as the confidant, consoler and reassurance of his parents, as well as an erotic and narcissistic plaything.

Within the analytic work with Jep, the first tasks were to survive his attacks on objects, his provocations, his limitless activity, his oppositionality, and his adamant refusal to listen. Later, he brought to sessions his self-destructiveness and his need to be comforted, both expressed in direct action. Through engagement in the play themes, calm acceptance of the activity, and a readiness to be used in the variety of ways which were demanded by Jep, the analyst was slowly able to articulate, in play and in words, some of the tremendous tensions from outside and inside to which this fragile child's mental apparatus was exposed. Treatment was prematurely brought to a close by the violent death of his father, which was followed soon afterwards by the death of his sister from cancer.

DISCUSSION

For both Clare and Jep, the ability to engage in the process of imaginative play represented a critical therapeutic point in the analysis. Both had been affectively and adaptively unable to find a means to represent for themselves, as much as for others, the content of their distress. Jep relied on the distractive whirl of his activity, while Clare took refuge in her insistence on sameness and structure. For each, the medium of imaginary play facilitated the therapeutic work, and in their play both found the words for their deepest dilemmas. In each instance, the primary goal of the analytic work, at least in the beginning and middle phase of the analysis, was to create a place in which each child could begin to play imaginatively. Interpretive work centered around those issues that made it difficult or overwhelming for either child to enter the imaginary world, and only later was it possible to translate interpretively the content of the imaginary world back to the child. Clare and Jep differed dramatically in their use of play. For Clare, the imaginary world was a place where she could more expansively and clearly communicate her troubles, while for Jep the play space was the place where he could safely represent the fears, excitement and dangers that were as much a part of his external as his inner world. Therapeutically, for Clare, play was liberating, while for Jep it served as an important protective haven where the horrors of his world could be more safely examined: Both children also seemed to improve in their day-to-day lives as their ability to play imaginatively within the analysis emerged. How play serves such an apparently restorative function is a crucial issue for understanding the role of imaginary play in the therapeutic work of child analysis.

From the vast domain of observation and experience of children in treatment and in other settings, child psychoanalysts have acquired multiple senses of the mental processes that underlie children's play. The psychoanalytic theory of play is not a formal, deductive set of hypotheses, but an orientation to the complex geography of the child's inner world. Within the inner life of the child, play is a mental process which takes its stand along with, intermingles with, builds upon and integrates with many other mental processes in the developing child's mind—thinking, imagining, pretending, planning, wondering, doubting, remembering, guessing, hoping, experimenting, revising and working through. The child at play makes use of these varied mental processes. In turn, the emergence of more sophisticated mental capacities that allow the child to appreciate the distinction between his subjective mental world and that which is directly perceivable make possible increasingly elaborate, sophisticated fantasy play (Mayes and Cohen, 1992). While playing, the child integrates his past experiences and his current feelings and desires. Using the capacity to play, he or she explores the inner and outer world, investigates hypotheses and possibilities, and moves ahead in personal development. In the repetitions of play, the child masters what he has experienced; through the creativity of play, through internal playfulness and external play, the child reviews, advances and conquers past and new territories. Further, through the act of imagination and fantasy within the play, the child is able to explore relationships with important others and to have others be as he needs them to be at that moment (Mayes and Cohen, 1992).

There are many meanings of play for children and for psychoanalysts who work with them (Erikson, 1987; Moran, 1987; Neubauer, 1987). Among these meanings are play as a representation and expression of the child's experiences and affects, and as a window into the child's self-representations and conflicts. Play as a communicative medium by which the child conveys his understanding of experiences is one basis for using play as a guide to interpretation and clarification. The intrinsic capacity for playing to serve developmental needs has been emphasized by Neubauer (1993, 1987) and Solnit (1987, 1993), and it is in this capacity that play serves as more than a guide to interpretation but is a part of the process of therapeutic change itself. The therapeutic, restorative functions of play within the analytic setting have been discussed by child psychoanalysts in a number of ways, beginning as early as 1927 with Anna Freud's lectures on child analysis. Sketching the outlines of a partial theory of therapeutic action, she spoke about children's play in analytic sessions as one of the important facets effecting change. Much later, as she explored the relation between capacities for play and later for work (Freud, 1965), she drew attention to the advances in impulse control and ego maturation which play apparently helps to consolidate; each again representing an area of change also related to the presumed therapeutic action of analysis. But, as (Downey, 1987) points out, between the 1927 lectures on child analysis and the later discussions of the indications for child analysis (Freud, 1945), the role of children's play within the analytic setting was defined and redefined many times and there was, for a time, a tension between playing and verbally interpreting. In part, the use of play by the analyst was caught up in the heated controversy between Anna Freud and Melanie Klein (Klein, 1932), in which each faulted the other for relying too much or too little on playing versus verbalization of the child's conflicts.

During the same period, (Waelder, 1932) defined multiple functions of play, including mastery, wish-fulfillment, and the assimilation of experiences and delineated play as an internalizing, healing, structure-building process in its own right that supported the emergence of children's gradual self-awareness. Through these synthetic functions, playing has the potential power to help move development forward by allowing the child to review his current situation, explore new possibilities, experiment with new solutions, and find new integrations. Play provides children with the earliest version of a self-reflective capacity. In much of Winnicott's work, too, there is the sense that playing, as such, may facilitate development, both in and out of therapy (Winnicott, 1971). Within the treatment setting, facilitating the play, particularly for Winnicott the spontaneous fantasy play in which both child and analyst are mutually involved, provides the significant contribution to therapeutic change: "[During the play] the significant moment is that at which the child surprises himself or herself: It is not the moment of my clever interpretation that is significant" (Winnicott, 1971, p. 51).

In therapy, as in life, it is sometimes not necessary, or even useful, for the psychoanalyst to interpret (in words) the child's play for this facilitation to proceed (Cohen and Cohen, 1993). The mobilization of the child's capacities for play, perhaps through the use of transference, may enable the child to do what is needed for his development to continue. For some children, such as Clare, additional verbalization outside, or during the play, may impede their embracing fully the necessity of playing and, paradoxically, slow their coming to use fantasy in the service of intrapsychic adaptation. The technical issue is when and how the analyst chooses to interpret the content of the play back to the child such that the child's playfulness is sustained even while he and the analyst step briefly outside the fantasy.

When the analyst chooses to interpret the content of the play vis-à-vis the story it conveys about the child's own wishes and worries, it is important to underscore the ways in which play does far more than merely repeat or symbolize the child's actual external experiences, or even his or her reactions to those experiences. In interpreting or understanding what a child is expressing in play, therefore, one cannot simply read the surface presentation of themes, affects or episodes. In their play, choirboys become gangsters; an oppositional, defiant 5-year-old takes on the role of a nursing mother; hurt and abandoned children are surrounded by a loving family; those who are well cared for attack dangerous enemies. Jep became a truck driver to try to keep his feelings in line and Clare used the playroom as her place to roam freely within her own story, as enacted by characters she had created. Children at play do not simply act out what they have seen or felt or even simply what they wish for—they imagine and try on, as Clare did in her repeated stories about regaining a lost infancy. Thus, any particular type of play—aggressive or loving, exhibitionistic or bashful, sexually provocative or sexually timid—must be read with caution as to its implications about what the child has seen, done or felt. More specifically, the play must be read, by the analyst, within the theory of transference, in which the preconscious moves towards consciousness and undergoes the transformations that we conceptualize as sublimation and displacement. The analyst's reading, however, is not a script that demands verbal interpretation, since sometimes little need be said about what the child is saying about himself. In many instances, more need be said about what does and does not make it possible for a child to play with a sense of pleasure and freedom, rather than what the play itself may or may not convey.

From the first years of life until the very end, a major part of mental life is devoted to trying to understand the life we are living. From childhood onwards, the mental processes which form the psychological substrate for play, as well as actual play that involves action and movement, is a special form of such self-understanding. The capacity for play provides both the child and adult with a powerful instrument for figuring out and coming to grips with mysteries and hardships (Cohen et al., 1087). The play of children who have been traumatized, just as the play of children with severe emotional disorders, may lose its vitality and openness and be unable to serve this process of self-reflective understanding. The play of children such as Jep, who are over stimulated and exposed to forces beyond their control or comprehension, may break through the structures in which play must be contained in order to distinguish it from the real world and real consequences.

Both Clare and Jep had difficulty finding the means to engage in pretending—one to engage at all and the other to contain the rush of overwhelming feelings within the pretend. As a result, both were stalled in their development. For Jep, life was too creative, spontaneous, exciting and unpredictable; there was no shortage of thrills, dangers or strong emotions in his life. He was the center of parental concern, a beautiful, adored, brilliant, magazine-cover child. His thrills were too much for a small child to contain, and his thoughts and feelings spilled over. In analysis, he found ways of creating some narrative structures through the close, patient engagement of an analyst who neither needed nor rejected him, who did not seduce or adore him, or forget that he was a child who could be hurt. His self-representation was fragmented and he was overwhelmed by his thrilling ideas and the dangers that he created for himself and for others who got in his path. In analysis, he was gradually able to give voice to a more childish need for protection and comfort but resisted this mode by self-stimulation. The attractions of thrilling overstimulation remained powerful influences on his activity within and outside of analysis.

For Clare, gaining access to a capacity for imagination and for play provided her with a communicative medium that far exceeded even her precocious verbal skills. She was able to express for herself through play that which was, at least for a time, beyond words. Caught in the universal and inevitable dilemma of being carried along toward independence and separation by the forces of maturation, Clare used every means at her disposal to resist those thrusts. The earliest marks of her character were organized around her stolid routines, which kept her on what seemed stable but developmentally unmoving ground. The stability was, however, an illusion, for with it came unsettling tensions and unhappiness. Like Jep, through the transferential relationship Clare could hesitantly let go of her anchors to reveal to herself as well as to the analyst the wishes and fears that were holding her back. The play became not just a safely displaced way to represent her developmental instabilities—the very spontaneity of the fantasy itself stood in stark and healing contrast to the restraints that she easily imposed on her actions and thoughts.

SUMMARY

From its inception, child psychoanalysis has used fantasy play as a window to both the content and process of children's inner worlds. Because of the link to action and primary process, young children's imaginary play is rich in symbolic expressions that facilitate analytic interpretive interventions addressing the conflicts impeding development. There are inevitable tensions between allowing play to emerge as a therapeutic process in its own right and the usual psychoanalytic emphasis on clarification, verbalization and, above all, interpretation within and about the transference. For many children, the very act of playing carries much of the therapeutic work aimed toward facilitating their return to developmentally appropriate and adaptive psychic functioning. The mobilization of capacities for play in the analysis allows children to do what is needed for their development to continue and makes use of the developmentally restorative functions of play in the service of therapeutic action.

ACKNOWLEDGMENTS

The ideas in this presentation reflect discussions of the Study Group on the Many Meanings of Play in Child Psychoanalysis sponsored by the Psychoanalytic Research and Development Fund and the work of the study group on play in the Child Study Center. We especially wish to acknowledge the contributions of our clinical collaborators and colleagues Catherine Cox, Albert J. Solnit, Peter Neubauer, Steven Marans, Phyllis Cohen and Matthew Cohen.

Chapter 8 The Development of a Capacity for Imagination in Early Childhood (1992)

Linda C. Mayes and Donald J. Cohen

There are no days in life so memorable as those which vibrated to some stroke of the imagination.
—Emerson, *The Conduct of Life* (1860)

Popularly conceived, imagination is the province of play, art, and scientific genius and properly belongs to children, artists, and the gifted few who are able to see old problems in a new light. These individuals are given a license to imagine for the rest of the world to respect and simultaneously contain lest such license carry its holder beyond the limits of accepted creative ambiguity. While imagination is seen as the opposite of reality and is as free and unlimited as logical thought is methodical and rule-bound, there are limits to what we intuitively accept as imaginative and what we do not. We praise the creative imagination of the artist or young child but are suspicious of the inventions

First appeared in *The Psychoanalytic Study of the Child,* Volume 47, eds. Albert J. Solnit, Peter B. Neubauer, Samuel Abrams, and A. Scott Dowling (New Haven: Yale University Press, 1992). Copyright © 1992, Albert J. Solnit, Peter B. Neubauer, Samuel Abrams, and A. Scott Dowling. All rights reserved.

of the conspirator and eccentric. We admire imagination in the service of resourcefulness and solutions to difficult dilemmas but may scorn the individual
who rarely has a product or settlement to show for his musings, however "imaginative" or novel they may be. We delight in the playfulness of a good storyteller, child or adult, but become uneasy when the fantasy becomes too fantas-
tic or violates too many veridical conventions.

Whenever a term with so many layers of meaning and implications is ab-
sorbed into a general psychology of mental functioning, its technical applications may be confounded and interwoven with its popular usage. Within psychoanalysis, imagination is broadly used as both verb and noun, as process and
product. It is the process of creating mental images in the service of wish fulfillment or defense but is evident in the products of dreams, symptoms, children's
play, parapraxes, and transferential phenomena, each of which represents the
data of the psychoanalytic process. It is seen as ubiquitous to all mental life and
at the same time special to the creative act (Lee, 1949). Imagination is often
used synonymously with unconscious fantasies, primary process, mental representation, or free association. As in the popular usage, there is an assumed optimal balance between the actions of too much and too little imagination in the
services of reality testing, the regulation of tension, and ego organization. Too
much imagination impairs the individual's capacity to judge reality and to use
thought as trial action, while too little imagination grounds that person in a
stale, rarely novel, affectively impoverished world.

Imagination then in the psychoanalytic frame of reference broadly encom-
passes a number of interrelated functions and concepts (Beres, 1960a; Beres,
1960b; Rosen, 1960), including the capacity to create a fantasy, the ability to use
such a fantasy in the service of affect regulation and/or defense, the synthesis of
memories and percepts into a mental image of a person or thing which is not
present, and the inner world of mental representations as opposed to the external world of sensory perceptions. From the psychoanalytic point of view, imagination involves the creation of an inner world of subjectivity against which
one judges (consciously and unconsciously) the objective, veridical world and
in which there is the freedom to perceive and remodel others as one wishes or
needs them to be. Implied, but not directly highlighted, by this broad application of the term is how the capacity to imagine the other in multiple ways is a
central precondition for the creation of the self-defining fantasies characteristic
of the oedipal phase.

For example, in the following brief fragment of play, a 5-year-old girl uses her
imagination to try on multiple roles for herself and her relationships with oth-

ers. As she quietly arranges furniture in a doll-house, she introduces a family including a little girl, the father, a baby brother, and a mother. She arranges and rearranges the dolls, first placing the two children together between the parents, then the baby brother with the mother, the little girl with the father, then the father and mother together with both children off to the side. She sings and whispers to herself as she places her characters in their assigned beds. Abruptly, the little girl takes her baby brother, and they leave to go on a very long trip to a magic place. They take few supplies, but the little girl is very resourceful. She knows where to look for food and how to take care of everyone, including her baby brother who feels quite lonely and hungry. The little girl reassures her brother that she can do everything just like their mother. The parents are very worried and do not know quite what to do. The mother tries several times to find her children but stops her search when it gets dark. Only the father is able to make it through the cold snow, dense forest, and other continuously appearing tests of endurance to find his two lost children. He praises the little girl for her resourcefulness and for how grown-up she is and promises her that he will protect her always, even from her mother's anger at her for going away.

The capacity to tolerate multiple, often conflicting views of the object world is made possible by a capacity to imagine; and the ability to represent wishes and desires vis-à-vis multiple others characterizes the fantasy play of the oedipal-aged child (Cohen et al., 1987; Marans et al., 1991). These fantasies move development forward, for it is through them that the child develops a view of himself in relation to others and is able to try on and act out the consequences he anticipates from the imaginary relationships he creates. In turn, the capacity to imagine the other requires the integration of a number of specific neurocognitive functions that also mature between the third and sixth year of life, e.g., distinguishing thought from action and understanding that others as well as oneself are motivated to act because of mental states such as feelings, beliefs, and fantasies (Wellman 1988, 1990).

In this paper, we offer an integration of observations from psychoanalytically informed studies of the emergence of fantasy play in the oedipal phase with findings from recent work on how children acquire an understanding of their own and others' mental processes (reviewed in Astington et al., 1988). Based on observations from our ongoing studies of the play of oedipal-aged children (Cohen et al., 1987; Marans et al., 1991), we mark out the preconditions for one aspect of imagination, that which is involved in the creation of an internal object world. Imagination as a mental capacity is part of a line of development that begins in the earliest symbiotic interactions between mother and infant, takes further shape as the child moves from dyadic to triadic relations, and culminates in a fully mature capacity to reflect upon in thought one's wishes and feelings vis-à-vis multiple others. We suggest that particularly for the 3- to 5-year-old child, imagination represents a special mode of mental functioning which allows him not only to demarcate the physical (or perceivable) and the mental (or fantasized) world, but more importantly expands his internal object world and motivates him toward increasingly complex relationships with others.

With a capacity for imagination, relationships with others are colored both by the child's previous experiences and by his imagined wishes and beliefs. The capacity for sustained imaginary play emerges in parallel with the child's acquisition of an understanding of how the actions and words of others reflect and are motivated by their feelings, beliefs, wishes, and memories, each actions of mind. Such an understanding allows the child to imbue the persons in his imaginary play with complex feelings and desires toward others, and to create the stories, or an inner world, by which he defines himself and through which he will continue to view and define his external world.

THE PREVERBAL ROOTS OF THE MENTAL CAPACITY FOR IMAGINATION

The verb imagine and its related derivatives imagination and imaginary have their origin in two related words, the Latin verb *imaginari* and the noun *imago.* The combination of these two root words gives a fundamentally object-related quality to the process of imagining for *imago,* especially in the plural, referred to portraits of ancestors which were placed in the atria of Roman homes or carried in family funeral processions (Glare, 1982). As a verb, *imaginari* implied the act of picturing to oneself. Later usages of imago by poets such as Virgil and Ovid conveyed the notion of a mental image, an idea, or pretence, most often of another person. With time, the word imagine came to mean the creation of a mental image of something never before wholly or similarly perceived in reality by the imaginer, or the capacity to form concepts beyond those derived from external objects (Oxford English Dictionary, 1989).

Freud never discussed imagination as a process per se but did use the term generally to imply the creation of mental images and the use of fantasy in the service of wish fulfillment and the mastery of anxiety. In *Beyond the Pleasure Principle* (Freud, 1920) he described his observations of an 18-month-old child who responded to a parent's absence by playing a disappearing game with an object on a string. The child actively and pleasurably made the object vanish and then reappear by pulling on the string. By so doing, he turned his passive experience of anxiety and sadness at the disappearance of important objects into active pleasure at being able to make the toy disappear and reappear at will. As Rosen (1960) also points out, such play in action is analogous to the difference between passively perceiving an object when present and actively evoking the memory, or later imagining the scene, when the object is absent. In her concept of developmental lines, Anna Freud (Freud, 1965, 1973) did not specifically discuss imagination or the process of being able to create actively a fantasy in the service of anxiety regulation. She did, however, outline the line of development that proceeds from the physical to the mental world, which includes the progression from play with body to play with fantasy and from direct somatic expression of wishes and conflicts to the capacity to express the same in thoughts and language. While this particular progression captures some of the manifest qualities of the development of an imaginative capacity, it does not expand upon how the capacity for imagination develops out of a social matrix and how, in early development, imagination is essential for the child's appreciation of an increasingly complex social world.

Stated simply, the need for an imaginative capacity comes into being as the child wants or desires those individuals whom he does not or cannot have at that moment. The fantasies of the oedipal-aged child express, and in some ways gratify, these desires, but there are a number of functional preconditions for the characteristic oedipal-phase fantasies. In the first three years of life for normally developing children, several perceptual, neurological, and cognitive functions mature in such a way as to allow the child increasing separateness from the parent. These functions involve minimally the capacity to evoke a mental image of the other, to remember previous experiences with that other, and the ability to modulate one's own states of anxiety in the other's absence. Evoking a mental image of the other is part of the ability to know that the other is absent and to look for that person. For example, Piaget (1937) outlined how the child's understanding of objects in their absence progresses from the 3-month-old's visual tracking the path of a disappearing object without further searching after the object is out of sight to the active searching of an 8- to 10-month-old along the path of displacement. By the beginning of the second year, the child takes into account sequential displacements of an object and will search for it where he last saw it. Finally, by the latter half of the second year, children are able to deal with invisible displacements, that is, they are able to search for something without perceptual reinforcements. Presumably, at this age, the child has a mental representation of the object that exists apart from immediate perception, and is capable of true evocative memory with few to no perceptual cues.

The coming together of these various perceptual and early neurocognitive functions into a capacity first to remember the other in his or her absence (and later to imagine the other in whatever ways the child wishes) fosters the child's increasing independence and moves toward separation and allows him to tolerate the frustration, fear, and sadness engendered by such separation. The infant's move toward a definition of other as distinct from self and the development of a capacity for imagination are tandem processes. Each depends upon the other, and each depends upon the integration of maturing perceptual and neurocognitive abilities to perceive persons as distinct and to remember them.

A central contribution of the psychoanalytic theory of early development has been the conceptualization of the related processes of self-other differentiation, individuation, and internalization, each firmly rooted in the earliest interactions between infant and mother (Loewald, 1977b; Mahler, 1971, 1974; Mahler et al., 1975; Mahler and Furer, 1968; Ritvo and Solnit, 1958; Weil, 1970). In brief summary, the elements of that early mother-infant matrix essential for a developing imaginative capacity involve the connections between the affective experience of the infant and the creation of a representational world (Loewald, 1977b). At the beginning of psychological life, from the infant's point of view, the outside world consists mainly of mother, or perhaps of mother not as person but as the source of food and warmth. At this stage, mother represents the world that acts contingently on the infant's needs, but she exists intrapsychically only inasmuch as the infant needs physically. Such a stage cannot exist for long since the infant soon experiences the frustration engendered by the mother's inevitable absences and delays. Frustration and the ensuing discomfort represent a first break in the sensation of immediate gratification and the first experience of the infant with the separateness between states of physical need and satisfaction of such needs. Through such inevitably repeated experiences and the beginning feelings of separateness, desire for another takes shape for it is that other who can alleviate discomfort.

The contingency of a mother's nurturing acts on the infant's discomforts and the association between her absence and the infant's sense of frustration establish referencing links between the mother's behavior and the affective outcome for the infant. These links in turn contribute to the beginning of a representational world. Through these repeated experiences, both frustrating and gratifying, in the presence of another, memories laden with affective traces are created, and the other of the inner, representational world gradually takes shape (Loewald, 1977b; Mahler and Furer, 1968). In the psychoanalytic frame of reference, we say the infant has begun to internalize a sense of the other through the collective memories, now beginning representations, of repeatedly satisfying (or frustrating) experiences. In the neurocognitive frame of reference, we say the infant has developed a set of schemas based on previous experiences with another person, and such schemas are the basis of his expectations that the other will reappear and behave toward him in certain predictable ways (Lewis and Goldberg, 1969).

Internalizing a sense of the other (or developing experiential schemas) is the essential precursor for developing a capacity to imagine the other, since rudimentary fantasies about the specific (and general) other are created from these early experiential representations. With time, the infant is able to draw on these beginning representations in moments of discomfort or frustration and evoke memories of previously gratifying moments with mother (Loewald, 1972b). Consider, for example, how the crying, hungry infant is temporarily soothed by the sound of his mother's voice calling out from another room, or at times even by the familiar sounds of mother preparing the bottle. We presume with the facilitation of perceptual cues, the infant is "remembering" previous feeding experiences, and these memories are briefly as comforting as the actual experience itself. The capacity to evoke memories of the other is a precursor for the capacity to imagine the other inasmuch as the memories serve to organize the infant and regulate states of tension. Further, in evoking a memory of the other, the infant "uses" a mental activity to re-create the other in mind and to regulate a heightened state of arousal.

The ability to store perceptions in memory and to evoke those memories with appropriate stimuli is a central prerequisite not only in a developmental line for imagination but also in our psychoanalytic models of the self-other differentiation. How early is it apparently possible for the infant to "remember" a previously experienced condition or person? In the studies of contingent learning, 8- to 12-week-old infants evidence recognition memory for certain situations, particularly if those situations were pleasurable (Rovee-Collier and Fagan, 1981; Rovee-Collier et al., 1980). Within the first month of life, recognition memory tasks demonstrate that infants remember non-familiar speech sounds for up to two days (Ungerer et al., 1978), and within the first 6 months, infants require both less exposure time to encode the information and evidence longer retention (Rovee-Collier, 1987). Whether or not young children have a similar capacity for evocative memory is a more difficult empirical question (Nachman and Stern, 1984). It is important to note that while we assume clinically that young children do have the capacity to evoke a memory of the other long before they can describe a memory in words, the empirical evidence for this is unclear.

Beginning to create a sense of the other as separate from self with the attendant emergence of a representational world requires the integration of a number of basic perceptual and neuroregulatory functions. In the first six months, these include the capacities to quiet oneself and to maintain a sustained alert state, to attend to selected elements of the environment, and to make the auditory, visual, and tactile discriminations that are critical for interactions in the animate world (Mayes and Cohen, 1995). For example, within the first three months infants are able to discriminate visual patterns of increasing complexity and contour density (Banks and Salapatek, 1983) and to discriminate changes in the pitch of a speech sequence (Kessen et al., 1979), both essential abilities for social interaction. Similarly, between one and three months, infants evidence the ability to distinguish among different facial affective expressions (Nelson, 1987) and show visual scanning patterns that permit definition of the external boundaries of a face as well as selective scanning of internal features such as eyes or mouth (Haith et al., 1977). Capacities such as these make it possible for the infant to "metabolize" the input from the social world and to begin to form early representations (or schemas) of experiences. Further, these early perceptual experiences with others are necessary not only for the creation of mental representations of others but also for the later ability to use percepts of people in novel ways in the activity of imagining. For example, the young child's pleasure in playing with incongruently matching types of voices to characters is built upon an early perceptual capacity to match congruently voice and facial expression (Walker, 1982). If the saliency of social cues is not reinforced experientially or is diminished because of constitutional impairments (e.g., congenital blindness or deafness), then early disturbances in self-other differentiation result (Fraiberg and Adelson, 1973) with the attendant impairments in later imaginative activity.

In the latter half of the first year and beginning of the second, infants respond with a greater specificity and directedness to their social world, a circumstance that speaks to the increasing fidelity of their mental representations of others and a developing sense of self as agent. The infant becomes the active initiator of more and more communicative exchanges, which also become more specific and differentiated (Bullowa, 1979). The infant draws his mother's attention to a situation—e.g., "joint attention" (Bruner, 1975) and she in turn provides the contextual meaning for the situation and for the infant's actions.

Through their joint efforts, the infant learns to use his feelings and actions to engage others (Shotter and Gregory, 1976) not just for comfort and care but now for play and shared communications. During this time, infants delightedly respond to and sometimes seek out disappearing games such as peek-a-boo that enact with shared pretense the brief comings and goings of the other. The ability to tolerate such games and even to seek them out with pleasure precedes (and is a necessary precondition for) the capacity to create similar situations in thought, that is, to imagine the comings and goings of another. Also, the infant's pleasure with such games contrasted to his distress with actual separations during this period suggests that there is a rudimentary sense of pretense, that he "knows" mother is really there and both parties "know" the external reality. Being able to engage another in a playful context, or more accurately, to pretend to alter the external conditions is another precondition for imagination in which reality is playfully altered in thought.

Another transition in the infant's concept of self and other evident in the latter half of the second year is the infant's looking to parents for affective guidance in situations of uncertainty or novelty (e.g., social referencing; see Sorce et al., 1985). Parents' affective responses to such bids do alter the infant's exploratory behaviors. When their mothers intentionally display negative affective expressions, 12-month-old infants are less friendly to strangers (Feinman and Lewis, 1983), and inhibit playing with specific, novel toys (Hornik et al., 1987). Conversely, positive affective signals from the parent facilitate and encourage exploration of novel objects, people, or situations (Feinman and Lewis, 1983; Gunnar and Stone, 1984; Hornik et al., 1987).

Social referencing suggests minimally that the infant has developed a sense that information from the parent has meaning for him vis-à-vis his own activities or feelings in the face of novel situations and persons. The infant's social referencing activities engage the parent in a shared experience based on both parties' assumption that one understands at least in part the other's request. Assuming that the feelings of others have meaning vis-à-vis one's own behaviors is a step toward differentiation of self and other and is essential for later imaginative activity in which the child imagines how others might respond to him. Later stages in neurocognitive maturation enhance the child's ability to conceptualize others' feelings and beliefs (see below), but social referencing is the first evidence that the child actively seeks the different affective responses of others to regulate his own actions.

The differentiated meaning of the parent to the child also is seen during this period by the child's reaction to both a parent's absence and a stranger's pres-

ence. The child's dysphoric change in state (crying or angry protests) on anticipated separation and excited pleasure on reunion is evidence that the child is
beginning to make at least rudimentary connections between his own feelings
in relation to his parents and their actions and to understand that others are
available to appreciate and care about the child's distressed states.

Situations such as the response to separation and the child's social referencing in response to novelty or uncertainty are paradigmatic for the increasing
differentiation of self as agent and for the increasing need for an imaginative capacity. Not only is the child able to draw on the stored representations of early
experiences with the other but now encounters himself as an active agent in engaging the other. At this point, wishes, desires, and expectations for the other
are not only possible but also the beginning understanding that one possesses
an inner subjective world. The self-object world has begun to fill out and move
beyond the bounds of pleasurable or unpleasurable experiences or of simply
regulating tension states. It has acquired the dimensions of causality and intentionality, of agency, and the infant's appreciation that other individuals have
differentiated feelings is more evident. From the psychoanalytic point of view,
these shifts or maturation in the definition of self are manifest in an increasingly elaborate inner world of differentiated wishes toward another. Others increasingly populate the child's internal world, and he draws on them, remembers them, and experiences differentiated feelings in response to his memories.
In part, the infant's more active efforts to engage the other also are motivated by
the wish to share experience with that other, whether the experience of the infant's uncertainty or his pleasure in discovery. It is the earliest form of sharing
with another one's inner experiences or fantasies in the form of affects. Later
with the emergence of a capacity for imagination, the child will engage others
not just with affects but with the more elaborate fantasies and wishes which his
capacity for imagination makes possible.

In summary, these developments in the first eighteen months of life are the
underlying substrate for, and beginnings of, a capacity for imagination. Once
the very young child has acquired the capacity to use memory in the service of
self-other differentiation, that is, to be able to evoke the memory of satisfactory
past times in the other's absence, the next step is to imagine the scene as one
might wish it. Imagination draws upon, but is not equivalent with, evocative
memory or the creation of mental images of others. Between 24 and 36 months
of age, a number of maturing neurocognitive capacities are necessary for the full
integration of an imaginative capacity and for this next step to occur. At the
very least, imagination requires that the child grasp the difference between the

physical and the mental worlds and understand that thinking about something or someone is an action of mind which is different from being physically with that person or possessing the toy. To imagine is to recognize a difference between the subjective and objective worlds and to appreciate that mind, mental activities, or thoughts define a world different at least in part from sensory perception. Further, in the act of imagining another, the child not only demarcates an inner world of subjectivity that is understood to be different from the objective, veridical world, but he also creates a world in which people behave toward him because of certain feelings which he imagines them to have. In short, he not only looks to others for their affective reactions as he did in the first two years, but he now attributes beliefs and feelings to the others of his inner world. He imbues them with mental states that guide their actions toward him, and ultimately his actions toward them.

Consider the following scene. A 4-year-old boy waits for his mother to pick him up after nursery school. Though he is playing outside with several of his friends, he closely watches the sidewalk beside the playground where his mother will be walking. Maybe she will be late, who else might she be with, perhaps she is with his father, what might they be doing? He begins to imagine a story in which he sees her in his mind rushing out of the house to the car. He imagines her humming to herself in the car as she drives to the playground, he thinks about her smiling as she comes down the sidewalk and hugging him when she gets close. He thinks how good she will smell, how she will laugh and ask him about his day, maybe even race him to the car, and then they will have a very special ride home, just the two of them. Suddenly he looks up and she is there smiling just as he had imagined, and it is as if he had not been waiting even for those few minutes.

Several features of this story reflect aspects of the integration of neurocognitive and psychic processes that emerge between 24 and 48 months and are a part of the maturing capacity for imagining. For one, the story is a combination of remembered and created elements. Like the infant's evocative memory activity at moments of frustration, the boy's imagination has been brought into the service of easing his loneliness and the anxiety of his waiting. But unlike the infant, the boy does not rely solely on his memory of when his mother has come before. He adds to the story and creates images of what his mother must do in order to come for him. He is engaged in a higher order of mental activity. He brings his mother there in his mind, he holds her mentally even before he holds her physically, but he uses his imagination to delay his need for action and for physical contact with her. Second, he creates a context for his scene that is not necessarily exactly as it will happen. He imagines his mother running to the car or walking down the sidewalk. He holds a belief (e.g., a mental state) about what she will do and imagines it accordingly. Third, he imagines that his mother wants to come for him, to have a special time with him. She is not there at that moment, but her love and desire for her son, which he imagines, will bring her to him. He attributes to her the mental state of loving him which motivates her actions toward him. And fourth, he imagines that she leaves others with whom she also wants to be to come to him, that there are other persons in her life toward whom she also has feelings and wishes. He understands her separateness from him and fills in that separateness through the act of imagination.

The separation between the mental and physical worlds and the relation between action and mental states for both mother and boy are the neurocognitive underpinnings of his imaginative activity and are necessary for the creation of a full inner fantasy life that can be used for affect regulation. Only when the child has acquired a concept of mind can he "understand" that he is imagining that which he does not have. Acquiring a concept of mind is both a subtle and a crucial step in providing children the mental tools for understanding that imagination demarcates a subjective, pretend world. It is the step that heralds the beginning of the fantasy play of the oedipal-aged child (Cohen et al., 1987; Solnit, 1987) and is a necessary precondition for the child's entry into full and complex loving relationships with others through the deepening of a capacity for imagination.

A DEVELOPMENTAL LINE FOR AN
IMAGINATIVE CAPACITY[1]

The relation between an integrated capacity for imagination and adaptive development is particularly evident in those children who are able to create rich and complex inner worlds despite their external experiences. Children from socially impoverished or disorganized environments or those experiencing early traumatic events who are nevertheless able to build up a richly sustaining world of internal objects show how a capacity to imagine takes as substrate the child's wishes and desires even in the absence of external gratification to create the idealized objects of inner world. For children whose early experiences do not necessarily provide them the experiential, external raw material for creating through imagination an enduring inner world, the capacity to understand the mental states of oneself and others is critical. When the external world is impoverished, the beliefs and feelings of the others of the inner world become sustaining. The idealized mother, the family romance, even the wishful daydream come out of the capacity to imagine others' feelings and beliefs which, once possible, rely only partially on memories and percepts and are fueled by instinctual life. Once in place, an imaginative capacity allows the child (and adult) to populate his or her own mind with objects who then influence conscious life and perception and permits him to be in the company of others even when externally alone. In this way, imagination is developmentally adaptive, growth-promoting, and allows children and adults to be alone without being incapacitated by loneliness. Conversely, it is exactly this ability to create through imagination an inner world populated by others that permits the child to be separate and alone even in the company of others, for through his imaginary inner world he is never really alone and can thus remain a separate individual (Winnicott, 1958).

Recognizing that an understanding of mind and of mental states is fundamental to the imaginative process and to the ability to use imagination adaptively also helps us understand what is functionally required for the child involved in the analytic process and raises a number of empirical issues. There is an implied, but necessary, understanding between child and analyst that the play in which they are jointly engaged through its imaginative activity conveys the child's desires and beliefs about his own world. Such understanding makes interpretive activity possible. Indeed, it is often when fantasy is not produced by an integrated imaginative capacity that it seems least communicative and most cut off from the child's world of relationships. In the child's acceptance of imagination as a communicative process, he understands that the analyst also "knows" that what the child is presenting is a product of mind. And just to be sure the lines are clear to all participants, young children commonly begin their play with context—demarcating statements such as "let's pretend" or "not really." How, or if, imagination contributes to observable psychic change in an analysis and how the imaginative process becomes involved in self-awareness and self-reflection are serious questions for clinical analytic study. But at the very least the capacity for imagination becomes linked to reflecting upon one's own wishes and beliefs since the child is in the company of another who reflects back to him in the language of mind and mental states what the child says in his imaginative play.

SUMMARY

The capacity for imagination represents a synthetic ego function that emerges through the integration of several neurocognitive capacities into one mental activity which results in a psychic product (e.g., fantasy) that serves a psychological function (e.g., affect regulation). The capacity for imagination develops in tandem with the child's increasing differentiation and separation from others and provides a way for the child to be a separate individual while at the same time creating an inner world filled with others. The process of imagination is distinctly different from memory inasmuch as imagination creates the object world as one wishes it to be. Although part of the imagined situation or person is based on previous experience, the imaginative process extends and revises that experience. The imaginative process is given full shape and depth with the ability to understand the nature of the subjective world and the nature of other's and one's own mental states. With the achievement of an understanding of mental states, of the relation between mind and action, and, hence, the emergence of an imaginative capacity, the child has opened to him a vastly enlarged world not only for fantasy but also for deepened relationships with others.

Part Five **No Safe Haven: Aggression, Violence, and Trauma**

Chapter 9 The Social Matrix of Aggression: Enactments and Representations of Loving and Hating in the First Years of Life (1993)

Linda C. Mayes and Donald J. Cohen

There is nothing we value and
hunt and cultivate and strive
to draw to us but in some hour
we turn and rend it.
—Emerson, 1836

Considerations of aggression readily lead to polarities—love and hate, war and peace, creativity and destruction, synthesis and fragmentation, affection and hostility. Dichotomies such as these common in the popular worldview of aggressivity parallel the prevailing classic psychoanalytic premise that aggression is an instinctual drive directed toward destruction and ultimately death. Posed as the counterforce to life-sustaining libidinal instincts, aggression and its apparent drive derivatives are a ubiquitous presence in day-to-day life; and the manifes-

First appeared in *The Psychoanalytic Study of the Child,* Volume 48, eds. Albert J. Solnit, Peter B. Neubauer, Samuel Abrams, and A. Scott Dowling (New Haven: Yale University Press, 1993). Copyright © 1993, Albert J. Solnit, Peter B. Neubauer, Samuel Abrams, and A. Scott Dowling. All rights reserved.

tations of aggression occasion respect and admiration as well as dread and caution in the observer and often the aggressor. Fictional and historical accounts as well as stories from the consulting room are replete with tragic individuals apparently driven by a dark, aggressive force impelling them to destroy much that is good and restorative in their own lives and those of close and distant others. As Proust's Marcel observed, pondering once again the tortuous interminglings of love and hate, "At the heart of our friendly or purely social relations, there lurks a hostility momentarily cured but recurring by fits and starts."

However, despite its ubiquity, psychoanalytic considerations of aggression have regularly led to theoretical quandaries.[1] The recurrent dilemmas involve a number of issues, each of which reflect in part the problematic legacy of Freud's dual-instinct model as put forth in *Beyond the Pleasure Principle* (Freud, 1920). Many analytic theorists have highlighted the inherent problems in considering aggression as an instinctual force on equal theoretical as well as functional footing with libidinal drives (e.g., Gillespie, 1971) or in directly equating aggression either with destruction (e.g., Stepansky, 1977) or with a death instinct (e.g., Stone, 1971). In addition, others have emphasized the apparent paradox that aggression is essential for individual and species survival despite its inherently hostile, destructive, perhaps fatal implications (e.g., Spitz, 1965; Stechler and Halton, 1987). Several have proposed different categories of aggression, which allow for constructive derivations such as mastery as well as the more traditionally implied hostile aspects (e.g., Marcovitz, 1982; Parens, 1979). Those struggling to provide a biological grounding for the aggressive instinct that parallels the biology of libidinal drives have linked aggression with physical states of frustration and tension (Dollard et al., 1939) and in so doing, have vested it with a less negative cast.

Perhaps what has been most troubling theoretically for psychoanalysis is the different nature of aggression in the developing young child compared, for example, to the rageful, melancholic, suicidal or masochistic adult. In very young children, aggressivity is more frequently and directly expressed, less apparently destructive or hostile, and more apparently pleasurable or constructive, at least in the first four or five years of life. Indeed, from the perspective of the child analyst, "aggression looms larger than sex in child analysis, dominates the child patient's acting out and transference behaviour" (Freud, 1972a, p. 168). Yet a developmentally framed theory of aggression exists only in bits and pieces in various approaches to early development.

In this paper, we address one specific aspect of aggression in early development—the role of aggression in the child's moves toward individuation (e.g., Mahler et al., 1975; Winnicott, 1950) and in the shaping of the child's sense of self. How aggression toward another mixes with desire for another in the formation of early capacities for object relatedness is a central question for any developmental theory of aggression, for, at its core, aggression is directed toward others, whether they be in the individual's internal or external world. The child's instinctual strivings for both loving and hating are given form and meaning in the child's earliest relationships with important others (Loewald, 1978a); and early aggressive strivings are modified and transformed in the context of those relationships (e.g., Solnit, 1972). Conversely, the very presence of aggressive strivings in the child's relationship with others makes possible deepening libidinal ties, that is, aggression is a necessary component of the child's capacity to love others and to hold others in mind in their absence. As Downey (1984) and Loewald (1960) have also indicated, aggression makes it possible for the child to be a separate individual who is then capable of the identifications, introjections, and partial mergings so characteristic of love relationships. The very separateness fostered and facilitated by the child's early aggressivity allows the child the capacity to be close without losing his hard-won, separate sense of self. Thus, the early developmental transformations in both the frequency and character of the child's aggressivity reflect, at least in part, the child's individuation and emerging self-definition.

Most importantly, we outline how the child's maturing neurocognitive capacities for attributing affects, beliefs, and other mental states to others not only is a part of self-object differentiation (e.g., Mayes and Cohen, 1992; Mayes and Cohen, 1993a; Mayes et al., 1993) but also contributes to the transformation of aggressive as well as libidinal strivings into the balanced form essential for mature object relations. The capacity to reflect upon thoughts and feelings in oneself and others provides children with a fuller range of responses to their own and others' perceived aggression. The mental capacities for remembering, for fantasy, and for trial action allow the child to contain the aggressive act or wish in thought and attribute aggressive motives and affects to others while at the same time maintaining both his libidinal ties to the other as well as his separateness. With an emerging appreciation of the distinction between the external world of action and perception and the inner, subjective world of thoughts and fantasies, aggressive and loving feelings are potentially more peaceably intermingled since hate contained in fantasy, thoughts, and feelings allows at least the possibility that important others remain intact.

PSYCHOANALYTIC VIEW OF AGGRESSION

At the conclusion of the 27th International Congress, Anna Freud (1972) observed that frequent debates and discussions to that point had failed to remove "uncertainties concerning the status of aggression in the theory of drives, or the clarification of some urgent problems, such as the part played by aggression in normal infantile development; its involvement with the various agencies in the psychic structure; its role for character formation" (Freud, 1972a, p. 163). She went on to outline the reasons that aggression appeared so problematic to analysts despite its centrality in everyday life and its inescapable presence in the lives of young children. Aggression explicitly entered analytic theory late. Long after the erotic, relationship-building, libidinal drive had been securely placed in the context of mental functioning, Freud (1920) introduced the dualism of life and death to instinctual life.

Like a younger sibling being compared to all the achievements and characteristics of the older sibling, the aggressive drive was inevitably shaped to match the libidinal component. As a separate drive standing in parallel with the well-defined libidinal instinct, aggression needed to meet the criteria of stage development with specific body zones and to have a source, aim, and object-criteria that have been difficult to fulfill. The reasoning was essentially backward. Seeking to fit clinical observations of aggression into the framework of libidinal instinct theory did not validate aggression as a parallel, but independent drive (Freud, 1972a; Solnit, 1972). The presumed symmetry was misleading and inaccurate and led to the conceptually troubling legacy of a parallel, separate instinct that was nevertheless not quite parallel inasmuch as the aim was manifestly not pleasure or tension reduction but fragmentation and ultimately destruction.

Such was the dilemma for understanding aggression in children where destruction and hostile intent, although present, were not apparently primary. Possibly constructive, positive functions for aggression in early psychic life were obscured by the negative valence. Understanding how such a dichotomy evolved in psychoanalytic theory is not within the scope of this paper (see, for example, Stepansky, 1977), but it is useful to explore briefly the role of aggression in psychoanalysis before it was given explicit, elevated status as a separate instinct.

Aggression was a vital, albeit implicit, presence in early psychoanalytic theory as one of the large number of functions dedicated to preserving and protecting the intactness of the self, a role that more closely approximates clinical observations of aggressivity in early childhood. Before the structural theory, aggressive impulses were subsumed under derivatives of a drive for sexual mastery (Freud, 1905). By 1915, aggressive strivings were singled out more conspicuously as primary components of a drive for mastery or self-preservation and self-non-self differentiation. However, this singular constructive place for aggression was short-lived, for within the decade, with the introduction of the structural theory, the ego was no longer equipped with drives of its own (Bibring, 1941; Hartmann, 1948). With *Beyond the Pleasure Principle* (1920) Freud attempted to deal with a dilemma increasingly evident in the consulting room as well as the world at large—manifestly hostile acts were not self-preservative and patients were often caught in self-destructive and self-punitive trends and cycles of self-blaming, unrelenting depression (Brenner, 1971). These repeatedly occurring manifestations of aggression in the unconscious minds of individuals in analysis in the decade of 1910–20 seemed beyond any theories of a self-protective function. Many have speculated too upon how much to emphasize the impact of either the carnage of the World War or of his daughter's death on Freud's changing view of aggression (Gay, 1988). However, in ultimately and despairingly insisting that there was an eternal antagonism between the demands of human instinctual nature and those of civilization, Freud remained true to his nineteenth-century Enlightenment views and to his profound Darwinian influence (Rochlin, 1982). In 1930, physically ill and psychologically resigned, he wrote, "I adopt the standpoint . . . that the inclination to aggression is an original, self-subsisting instinctual disposition in man, and I return to my view that it constitutes the greatest impediment to civilization" (Freud, 1930, p. 122).

In this crucial transition, Freud chose not to accept aggression in and of itself as constructively essential for normal psychic development. He placed it outside not only the pleasure principle but, perhaps more importantly, outside the shaping influences of early experience and outside any developmental framework. But, paradoxically, as Freud marked aggression the darkly primitive, ever-present destructive force always threatening to disrupt or destroy more constructive, progressive developmental gains, his students and contemporaries continued to place great weight on the role of aggression in fantasy and action as a central shaping factor in early character formation, as Freud himself had done in an earlier period (Freud, 1909). For example, Abraham (1923, 1925), Reich (1933), and others grounded the analytic theory of character formation in the earliest body-based aspects of infantile experience related to aggressive, not libidinal, derivatives (e.g., the paradigmatic relations between biting or oral sadism in the infant or anal sadism in the toddler and later character structure).

Others too struggled to preserve the dual-instinct model while at the same time maintaining a more constructive role for aggression in the analytic theory of early character formation (e.g., Bibring, 1941; Fenichel, 1945; Waelder, 1956). Like Freud in the earlier theories (1905), Hartmann et al. (1949) argued for the role of aggression in object-preserving needs and for the importance of the modification of aggression through fusion with libidinal instincts. In addition, they suggested there were at least three other routes for the modulation of aggression (sublimation, displacement to other objects, and restriction of the aim) so that aggressive impulses were available for psychic structure formation (e.g., superego). With the albeit somewhat difficult concept of neutralization, aggressive strivings became available again for the service of adaptive development, and a measure of ego integrity and strength was the ability to "neutralize large quantities of aggression" (p.24).

For those analysts steeped in the tradition of infant observation and direct work with very young children, aggression is an evident and early presence in the lives of very young infants and has been considered central, if not paramount, to the infant's differentiating sense of self (Klein, 1957). Aggressivity and aggressive feelings are rooted in the earliest and most basic biologically determined patterns of behavior designed to protect the child and bring others to him in times of need. For example, the infant's cry is almost always perceived by adults as unpleasant and aversive yet indicative of need, and it generally arouses in the parent a sense of urgency to respond (Lester and Boukydis, 1984). Similarly, when infants look away during stressful interactions, they actively block out the situation that is distressing or overwhelming (e.g., Mayes and Carter, 1990). Or early motor activity and motility are manifestations of the nondestructive aspects of aggression that are a part of the process of experiencing self as effective and autonomous (Greenacre, 1971; Parens, 1979; Spitz, 1969)—the toddler's vigorous struggling or running away while being dressed or his gleefully and persistently pushing a toy off a table. Motoric activity also contributes to self-definition and the individuation process, for when the infant's and young child's vigorous muscular activity is met by normal opposition during moment-to-moment physical care routines, the child gains a sense of body and of what is real (Winnicott, 1950).

These and other body-based modes of protecting self and expressing one's own effectiveness become the persistent, readily available schemas for how the child (and adult) experiences and responds to internal or external senses of danger, real or imagined. If the psychoanalytic theory of object relatedness has its biological rootedness in the infant's adaptiveness to perceive, react to, and process socially based information (Mayes and Cohen, 1993a), the psychoanalytic theory of character formation is firmly grounded in these early modes of expression of aggression (Cohen, 1990). Furthermore, when the parent in Winnicott's terms (1950; 1969) "survives" the infant's earliest aggressive (e.g., motoric) strivings, he or she becomes more differentiated as an external object with whom the infant has a shared reality. In this sense, aggression precedes a capacity for loving (Downey, 1984). Aggression, more than the internalization of consistent nurturing, fosters individuation, self-object differentiation, and the young child's recognition of object permanence and an external reality shared with the parent (Winnicott, 1945a, 1969, 1971). With such recognition, a sense of trust in the object develops and a feeling that it is safer to hate and rebel against a mother whom the child also loves.

How the child's experiences with others further shape the process of the transformation of aggressive motives and fantasies into more complex and adaptive ways of relating to the world represents a later contribution to the analytic theory of aggression and character formation—and a central paradigm shift in the theory of instincts. Loewald (1978a) places the origin of instinctual life—both aggressive and libidinal—in the social context of interactions between mother and infant. The infant experiences himself as more or less aggressive in relation to the mother's experience of those and other behaviors just cited. When the 4-month-old infant vigorously sucking at the breast abruptly bites, how much the mother reacts to her unexpected pain as an aggressive attack versus a surprising but notable measure of her child's assertiveness and mastery will influence how the infant experiences such moments later on. Or when the 18-month-old about to run off to explore a new place or person looks back for his mother's reaction (e.g., social referencing; Sorce et al., 1985), his excitement and pleasure will be reinforced by his mother's encouragement or dampened by her look of fear or anger. Stated another way, how much separation and moves toward autonomy or mastery come to be experienced intrapsychically by the child as pleasurable or aggressive and hurtful depends in large part on the parent's experience and reaction.[2]

Thus, from the beginning of infancy, any aggressive act or fantasy is embedded in a social matrix. What an individual child comes to interpret and experience as aggressive and later patterns of assertiveness, self-protectiveness, and the modulation of anger and hostility toward others are rooted in these earliest interactions with others. Likewise, how much aggressivity is experienced by the individual as essential, positive, and adaptive and how much aggressive feelings and wishes in oneself and others are feared and dreaded is given initial form early in the first 12 to 18 months. To be sure, aggression and aggressivity are closely tied to biological processes. There are basic neurobiological contributions to individual variations in the degree of hostile, destructive impulses, and at some point in situations of danger and mortal threat, protective biological response processes (e.g., fight or flight, rageful attack) take over both for children and for adults (Alpert et al., 1981). Indeed, driving away predators and protective destructiveness are fundamental biological processes present in all species. But what comes to be symbolized and represented in the human mind as predatory or dangerous, what kinds of events are perceived as threatening and hostile, and how aggressivity assumes adaptive and nonadaptive forms are defined and refined in the context of the child's earliest experiences. The basic biology of assertiveness and protective destructiveness is channeled by object relations, and these early patterns of experiencing the aggressivity of self and others as constructive or destructive remain available as mental representations throughout life (Loewald, 1978a).

On the other hand, because much of the psychoanalytic view of aggression in early childhood implicitly focuses on the child's internal experiences of aggression—his own and others', what has been less often addressed has been (1) the specific nature of the transformations of aggressive behaviors in the first five years (e.g., are there observable differences in the types of aggressive behaviors in young children that permit a more differentiated developmental theory of how aggressive patterns are established early in life?); and (2) how maturing cognitive capacities for abstraction, symbolization, and fantasy underlie the child's ability to understand and differentiate his own and others' aggressive intentions and states. Such capacities are the neurocognitive underpinnings that make possible the transformation of early aggressive strivings contextualized by the child's experiences with important others. Studies of aggression from disciplines outside psychoanalysis provide some insight into these issues.

OBSERVATIONAL STUDIES OF AGGRESSION
IN CHILDREN

From the late 1920s on (e.g., Goodenough, 1931; Green, 1933), aggressivity in early childhood was a topic of empirical interest. In contrast to the psychoanalytic views of aggression in unconscious fantasy life, particularly from the views of the British school (e.g., Klein, 1957; Winnicott, 1945a, 1950), empirical studies of aggressivity examined the external conditions and manifestations of aggression in the child's early behaviors. Taking their cue not only from drive theory and models of frustration/tension release (Dollard et al., 1939) but also from ethological studies of animal behavior (Lorenz, 1966), many investigators sought to understand what role aggressive behavior played in the child's earliest socially adaptive development and how the child's environment shaped and modified aggressive behaviors (for a review, see Parke and Slaby, 1983). For example, was rough-and-tumble play, seen in the young of many species, an anlage of the older child's and adult's capacities to deal with aggressive interactions with their peers (Harlow and Harlow, 1965)? Similarly, the tantrums of early childhood were proposed as a template for children's learning the efficacy of both aggressive action and inhibition (Etzel and Gewirtz, 1967).

Investigators attempting to understand the roots of aggressive behavior in early childhood found that aggressivity was less often regarded as the result of a primary drive or instinct and more often, at least in its earliest manifestations, as a more or less differentiated response to frustration of wishes and needs or to the demands of the social world on the child. For infants, these frustrations arose out of physical needs, while for older children disappointing interactions with others were sufficient sources of frustrating experiences. Stimulus-response models guided much of the early work on childhood aggressive behavior, and the transformations of aggressivity with maturation were viewed through the frame of behavior modification and learning theory (Bandura, 1973). Whether or not aggressive behaviors led a child to his or her goal and how children responded to the evidence of their own destructiveness or the overt pain of the injured person were viewed as paramount events in the shaping of aggressivity. Later studies placed childhood aggression in the context of social cognition and in parallel with the emergence of capacities for empathy in the first three to five years of life (Cummings et al., 1986; Dodge, 1986; Quiggle et al., 1992). The child's ability to understand, respond to, or identify with the person injured by an overtly aggressive act modifies acceptable patterns of aggressivity. The social cognition model in particular permits study of how the child's social information-processing capacities across development alter his or her own aggressive behaviors as well as his responses to those of others.

Regardless of the theoretical frame of reference, a central contribution of empirical studies of aggressive behavior has been the various attempts to clarify what does and does not constitute aggression in young children. At the very least, from the standpoint of observational studies, aggressive behavior is usually assumed to involve injury (real, anticipated, or imagined) to a person or inanimate object (Buss, 1961; Feshbach, 1964), but any definition of the phenomenology of aggression in early childhood needs to consider at least five definitional issues: (1) What are the behavioral manifestations of aggression in early childhood and do these manifestations change with maturation and with the responses of the environment? (2) Are aggressive acts directed toward persons different from acts involving inanimate objects? (3) What are the instigating events leading to aggressive acts, e.g., deprivation, personal injury or attack, humiliation, or fright? (4) Are aggressive acts that are apparently responsive to the aggression of another different from aggressive behavior instigated by the child? (5) What are the goals of an aggressive act in children? How can aggressive behavior motivated by the intention to harm and destroy be distinguished from aggressive acts in which the goal is not injury but the achievement of a manifestly nonaggressive intent (e.g., to gain another's attention, to reclaim a favorite toy, to win in a game).

A number of observational studies address different aspects of these questions and have documented changes in the overt behavioral manifestations of aggression in the first five to six years of life. However, it must be noted that despite decades of study, there is still a relative paucity of data to address the issues of both developmental transformations and individual differences in aggressive behavior in preschool children (see Parke and Slaby, 1983). Aggressivity in very young children is most often manifested physically by hitting, biting, shoving, or kicking, but physical aggressivity decreases markedly after the third year of life, while verbal aggressivity (e.g., shouting, name-calling) increases between ages 2 and 4 (Goodenough, 1931). Generally, all types of aggressive acts decrease as children approach 4 to 5 years of age (Cummings et al., 1986, 1989). In comparing 4- to 6- and 6- to 7-year-olds, Hartup (1974) found that younger children were more aggressive than older children and that the difference was due to more frequent incidences in younger children of aggressivity focused on acquiring or reclaiming desired objects, that is, in asserting needs and wants.

Similarly, within the 2- to 4-year-old age group, struggles over acquiring objects decrease as the child matures (see review in Hay, 1984). Perhaps most importantly, when aggressive acts are divided into initiated and responsive, the incidence of child-initiated aggressivity decreases as children become older, a finding interpreted as consistent with the social learning theory of aggression (Dodge, 1980; Dodge and Coie, 1987). With age, children learn what types of aggressivity are permissible in what type of situations (Cummings et al., 1989). By school age, aggressivity is more often personally directed, is instigated by threats to the child's self-esteem, and is more often overtly intended to harm the offending other. Aggressive acts intended to gain or preserve possession in which injury to another is only secondary are far less common for school-aged children (Hartup, 1974). Thus, paradoxically, as the child matures, aggressivity becomes less frequent but more often socially directed and apparently motivated by an intent to harm or injure. The instigating actions are also less often overt attacks by another, such as a toy being stolen, and more often involve perceived violations in the rules and expectations of social interactions (e.g., insults, criticism, ridicule).

Throughout these observations, however, the issue of intent or some other motivational construct remains problematic. As suggested above, the goal of an aggressive act may be as much to gain a wished-for person or achievement or fulfill an ambition as it is to harm and injure. For example, when the toddler hurls a toy across the room, breaking both the toy and damaging the wall, the act is overtly aggressive but may or may not be aggressive in its intent to do damage or harm. On the other hand, if intent is excluded from the definition, certain acts that are manifestly but nonintentionally aggressive will nevertheless be considered aggressive and hostile. When a mother quickly grabs and holds her child tightly to prevent him or her from dashing out into a busy intersection, the act is manifestly aggressive though intentionally protective.

In answer to this dilemma, a number of observational schemas have attempted to distinguish various states of intentionality in aggressive acts and have divided aggressive behavior into "hostile" and "instrumental" aggressivity (Buss, 1966; Feshbach, 1964). The former is usually person-directed and requires inference by the child that the other person has behaved with the intention to hurt or harm. In acts of instrumental aggressivity, the intent is to achieve a nonaggressive goal. In the course of the act, harm to another may occur, but this is not the original intent of the act. Thus, manifestly aggressive behaviors may serve the purposes of assertiveness and protection of self and others as well as the expression of hostility and the intent to do harm—again the dilemma of constructive versus destructive goals of aggression. For young children, it is instrumental aggressivity that diminishes as the child approaches school age while acts of hostile aggressivity become more prominent (Hartup, 1974). However, the distinctions between instrumental and hostile aggressive actions are easily blurred. Both may occur in the same interchange—the mother's vigorous hold on her struggling toddler is person-directed but is not with intent to do harm. Moreover, hostile aggressive acts are not without instrumental value. Attacking a teasing, taunting child restores the self-esteem of the initially injured other, a goal as constructive and worthy as the young child's vigorously seeking to regain his lost toy.

The deeper issue in distinguishing the goals involved in an aggressive act is understanding how children come to be able to judge the intent of their peers and of adults when they feel aggressed upon and what are the given conditions for any individual child that lead to his experiencing his own or another's actions as aggressive. The judgment of hostile or injurious intent is not confined to observational paradigms dedicated to the categorization of aggressive acts but is also a fundamental aspect of the child's knowing how to respond to the perceived aggressive act of another. Children and adults commonly make errors in judgment regarding the level of intention to do injury and harm that is contained in another's actions. Distraught mothers interpret their child's lusty "no" as a call to battle just as many lovers count the hours between telephone calls as irrefutable evidence of intended, wounding rejection. Some children and adults hear only the aggressive intent in an ironic or sarcastic statement and respond in kind, while for others only a direct and sudden physical attack is perceived as threatening and dangerous.

Developmental shifts in the attribution of aggressive intent have been described for school-aged children. Boys 7, 9, and 12 years of age were presented with a variety of aggressive incidents, some involving a child accidentally attacking another, while others were more evidently intentional (Shantz and Voydanoff, 1973). The younger the child, the less able he was to distinguish between levels of intention and accident and the more likely he was to react similarly to accidental or intentional provocation. When children are presented with unambiguous information about the intentions behind the aggressive act, even preschool children are able to alter their response based on the aggressor's intentions (Rule et al., 1974). But in naturalistic situations where cues are often subtle and ambiguous, the younger the child, the more difficulty he or she has in inferring intentionality and using such inference to guide his or her behavior (Rotenberg, 1980).

Understanding another's intentionality in any action reflects a complex series of neurocognitive operations that mature between 3 and 5 years of age and involve the child's emerging understanding that the actions of others are a reflection of the feelings, beliefs, and thoughts of others, that is, that mind or mental states guide actions and behaviors. Appreciating and interpreting the intentionality of another is a part of children's acquiring an understanding of their own and others' mental processes. Elsewhere, we have described how the capacity to understand the notion of a subjective mental world and the link between that world and the world of directly perceivable action also makes possible both the increasing differentiation of self and other and the use of the mental process of imagination in the service of deepening capacities for relatedness

(Mayes and Cohen, 1992; Mayes and Cohen, 1993a; Mayes et al., 1993). Being able not only to attribute aggressive intentional states to another but also to attribute aggressive intentions different from one's own reflects another aspect of what is now frequently labeled the child's emerging theory of mind (reviewed in Astington and Gopnik, 1991; Astington et al., 1988; Wellman, 1990; and Baron-Cohen et al., 1992).

THEORIES OF MIND AND THE MODULATION
OF AGGRESSION

In the first three to five years of life, the child's orientation to the world of others dramatically shifts. He gradually acquires some understanding that being separate from another is fundamentally related, in part, to having a private, subjective world defined by acts of mind. He is aware not only of other minds but more importantly that the mind of others (e.g., their beliefs and feeling states) may be different from his own. With such an appreciation, the child understands that he and others act in ways that are interpretable on the basis of these thoughts, beliefs, desires, and feelings, that is, we do something because we love (or hate) someone or believe that another person feels toward us in a certain way. Achieving such understanding reflects a major shift in the child's capacity for metarepresentation, for now he is able to allow one thing to stand for another in his private, subjective world and to attribute states he cannot directly perceive to others in his world.

Before the achievement of an appreciation of the mind of other persons, the child's understanding of the motives of others toward him is not differentiated. He believes that they act because he needs or wants, and failures on the parts of others are experienced as depriving, frustrating and threatening. As the child begins to understand the notion of mind, he is able to explain the other's emotions and attitudes and to act or feel accordingly. The 5-year-old oedipal-aged child's move from dyadic to triadic relationships is facilitated by his newly emerging capacity to attribute complex feelings, beliefs, and intentions to multiple others, which in turn makes it possible for him to be concerned about the differing, often conflicting, beliefs and feelings of more than one other person in his world. In the act of trying to understand or image the mental world of other persons, the child not only demarcates an inner world of subjectivity that is understood to be different from the objective, veridical world, but he also creates an inner world in which people behave toward him because of certain feelings which he imagines them to have (Mayes and Cohen, 1992). Similarly, an understanding of the other's mind allows the child to imagine the other's feelings toward him and to envision how things might be were such feelings and beliefs different.

As he begins to appreciate the subjective nature of the mental world, the 4- to 5-year-old child acquires an understanding that, stated most simply, things are not always as they seem (Mayes and Cohen, 1993a). In that context, he recognizes the notion of false belief—that someone may act on the basis of a belief that is presently incorrect or false because external conditions have changed. Exactly because he is acquiring an understanding that individuals may hold to different beliefs even if the external, directly perceivable conditions appear the same, he is capable of jokes and of deception (Chandler et al., 1989). Children between 4 and 5 years of age also become able to understand that others (as well as themselves) may hold to two or more beliefs that are manifestly contradictory. They understand that someone may want or desire something very much but believe incorrectly that he knows the exact location or way to satisfy his desire (Mayes and Cohen, 1992). Similarly, they gradually acquire the understanding that persons may feel differently about the same person at different times, or that it is possible to both like someone and be angry at them, to love and to hurt the same person.

Knowing that beliefs and feelings do not always correspond to externally perceivable conditions is crucial in being able to appreciate varying levels of intentionality in an aggressive act. For example, in a group of preschool children, there often are vigorous, competitive efforts to be close to a favorite teacher during story time. When one child pushes another out of the special place, the 5-year-old child is better able to appreciate the teacher's explanations that his friend did not mean to hurt him but only wanted the special place for himself. His 3-year-old counterpart would have far greater difficulty understanding or acting on such an explanation and would be far more likely to respond to the aggressive act in kind. Similarly, allowing for the possibility that manifestly contradictory beliefs, affects, or thoughts may be held by and about the same person is a fundamental step toward the capacity for modulating one's own aggressivity and understanding another's aggressive intents. Appreciating that another may at one moment behave with the apparent intent to hurt and at the next moment be apologetic and loving allows the child to hold in closer proximity aggressive and loving feelings. That these capacities emerge around the same time observational studies report marked changes in the nature of children's aggressive behavior may be viewed as converging evidence for the necessary role of a capacity for attributing intentions to others in the transformation of early aggressive strivings.

In addition, the appreciation of a mental subjective world in others as well as in oneself allows the child the space of fantasy in which to play with the transformations of aggressive strivings. Feelings of neglect or disappointment that for the toddler may have contributed directly to the physical enactments of aggression may now be tempered in the child's fantasy life. Hostile, angry, destructive feelings experienced first with important others may be placed at least temporarily in the security of imaginary play and various solutions to such feelings tried on while the child is safely protected by his loving ties to the same person with whom he is angry. Parenthetically, it is particularly in this way that libidinal ties help transform and modulate aggressive strivings by providing safety as it were during the storm (Solnit, 1972). Within psychoanalysis, a fundamental premise of unconscious fantasy life is that the attribution of hostile, destructive intents first occurs with one's primary objects (e.g., Klein, 1957; Winnicott, 1945a, 1950). The understanding of a notion of mind that allows for contradictory mental states allows the child at least the mental capacity to hold both hate and love side by side in his representations of important others. With the capacity to allow for differing beliefs and feelings in one's own and others' minds, there is the possibility that what could previously be contained only in bad and good part objects can now be more readily mingled.

CLINICAL ILLUSTRATION

Sophie, aged 38 months, entered analysis four times a week because of stool withholding, a symptom that her parents felt had worsened as Sophie had had increasing difficulties with separation from either of them for almost any occasion (Mayes and Cohen, 1992). A bright, verbally gifted child, Sophie seemed increasingly thwarted and confused by the many levels of separation demands being maturationally thrust upon her. During her first year of analysis, Sophie frequently and abruptly interrupted her play with angry outbursts of yelling and vigorous hitting. These incidents sometimes appeared connected to times when the analyst had been unable to fulfill quickly enough something Sophie wanted immediately, but more often it seemed as if Sophie had been swept over by powerful feelings that she both anxiously and aggressively warded off in her physical attacks. Immediately after her outbursts, she would retreat to a far corner of the room, curl up with her blanket, and demand that the analyst not look at her. The warning about looking seemed to contain the fear that she was so aggressive that she would be left alone with no one looking at her, as well as a fear of the aggressive intent of looking as if the very act of visual contact would hold her and the analyst too dangerously close.

Interpreting Sophie's fear of her own angry feelings and her worry that she or her analyst might not survive her attacks unscathed seemed to help her return from her hiding place and resume the play she had abruptly interrupted. Gradually, her outbursts diminished; her play became more sustained and the themes more aggressive. She often pretended to be a demanding, imperious baby whose every wish was fulfilled immediately by the "slaves" she kept close by. When her "slaves" did not respond quickly enough, she feigned indignant anger and pronounced destructive, vile threats to their bodies and very lives. Not infrequently, Sophie would interrupt stories such as these to seek out once again a safe corner in the playroom for fear that, as she clearly expressed, the bad "pirates" feelings would cut a swath of indiscriminate destruction across the playroom toward her and the analyst. During these moments, though contained within her fantasy play, she earnestly insisted that the analyst too must seek cover for there was no predicting either the appearance or the wanton destructiveness of these "pirates" once released.

Through the characters and stories Sophie created in her play, it became clearer that her struggles with her aggressivity related to both her wish, need, and demand for an evenly attentive, always available care from others, and her concerns about how her aggressive feelings damaged others or drove them away. In one of her stories, a 4-year-old dragon character eagerly invited close friends to his birthday party only abruptly to hit and bite them. Puzzled and hurt, he asked his mother why his friends left the party. The mother explained how his friends did not understand why he was hitting and biting them when they were friends—they interpreted his intentions as hostile. In another story, a mother, on finding out that her baby had been quite demanding and bad during his visit to another family, says summarily, "Just throw him in the garbage." And in a third story an indiscriminately evil character who stole from families was abruptly left alone and poignantly searched for friends. Even the revenge heaped upon him by the family he had previously injured paled as Sophie embellished the story of his lonely search for others like him. Suddenly he was lovingly taken in by the very family he had so grievously injured. As she explained soberly to some of her dolls, it was possible to be angry with someone they also loved; and even when they were angry, they could also be close.

Each of these examples illustrates Sophie's profound, deeply felt struggles to understand how it was possible to have aggressive feelings toward those she loved and depended upon. As she gradually acquired the ability to appreciate and represent the differing thoughts and feelings of others and their different states of aggressive intention, she began to wonder and worry about the responses of others to both her fantasied and enacted aggression. Her play acquired a new depth and her characters, assuming more complex, multidimensional mental lives, became simultaneously emancipated and tragic. Through their aggression, they established for themselves a world in which they were feared, dreaded, and able to do whatever they wished but where they were left alone and denied the closeness they had so deeply desired. With a maturing capacity for attributing meanings, feelings, and different states of intention to others, Sophie was able to experiment with a multicausal view of aggressivity. Not only was it essential for the ongoing shaping of her own sense of self, but now she could see aggressive thoughts and wishes, as well as behavior, through the eyes of others and explore how love and hate exist side by side.

Children such as Sophie or Winnicott's Piggle (1977) illustrate not only how aggression fuels individuation and a sense of separateness but also how it contributes to the shaping of psychic structure. With a deepening understanding of one's own aggressive wishes and fantasies and an appreciation of the same in others, there comes also the fuller recognition of the potential impact of aggressive acts on others. Accepting a growing sense of personal responsibility for one's intentions, wishes, and fantasies is a part of the ongoing definition of self (Loewald, 1978a) and a part of the building up of the superego and the experiencing of guilt for one's own potential destructiveness toward others, especially those we care the most about. Concern for and about the other modifies and shapes the child's experience of his own aggressiveness. Libidinal and aggressive wishes are intermingled as the child struggles to repair what he perceives and accepts as the results of his aggressivity. In this sense, the building up of superego functions, like the capacity for loving, is deeply rooted in the child's sense of his own aggressivity and the effect on others. Once again, individual variations in the child's internal representations of the values and rights of others have their roots not only in libidinal ties to parents and in the working through of oedipal love (Hartmann and Loewenstein, 1962), but also in how much aggression has been experienced as constructive or destructive in the context of relationships with others.

SUMMARY AND RESEARCH IMPLICATIONS

The capacity to attribute aggressive intentions and motives to oneself and to others represents a synthetic ego function that plays a significant role in the transformation of aggressive strivings in the preschool child and in the more differentiated use of aggression in the service of both self-definition and relations with others. Aggression is experienced, shaped, refined, and remodeled in the context of loving relations, and it is a central psychoanalytic observation that young children first experience their own aggressive feelings in response to and in the presence of those whom they love the most. With the maturing ability to understand and reflect upon one's own and others' mental states, the experience of being or feeling aggressive toward another gains new meaning.

Observational studies indicate that aggressive behaviors change markedly in the preschool years, or in the terminology of psychoanalytic observation, direct discharge of aggressive drive derivatives is muted and shaped by the child's relations with his parents or with those who most actively care for him. Children become less physically aggressive and aggressive responses to frustration of physical needs or desires are less often the eliciting events. However, paradoxically, by 4 to 6 years of age, while generally less aggressive, children more often direct their aggressivity to others and are more often aggressive in response to perceived threats to their sense of self. At the same time, because of maturing capacities for symbolization and abstraction, children are able to use pretense and fantasy to work out their experiences of their own and others' aggression. For the oedipal-aged child, the transformation of aggression and the blending of aggressive and libidinal wishes toward the same person are made possible by the ability to understand the nature of one's own and others' mental states and of the relation between mind and action. In a very real sense, understanding aggressive states of mind and intentions is a more difficult, or at least equally essential, task in the child's developing and expanding relationships with multiple others. Appreciating the neurocognitive contributions to the transformations of aggression makes possible more detailed studies of how children may fail to use aggression constructively for self-other differentiation, of the environmental contributions to the early transformations of aggressive strivings, and the individual differences in how much children or adults attribute hostile intentions to the actions of others.

The latter point brings us back to the psychoanalytic theory of the role of experience in mediating the child's sense of his own aggressiveness and raises several areas for investigation. The theory presented thus far for the modulation and transformation of aggressivity in the preschool-aged child permits us a conceptual frame for thinking about the circumstances in which the child's external world is chronically violent and/or depriving and physically hurtful. Young children who are chronically ill or physically restrained in the first months of life because of illness have both the experience of being hurt by others and of having fewer and different opportunities to use their bodies to assert their needs or protect themselves. Or when the child's normally occurring assertive or aggressive acts (e.g., the toddler's tantrum) or even fantasies of aggression are met by real, often life-threatening aggressive responses, the child's experience of himself as aggressive is shaped in ways that are dramatically different from those which contain and accept his aggressive assertiveness. Similarly, children who are the habitual witnesses of physical violence both to those they love and to those who randomly pass through their world will likely experience a greater and earlier sense of danger when confronted with their own aggressive feelings and wishes. Or they may experience their own aggressivity and fantasies as compatible with that which commonly occurs around them and permissible by those whom they have experienced as equally violent and destructive.

How each of these situations influences the transformation of aggression as the child gradually acquires more sophisticated capacities to reflect upon his and others' aggressive intentions is a question most relevant to psychoanalytically informed investigations. For example, relationships with important others that are marred by explicit violence and abuse may bring the child face to face with the mind of another that is too frightening and dangerous to try to understand. In such cases, despite maturational readiness, the capacity to understand others' minds and different states of aggressive intention may be seriously impaired. In addition, when the child's mode of experiencing the world early on has been predominantly colored by aggression, danger, and hurtfulness, it is not clear how, or if, the capacity to attribute beliefs and intentions to others allows the child to imbue those others or himself in fantasy with less aggressive, hurtful minds. In other words, in these instances, how much is the child able to work out his real experiences of destructiveness and rage through his play and in the privacy of his inner subjective world? And even with the capacity to reflect upon the aggressive wishes and fantasies of self and other, children exposed to chronic, intense violence will likely have a different sense of their own intentionality and responsibility.

Questions such as these are deeply germane to child psychoanalysts who are increasingly called upon to care for the children from substance-abusing homes and neighborhoods and children of the inner city whose external worlds are so unsafe that their inner fantasies are daily given voice and reality in their immediate and observed experiences (Marans and Cohen, 1993; Mayes and Cohen, 1992). Such questions also provide us with the broadest outlines of a theory that distinguishes between the conduct or disruptive behavior problems of young children bounded by anxiety and fear as with Sophie and those who seem unmoved by their effects on others. Finally, from its earliest beginnings, psychoanalysis has been profoundly concerned with the experience and nature of early trauma and how that experience is mediated and modified by the child's inner fantasy and shapes the child's ongoing modes of apprehending the world. When children are still evolving a sense of what is inner and outer, pretend and real, and what it means to hold aggressive wishes and feelings toward those they love and depend upon, early exposure to violence and deprivation shapes their view of themselves in relation to their own and others' aggressivity and their view of the world as hostile or protective, constructive or destructive, forgiving or punishing, loving or hating. In these ways, aggression remains central to the psychoanalytic theory of character formation and to the child's developing ability to integrate and synthesize loving and aggressive feelings in the service of deepening relations with others.

ACKNOWLEDGMENTS

The authors gratefully acknowledge their discussions on this topic with their colleagues Steven Marans and Albert J. Solnit. This paper is dedicated to Dr. Sally Provence, whose work exemplifies how careful observation of infants and their parents enriches our understanding of inner lives.

Chapter 10 Child Development and Adaptation to Catastrophic Circumstances (1996)

Steven Marans, Miriam Berkman, and Donald J. Cohen

Children who live in nations torn by war for many years feel that their neighborhoods are dangerous and their world unsafe. They cannot walk the streets with a sense of mastery, ownership, and security. Instead, the sight of wounded and dead bodies on the sidewalk and the sounds of nightly gunfire are daily reminders of the hazards they must negotiate; friends in caskets are evidence of what could happen to them. These children also sense that their communities are surrounded by a safe, prosperous society from which they are excluded. They often lack the supports of family or of the community and its institutions to help them deal with their anxiety and despair. It is a horrifying fact that much the same can be said of children in the American inner city.

The statistics regarding the incidence of assaultive violence are disturbing testaments to the scope of the danger confronting so many

First appeared in *Minefields in Their Hearts: The Mental Health of Children in War and Communal Violence,* eds. R. J. Apfel and B. Simon (New Haven: Yale University Press, 1996), 104–127. Copyright © 1996, Yale University. All rights reserved.

American children today.

- From 1984 to 1993 there was a 51 percent increase in violent crimes (murder, forcible rape, robbery, and aggravated assault) in the United States (Justice, 1994).
- In 1993 there were 24,526 murders, 104,806 rapes, 659,757 robberies, and 1,135,009 aggravated assaults nationwide.
- Between 1983 and 1992 there was a 36.1 percent increase in arrests for possession of weapons.
- In 1991, 2.2 million people suffered nonfatal injuries from assaultive violence.
- Homicide is the second leading cause of death among fifteen- to twenty-four-year-olds.
- African-American male teens are eleven times more likely to be killed by guns than their white counterparts.
- From 1989 to 1990 Boston had a 45 percent increase in urban violence; Denver had a 29 percent increase; Chicago, New Orleans, and Dallas had increases of 20 percent (1991).

Studies of rates of children's exposure to scenes of violence produce equally alarming statistics.

- At Boston City Hospital it was reported that one out of every ten children seen in the primary care clinic had witnessed a shooting or stabbing before the age of six—half in the home, half on the streets. The average age of these children was 2.7 years (Taylor et al., 1992).
- In New Haven, 41 percent of a sample of sixth-, eighth-, and tenth-grade students reported having seen someone shot or stabbed in the preceding year (New Haven Public Schools, 1992).

Such exposure to violence was associated with feelings of depression and anxiety, higher levels of antisocial and aggressive activities, greater alcohol use, lower school attainment, and increased risk-taking.

Violence in America is only one of the many significant environmental factors that affect the lives of many American children. For example, each year more than 1 million children feel the effects of divorce and separation (U.S. Congress, 1989); over 1 million babies are born to unwed mothers (National Center for Health Statistics, 1988); and more than 13 million children live in poverty—over 2 million more than a decade ago. While most poor children are white, minority children are much more likely to live in a poor family: 44 percent of African American and 36 percent of Hispanic children are poor, compared with fewer than 15 percent of white children (Department of Commerce, 1990a). One indicator of the outcome of so many stressors is the fact that one in five American children between the ages of three and seventeen are reported by parents to have had a developmental delay, learning disability, or behavioral problems (Zill and Schoenborn, 1988). About 30 percent of ninth-graders do not graduate from high school, and about 500,000 youngsters drop out each year (Kaufman and Frase, 1990). In the nation's urban centers as many as half of all students drop out. Dropouts are 3.5 times as likely as high school graduates to be arrested and 6 times as likely to become unmarried parents (Schorr, 1988).

In addition, children and adolescents increasingly are becoming active participants in the violence that has contributed to the climate of social adversity and despair in which they have been raised. Nationwide juvenile arrests in 1992 included:

- 3,092 children and adolescents arrested for criminal homicide
- 4,750 arrested for rape
- 40,499 arrested for robbery
- 62,039 arrested for aggravated assault
- 138,713 arrested for simple assault
- 47,369 arrested for weapons offenses

Overall, between 1989 and 1993 juvenile arrests for violent crime rose about 36 percent and juvenile arrests for weapons offenses rose 67 percent. The vast majority of the children and adolescents accused of violent crimes are male, and a disproportionate percentage come from minority groups and poor families (Justice, 1994). Though these numbers are disturbing in themselves, statistics alone do not describe the nature of the disruptions that occur in the inner lives of children who are repetitively exposed to violence in their homes and communities.

CHILDREN'S EXPOSURE TO VIOLENCE IN A DEVELOPMENTAL CONTEXT

Children's exposure to interpersonal violence disrupts basic preconditions for their optimal development. Children who witness violence do so in the context of developmentally shifting modes of expressing their own aggressive impulses and feelings. Aggressivity plays a central role in development as a means of achieving a sense of power and competence; it is also a source of conflict between love and hate. Over the course of development, the more direct enactments of the toddler's hitting, biting, and kicking shift to the preschooler's fantasies and play of destructive power, to the competition on the school-age child's sports field, to the vicissitudes of affection and anger that are a part of adolescent and adult relationships (Freud, 1972b; Marans and Cohen, 1993). However, this capacity to move from enactment to more sublimated expressions of aggressivity is undermined when the basic preconditions for feeling competent—including physical safety, stable relationships, and success in achieving desired goals—are overwhelmed by poverty, family dysfunction, overstimulation, and threatened or actual physical danger.

In the lives of all children there are expectable experiences of aggression, violence, and bodily harm at the hands of parents, siblings, and peers, or in the context of accidental injuries. With optimal development, the child is able to distinguish between fantasy and reality, between wishes and enactment, and between projections and real dangers. Again, optimally, parents and other significant adults support children in their attempts to establish these boundaries. They help children feel that the world is basically secure and safe, that there are no demons in the shadows, that their wounds will heal, that there are limits to the expression of aggressive urges, that their wishes to harm others cannot cause accidents that may occur, and that they can express their scary thoughts without worrying that they will be hurt in retaliation.

The potential trauma that follows the child's direct exposure to violence does not simply represent a shock that happens from outside; its impact depends on the diverse personal meanings that a given external event may carry for children in terms of their own internal concerns, past experiences, and phase-specific development.

ACUTE AND LONG-TERM EFFECTS

When children witness or directly experience real communal violence, the line between fantasy and reality is blurred: their most powerful and potentially frightening fantasies about bodily injury, loss of relationships, and loss of impulse control are enacted before their eyes. In the face of stabbings, beatings, and shootings, children may be traumatized because they cannot contain the stimulation within existing mental structures that allow for accommodation and assimilation. When the capacity to anticipate and contain exceptional events of danger is lost, the child feels that dreaded aspects of internal fantasies are vivified and are overwhelmingly real. These traumatizing experiences cannot be adequately dealt with immediately by the usual behavioral responses (fight or flight), and at the same time, the mind is unable to prepare and to rely on familiar defenses (denial, repression, avoidance, intellectualization, and so on).

When these behavioral and mental systems are immobilized—when the child is rendered passive in the face of events that are threatening to his body and mind—a cascade of psychological and physiological processes ensue. The violent events are remembered differently from other events, and the experience is handled in a special fashion. In response to the potentially traumatic circumstances of exposure to violence, children may develop specific, circumscribed symptoms involving disruptions in patterns of sleeping, eating, toileting, attention, and relating, and may also experience generalized fearfulness, disregulation of the startle reflex, and flashbacks of aspects of the violent event (American Psychiatric Association, 1994). The child's avoidant behaviors and general hypervigilance may reflect attempts to guard against the anxiety aroused by persistent, preoccupying memories of various features of the violent event, or they may appear more episodically in response to specific traumatic reminders that derive from a range of circumstances and subjective phenomena associated with the original trauma (Pynoos, 1993). In addition, a child may resort to turning a passive experience into an active response in an attempt to regain a sense of power and control when the dangers of real violence provoke feelings of helplessness and fear. That is, rather than feeling the anxiety and humiliation of being the victim or feeling vulnerable to the aggression of others, the child may become the perpetrator. Like the other post-traumatic stress-related symptoms, oppositional behavior at home and at school may be a transient means for the child to reassert his power precisely when he is feeling most vulnerable. However, when the child is regularly exposed to the dangers of violence, symptoms may no longer serve the function of restitution and recovery but may reflect a chronic adaptation in which vegetative, cognitive, and affective capacities and optimal regulation of functions are severely compromised. In a similar way, the perpetration of violence may represent another long-term adaptation to the experience of being the passive, frightened victim and to chronic exposure to violence. Alterations in character development deriving in part from identification with the exciting and powerful role of perpetrator may become a reliable hedge against the feelings of and helplessness that were aroused by the actual experiences of overwhelming danger. When the most powerful models in the home and neighborhood exercise *their* potency at the end of a fist or a gun, aggressive enactments rather than sublimations may be an adaptive response to both internal and external sources of danger (Marans, 1994).

IMPACT ON FAMILIES AND COMMUNITIES

Adults are not immune to a range of similar responses when they are confronted by communal violence. Their inability to listen and attend to children's needs in the aftermath of traumatic events may be a natural consequence of their attempts at restitution and self-protection from feelings of vulnerability and traumatic disorganization. The potentially detrimental effects on individual and family functioning may also be mirrored in the larger community. Extended family, friends, and neighbors may be inhibited from listening to traumatic narratives and providing distressed individuals with appropriate support for reasons similar to those that inhibit parents from listening to children. In urban neighborhoods, where drug- or gang-related violence is particularly prevalent, many residents may have such a strong psychological investment in avoiding open discussion of their chronic fear and helplessness that there are few people in the community who are emotionally available to share the burdens of other community members at times of acute exposure to new episodes of violence.

Freud described the traumatic situation as one in which the individual has experienced helplessness in the face of a danger whose magnitude outweighs the "subject's estimation of his own strength" (Freud, 1926, p. 166). In many poor urban settings, the instability of families and the extended community places a special burden on existing social institutions that are called on to respond to both victims and perpetrators of violence. However, when service providers—mental professionals, medical providers, school personnel, protective service workers, and law enforcement officers—operate in isolation in their attempts to address the multiple needs of children and families caught in the cycle of violence, they too may find themselves overwhelmed and immobilized. Alternately, these seemingly disparate professional groups may attempt to regroup, capitalizing on knowledge gained independently, and consolidate their efforts developing new strategies for intervening in the cycle of interpersonal violence. If mental health professionals are to play a broader role in these efforts, then clinical expertise and research must be increasingly applied to a range of services that extend beyond the consulting room. While a violent event may precipitate a host of responses that compromise children's developmental potential, it may also provide a window of opportunity for introducing psychotherapeutic interventions and the application of what we have learned in the consulting room to the coordination of diverse services that have an impact on the daily lives of children and their families. New Haven's Child Development-Community Policing Program represents one such model of interdisciplinary collaboration (Marans and Pastore, 1995).

FROM THE CONSULTING ROOM TO THE
STREETS: A COLLABORATIVE RESPONSE

The Child Development–Community Policing (CDCP) Program was formed out of the joint recognition of leaders within the Yale Child Study Center and the New Haven Department of Police Service that police officers and mental health clinicians share serious concerns about the fate of children and families exposed to chronic urban violence, but that, for different reasons, neither group is able to intervene effectively. Though police officers are in daily contact with children who are victims, witnesses, and perpetrators of violence, they do not have the professional expertise, the time, or the other resources necessary to meet these children's psychological needs. Conversely, clinic-based mental health professionals may be professionally equipped to respond to children's psychological distress following episodes of violence, but the acutely traumatized children who are most in need of clinical service rarely are seen in existing outpatient clinics until months or years later, when chronic symptom or maladaptive behavior bring them to the attention of parents, teachers, or the juvenile courts. Valuable opportunities to intervene therefore are lost at the moment when professional contact could provide both immediate stabilization and bridges to a variety of services.

The collaboration between mental health and police professionals was born out of a common-sense recognition that police officers—who not only make house-calls twenty-four hours a day but are also first on the scene of violent events—are in a unique position to help children and families who are at greatest risk of becoming the psychological casualties of violence. Similarly, when mental health professionals venture beyond the consulting room they are much better able to learn more about the impact of violence on the lives of those who are most directly involved: children, families, and the professionals themselves. Working together, police and mental health professionals have combined their observations and knowledge from the consulting room and the streets in an effort to coordinate an array of responses for children and families whose exposure to violence threatens to compromise their development and functioning.

In beginning discussions between officers and clinicians, the issue of volume and the limitations of our isolated attempts to intervene on behalf of children exposed to violence became a jumping-off point for consideration of ways that they might work together. It became clear that each group felt defeated in their individual efforts to take charge and to intervene in ways that lead to an increased mastery for themselves and for those they hope to serve. Police officers, who are regularly exposed to disturbing scenes of violence, are especially susceptible to feelings of despair in identification with the children they encounter, or to fear about the dangers that may await *them* at the next call. In this context, it is understandable that officers defend themselves against such feelings by remaining anonymous, distant and perfunctory, turning a blind eye to the suffering of children, or feeling enraged and disdainful toward the adults who have exposed them to terror. Similarly, the clinicians described cases in which children's symptomatic difficulties in school, at home, and with peers brought them to the outpatient clinic at a point when psychotherapeutic intervention alone was no match for the long history of multiple traumatic experiences that had contributed to their compromised functioning. Clinicians were also confronted by the discrepancy between their recognition of the risk factors associated with children's exposure to violence and the numbers of children who would ever actually reach the consulting rooms. It was thought that a shared frame of reference developed out of existing knowledge from the streets and the consulting room could lead to increased understanding of the needs of children traumatized by their exposure to communal violence and the possibility that collaborative action might replace professional immobilization.

To consider their potential roles in responding to the needs of children exposed to violence, police officers would need to learn more about basic principles of development and concepts of human functioning. Similarly, clinicians would need to learn more about phenomena associated with acute incidents of violence and police practices. Both groups would need to learn about the range and limitations of the other's responsibilities.

Thus, a small group of supervisory officers was exposed to a variety of clinical services and liaison activities with social services. Clinicians spent time in "ride-along" tutorials in squad cars with the supervisory officers. Both groups participated in weekly discussions about principles of development and their application to clinical and policing practices. The practical issue of increasing collaborative responses to violence was addressed through the development of a twenty-four-hour on-call service that would allow officers to receive consultation and would provide immediate clinical response to violent crime scenes in which children were involved. In addition, the fellowships for clinicians and supervisory officers were formalized and a weekly meeting was begun to discuss cases referred through the consultation service. However, it was clear that if rank-and-file officers were to participate in this new endeavor, they too would need to establish a conceptual rationale for their collaborative work with mental health professionals, not simply follow orders from supervisors about making appropriate referrals.

DEVELOPING A COMMON LANGUAGE

In our efforts to increase the attention paid to the children exposed to communal violence it has been essential to establish a regular forum in which officers and clinicians can work out a common ground of concerns and a conceptual rationale for their collaborative work. In weekly seminars, officers and clinicians examine concepts regarding basic human needs; development of capacities for self-regulation and mastery; phase-specific sources of danger/anxiety; the link between behavior and underlying psychic processes (that is, the relation between anxiety and defenses); and individual variation with regard to potential life adaptations. It is crucial that the goal of these seminars is to demonstrate how officers' consideration of principles of development and human functioning can enhance the range of strategies in dealing with various situations and can help establish a more realistic appreciation for the impact they can have on the lives of children and families with whom they interact.

A series of ten seminars, co-led by clinicians and supervisory officers who have completed the fellowship, uses scenarios from the streets—ranging from experiences with parents and infants to involvement with adolescent gangs—to illustrate basic developmental concepts. While the discussions proceed according to a developmental sequence, they attempt to link the inner life of the child with manifest behaviors seen at the original phase of development and the ways that these phenomena may be observed throughout the life cycle. In turn, the seminars allow officers and clinicians to think about the meaning of behavior as an effective tool for determining strategies and as part of an effort to develop collaborative interventions between police and mental health professionals on behalf of children and families exposed to violence.

The convergence of principles of development and their application to policing strategies may be best illustrated in a description of a discussion that emerged in one of the seminar series about toddlerhood. Participants were asked to talk about their understanding of the salient features of the phase, and they responded with ideas about the "terrible twos," tantrums, toilet-training, and bossiness. These topics were elaborated in the discussion until participants began to make connections between how physical maturation, mastery, and the child's sense of omnipotence converge and at times clash with parental expectations and the notion of consequences. Issues regarding separation/individuation also entered into the discussion, as the behavioral assertion of strength, power, and well being could be more broadly understood in terms of the child's developing sense of self-worth and capacity for regulating/expressing urges and feelings. Again, the emphasis of the discussion moved toward the common theme of articulating the relation between observable phenomena and underlying motivation. The central importance of feelings of power, control, and mastery, and the defenses employed when narcissism is injured, was discussed as it applies to toddlers, older children, and adults. Concepts regarding displacement, turning passive into active, and reaction formations were illustrated in material brought from the streets by the officers in the class (Marans and Pastore, 1995).

One of the more powerful illustrations of the relation between anxiety and defense arose after a confrontation that occurred between police officers, a group of young drug dealers, and community members. Several of the officers, including the co-leader who had been involved, described the events. The day after the shooting death of a local drug dealer, a large group of teenagers gathered on a street corner. When two beat officers arrived, the group began jeering and moving toward them. The officers felt threatened and called for backup. Within minutes, squad cars were speeding into the area; the arriving officers formed a line, holding billy clubs at the ready, as the crowd grew more vocal and insulting. Other members of the community joined the crowd and tensions continued to rise until supervisory officers intervened. They first ordered the line of officers to put their billy clubs away and return to their cars. Officers assigned to the neighborhood were asked to wade into the crowd and talk with the most vocal participants they knew—drug dealers and community leaders alike. This group was invited to attend a hastily convened meeting in a nearby church. As the group moved away, the crowd slowly dispersed. Over the next several days, community leaders accompanied officers on patrol as a way of supporting the peace.

Following the description of the events, the officers in the seminar were divided into two groups—cops and crowd members. After meeting separately for several minutes, the groups recreated the standoff. They easily assumed their roles. The "crowd" threw insults at the cops as they moved closer to the cops on the "line." While first remaining very calm, several of the cops broke verbal ranks and began responding to the taunts. While at first they appealed to the crowd to calm down, the replies grew increasingly combative and incendiary.

One African-American officer replayed with another African-American cop on the line an interchange that had occurred when he had been at the original scene. He berated his fellow officer for being a "white man's nigger" and not knowing anything about what it is like to be a "real black man." True to the original scenario, the cop on the line argued that he had grown up in a similar neighborhood and that, unlike his tormentor, he had chosen to work hard and make a better life for himself, and so on. When the crowd member replied that the line cop was a "sellout," the mock pushing began, and the exercise was stopped.

In the discussion that followed officers spoke of intimidation, fear, humiliation, and the experience of being prejudged and insulted by people who do not even know them. In response to questions from the seminar leaders, "crowd members" spoke of their feelings of powerlessness in the face of unemployment and life in a blighted neighborhood—the sense of hopelessness and despair that finds some relief in the excitement and rage that gets targeted on a highly visible enemy. As the discussion continued, displacement and transference were addressed. The argument that developed around the issue of backing down in the face of a hostile crowd versus standing ground and demonstrating power and control was examined in relation to individual and group responses to various sources of anxiety, the degree of perceived danger, and the available capacities to defend against and diminish feelings of helplessness, fear, and humiliation. These themes and others are elaborated as the seminar moves through central concepts regarding the challenges and potential deviations of oedipal, latency, pubertal, and adolescent development.

As the seminars come to an end, officers increasingly refer to the scenes of violence and suffering they confront each day. Themes that commonly emerge in the discussions include sealing over—"getting used to it" and distancing themselves as best they can—displacing their frustration onto family members or citizens with whom they interact, viewing the world dichotomously (that is, us versus them), and heightening the sense of vigilance. These responses are discussed in terms of the defensive functions they serve—against feelings of fear, inadequacy, sadness, despair, and the like—as well as the interference they may pose in achieving the desired goals of their interventions.

Whereas the seminars on child development and human functioning are intended to develop a frame of reference for officers considering the relation between the child's inner life and manifest behavior, the consultation service provides direct support for officers in the field who are dealing with children and families exposed to violence and tragedy. The availability of immediate consultation has often allowed officers in the field to feel more effective in the face of tragedy. By brokering clinical services and attending to the emotional needs of the children involved, officers have a new way of "taking control" and becoming active in the aftermath of violence rather than simply feeling overwhelmed by it, sealing over, and quickly turning away from the scene. For many of the children and families, the referrals may not only offer accessible and responsive clinical services for the first time but may also reflect a new and different experience of officers and mental health professionals. In many of these situations both police and clinicians are not simply viewed as aloof and disengaged, providing too little, too late, but as benign figures of authority who are able to play a role in reestablishing a semblance of stability in the midst of the emotional chaos that often follows children's and families' direct exposure to violence.

INTEGRATING PERSPECTIVES AND INTERVENTIONS

In the first thirty-six months of operation, officers and clinicians together have seen more than 450 children through referrals to the consultation service made by community-based officers. The children, who range in age from two to seventeen, have been exposed to murders, stabbings, beatings, maiming by fire, death by drowning, and gunfire. They have been seen individually and as part of larger groups in their homes, in police substations, in emergency rooms, in schools, in community rooms of public housing projects, and at the Child Study Center. Because of the immediacy of the referrals, we have been able to observe children within minutes of a violent event. As each of these cases has been followed in the weekly Case Conference, we have been able to explore the effects of exposure to violence in terms of the specific characteristics of the event and its context within the family, the community, and the inner life of the child.

We have found, as have other investigators (Martinez and Richters, 1993; Pynoos et al., 1987; Pynoos and Nader, 1989; Pynoos et al., 1994; Terr, 1991), that beyond the obvious factors of direct physical injury to children and their parents, the psychological toll that violence takes on children is determined by an interplay of factors within the child and between the child and his or her surroundings:

- The characteristics of the violence itself—that is, the child's relationship to the perpetrator and victim, proximity to the incident, and response of the caregivers to the incident;

- The developmental phase of the child who is exposed, including preexisting vulnerabilities—that is, the status of emotional and cognitive resources available for mediating anxiety associated with objective and fantasized dangers;
- The familial and community context of the violent incident—that is, whether the incident is isolated and unusual or is part of a pattern of daily life; and
- The nature of responses to the possible effects of the child's exposure to violence by family members, school personnel, and community institutions.

In addition, while the configuration of these factors has varied, we have observed common immediate responses to violent events among the children seen through the consultation service. These include disbelief and denial of the outcome or even the occurrence of the violent event; intense longing for the presence of primary caregivers and concern about their safety (especially among children under age seven); concerns about bodily integrity and competence; revival of, and much talk about, previous losses, injuries, fights, and other episodes of violence; repetitive retelling of the events with ideas that might have altered the real outcome of the episode, described by Pynoos as "intervention fantasies" (Pynoos, 1993); attribution of blame to those not directly involved in the violence; or, alternatively, reveling in the excitement of the action of the violence with talk of the weapons used—who got "capped," "smoked," or "aired" (Marans, 1994).

Discussions about referrals from the consultation service frequently focus on the extent to which children describe the violent events they have witnessed in terms of the developmental phase—specific anxieties that are aroused. By observing the acute reactions and by listening to the stories from the child exposed to violence, we are able to better see what constitutes the specific danger that overwhelms that child, or what aspects and meanings of the event are experienced as exceptional and overwhelming—and therefore "traumatizing." For clinicians, direct observation of and interaction with children in the community who have just been exposed to incidents of traumatic violence, as well as regular collaborative contact with community-based police officers, has enhanced our understanding of the realities of these children's traumatic experiences, the environmental background against which acute episodes of violence take place, and the potentially therapeutic use that many children can make from their contact with police officers and other adults in the community. Increased understanding of acute traumatic reactions and environmental variables has, in turn, led to greater flexibility in the delivery of clinical services to families that might not otherwise make use of these resources. For officers, exposure to developmental principles and clinical consultation has expanded the range and specificity of their observations of children with whom they come in contact and has led to an expanded range of possible policing interventions, including referrals for individual clinical services, direct supportive interactions between officers and individual children and parents, and police involvement in community efforts to address neighborhood problems regarding the physical and psychological safety of children and families.

As a result of the ongoing collaboration and the establishment of trusting relationships among police and mental health professionals, both clinical and policing responses are increasingly informed by shared assessments of an individual child's perspectives, needs, and resources, as well as those of the family and community in which the violent events have occurred. In direct response to our increasing understanding of the multiple and interrelated stresses confronting the children and families referred to the consultation service, collaborative responses to acute incidents of violence have increasingly involved the coordination of multiple resources that have impact on the lives of children and families—schools, protective services, medical care, housing and the like. The following incidents illustrate these observations.

A STREET SHOOTING

Acute Responses

At noon on a late spring day, shots rang out. A school bus carrying eight children aged five and six was caught in the crossfire between rival drug dealers. The bus was hit by the gunfire, and a six-year-old boy was shot in the head. The bus went to a nearby middle school, where the children were met by police officers and emergency medical personnel. Officers trained in the CDCP program were the first to greet the children; they contacted members of the consultation service, whom they asked to join them at the middle school. The boy who was shot was taken to the hospital (he survived surgery and suffered neurological impairment for which he continues to receive rehabilitative services). The remaining children were taken inside the middle school building by police officers, who immediately began coordinating efforts to get the parents to the middle school. The officers described their central aim as protecting the children from the excitement surrounding the shooting (camera crews arriving, multiple police personnel, onlookers) and reuniting them with parents. Children were *not* interviewed by officers about the shooting. Officers explained that while this practice used to be part of the standard approach in an investigation, the reality was that any information obtained from the children was not immediately necessary and, according to the sergeant in charge of the scene, would only retraumatize the children, especially when what they needed the most was to be with their parents.

The CDCP clinicians arrived on the scene within ten minutes of the shooting. They were briefed by their police colleagues and were taken to the gym, where the children were sitting on the floor. Middle school personnel attempted to engage the children in a discussion about what they had seen, but the children remained quiet, clutching their knees and staring into the middle distance. The CDCP clinicians were introduced to the school personnel, who moved to the background as the clinicians began to work with the children. The clinicians had brought paper and markers. They sat down with two children each and asked them whether they would like to draw pictures. Each child quietly declined, but when asked whether they would like the clinician to draw something, the response was unanimously positive, as was the requested content of the pictures: "Draw my mommy." Each child was asked what sort of face the mommy should have and what words might fill the speech bubble that went along with the drawing of the face. The instructions for faces fell into two categories: happy and sad. The words alternated between "I'm so happy to see you!" and "I was so sad and worried about you!" After engaging in the drawings, the children grew more verbal, and each began to make inquiries about where their mothers were and when they would arrive. All of the children expressed concern that perhaps their mothers had been hurt and would not be coming for them. The senior police officer on the scene, a CDCP fellow, told the children and clinicians that all of the parents had been located and were on their way to the school.

One of the children then asked a clinician to draw a picture of a head. Whose head? "Um, a boy's head . . . that just got shot with a bullet." The rest of the children overheard this question and immediately turned their attention to the picture. The clinician requested details in order to complete the picture and asked whether any of the children wished to add something themselves. Three children scribbled the same ingredient with a red marker—blood, which soon covered much of the page. There were some questions about what was happening to the friend who had been shot, but most of the questions and comments had to do with bodily functions—How much blood does the body have? Can parts of the body fall off?—and talk quickly turned to a more spirited group discussion about the physical feats each could perform. The discussion was punctuated by sidelong glances to the door as parents began to arrive to pick up their children. Each parent was seen briefly by the clinician, given a telephone number to call with questions regarding their child's experiences, and asked whether they could be contacted for follow-up assessments.

While the crime scene was secured and the criminal investigation was begun, similar attention was paid to the emotional needs of the children who were caught in the experience of violence. All aspects of the response to the shooting—determining how to inform both the middle school and elementary communities about the shooting; briefing parents and school personnel; consulting with teachers, school administrators, and parents about how to respond to children in the classroom and at home; and making additional clinical services available—were coordinated and carried out by the CDCP Program in conjunction with the school system. Officers trained in the program were able to communicate information about the shooting in formal briefing sessions with parents and school personnel and informally in their encounters with children who approached them in the streets. They delivered information about the circumstances and background of the shooting, and they communicated their understanding about the meanings of adult expressions of rage and feelings of helplessness in a manner that indicated their sophistication about the complexity of responses to violence. The CDCP officers and clinicians were able to influence broader community responses to the shooting as well. They successfully argued that, while making some adults feel less helpless, using squad cars to escort school buses the day after the shooting would only exacerbate children's concerns about safety. In a similar vein, officers showed appreciation for children's anxiety and vulnerability by discussing their concerns about the children as they negotiated with the news people who gathered around the children's school. As a result, they helped to minimize the intrusiveness and associated excitement of cameras and the barrage of questions thrown at the children and families. Because of the CDCP responses to the shooting, the police in this situation were seen not merely as harbingers of tragic news and violence but as sources of effective authority, concerned about the safety and emotional well-being of the children and families affected (Marans and Pastore, 1995).

Clinical Follow-up

Five of the seven children received follow-up psychoanalytic psychotherapy because of enduring post-traumatic stress symptoms—disruptions in sleeping and eating; increased separation anxiety; and hypervigilance, generalized anxiety, and avoidant behaviors—that were not part of the premorbid history. Two vignettes offer illustrations of how a child's developmental phase and life circumstances determine the context and specific meaning of a disturbing external event and illustrate the effectiveness of preventive intervention for longer-term emotional and social growth. Each case example is a condensation of material that emerged during two to four months of weekly and twice-weekly treatment.

Beverly, five and a half years old, was sitting across the aisle from her classmate when he was shot. Her previous school functioning was good, as was her adaptation in an intact family (mother, father, and ten-month-old brother). Her developmental history was unremarkable. After the shooting, Beverly had difficulties with sleeping and eating, multiple new fears, and a need to remain close to her mother. These symptoms continued for two weeks before her parents agreed with the clinician's recommendation for individual work with the child in conjunction with guidance for the parents.

In her individual sessions, Beverly repeatedly returned to the scene of the shooting, reviewing an increasing array of details both in play with toy figures and in her drawings. Each narrative ended with Beverly stating that she felt scared or bad. Over time, the therapist probed these feelings—either within the action of the play or within the narrative that accompanied the pictures. Beverly would elaborate that she felt scared that the bullet might have hit her and very bad because her friend had been hurt. In one session, she drew the bullet tracking around her head on an eventual path to the head of her classmate. She grew quiet and looked forlorn. With the suggestion that there was a connection between her feelings and the story that lay behind the picture, Beverly revealed a secret whose telling spanned many sessions and was accompanied by a dramatic reduction and final resolution of her presenting symptoms.

The first part of the secret was that for several days before the shooting Beverly had been reprimanded by the driver for her behavior on the bus. Beverly thought that perhaps the bullet had really been meant for her as punishment. Later she told her therapist that she had been teasing and poking at the very classmate who was shot. The third part of the secret was about her baby brother. With great anxiety, Beverly reported that she teased the baby on numerous occasions and that, in fact, she often wished the brother were no longer around. With this confession, the cause of her worry and guilty feelings became clearer. She was able to articulate her fear that her bad wishes about her brother had come true in the shooting of her schoolmate and that her wishes would be discovered and severely punished. The therapist was able to point out that Beverly was behaving as if the reality of the scary elements had somehow been under her magical control. Her hostile wishes toward a rival baby brother and their displacement onto a school-mate were not unusual. However, for Beverly, the *realization* of these wishes—if only in the displacement—constituted the central source of her overwhelming anxiety and traumatization. In addition, her sense of magical control reflected both age-expectable phenomena augmented by reliance on magic for the pur-poses of restitution and recovery. That is, a belief in magical control would revise the original experience of traumatization or "absence of control" in the shooting, even if the belief in magic might also lead to a tremendous sense of responsibility for and guilt about the real and imagined event.

Another child, Miguel, age five, presented with multiple symptoms. Miguel was the youngest in a family of six. Both parents and a nineteen-year-old brother worked, one sister was in high school, and the other was in middle school. Prior to the shooting Miguel had no difficulties with sleeping or with leaving home for school or other activities. This changed dramatically after the shooting of his classmate. He insisted on sleeping with the light on throughout the night, departures from home were very upsetting for him, and in the re-maining days of school, he complained of sickness in order to avoid going. It took several weeks of treatment for Miguel to reveal in his play that he was ter-rified that the people responsible for the shooting of his classmate would come to shoot him and all of the members of his family. The fact that the shooters were in jail did nothing to alleviate Miguel's fears or symptoms. But his ability to express his central worry opened the door for further exploration, clarifica-tion of his thoughts, and greater mastery over a very frightening experience.

What lay behind Miguel's fear of being shot was his attempt to explain to himself why the shooting had happened and perhaps, with this explanation, to feel more able to predict similarly dangerous events. However, the explanation Miguel developed was limited by condensation and by the concrete thinking typical of his phase of development. Miguel was eventually able to explain to his therapist, and then to his parents, the following ideas: He had learned in school about how bad drugs are—that they do terrible things to the body, that they make people violent and are the cause of fights between drug dealers. When the shooting started and the bus was hit by gunfire, Miguel assumed that the shooting was about drugs and that if the school bus was being shot at, it must somehow be involved with drugs. If the school bus was involved in drugs and he was on the school bus, then he must somehow be connected with drugs, and if he was involved in drugs, then so must be his family. If he and the family were involved in drugs, then they too would fall victim to gunfire. While there was no indication that his family was involved with drug use or dealings, the dangers were brought home to Miguel as a powerful response to being shot at and to seeing his friend bleeding. While generating considerable fear, Miguel's explanation relied on the cognitive resources available to him and provided the basis for altering the traumatic episode. In the version of *his* making, Miguel was able to anticipate the danger—he expected assailants to come after him— and he defended against the danger by staying up at night, staying close to home, keeping family nearby. Understanding Miguel's solution in the context of phase-specific concerns and capacities helped him to clarify the distinction between his fantasy configurations and the factual information and led to a resolution of his developmental crisis and its attendant symptoms.

A ROBBERY AT GUNPOINT

Acute Responses

Whereas phase-appropriate concerns associated with the body, sibling rivalry, and magical and concrete thinking played a crucial role in understanding and addressing the nature of trauma for Beverly and Miguel, another incident illustrated an adolescent version of overwhelming, disorganizing anxiety. Mark, age fifteen, was robbed at gunpoint on a Friday evening. He had been walking with friends when two men put a reportedly large-caliber semi-automatic weapon in his face and demanded his money and gold jewelry. Mark had been walking behind several friends, and they were unaware of what occurred in an alley off of the main sidewalk. Mark later reported that men repeatedly shoved the weapon in his face and threatened to shoot him. After taking his valuables, the assailants fled, and Mark ran home. He ran into his room crying uncontrollably, hid on the floor of his closet and, in spite of his mother's urging refused to come out. After a while, Mark told his mother through sobs what had occurred, and she phoned the police. Each of the three officers who arrived had been trained in the child development seminars, and the supervisory officers had completed the fellowship. As one of the officers approached the bedroom, Mark began to scream. The officer told him that he had heard what had happened to him and that he realized that the hold-up was terrifying. Mark would not look at the officer and yelled at him to leave the room. The officer was about to leave when the supervisor pointed to his gun and utility belt. The officer then removed his holster and weapon, explaining to Mark that he would leave them outside the room, as he understood how frightening guns might be to him. Mark continued to sob and shake uncontrollably, but he allowed the officer to help him out of the room, and he accepted the suggestion that he go to the emergency room for treatment. The consultation service clinician was called and met Mark at the hospital.

Clinical Contact

During the interview, Mark was able to look at the clinician only after a comment that was made about how fear could make a person feel small and helpless—a very undesirable feeling for a fifteen-year-old guy. Mark began to talk about the events, repeating the scene and his assailants' commands to him over and over. The repetition began to include slight alterations in the details, and Mark protested that he should have "grabbed the gun and kicked each of the [attackers] in the balls." He described the gun muzzle as huge and insisted that he thought the attackers meant to kill him. As his shaking, hyperventilating, and sobbing subsided, Mark began to talk about the earlier part of the evening. He explained that before being robbed he had been "hanging back from his homeboys because they were with their ladies" and he had wanted to "give them space." He shyly told the clinician that he didn't have a girlfriend, and then he exploded with rage and broke into tears. He wanted to get a gun to kill the guys who "messed with him." He didn't deserve what had happened to him, he said—he was a good student and had just completed an important history paper. He explained that he had bought all of the thin gold chains he wore— emphasizing that he was not to be lumped with "low-life drug dealers." Mark began to cry again as he swore revenge. The clinician commented that it was humiliating to have to feel so terrified and suggested that Mark was wishing he could undo his experience. Mark replied that if he had had a gun or had disarmed his attackers he wouldn't have to feel as though he'd "wimped out." The clinician agreed that feeling powerful would certainly be the opposite of what he had experienced with a gun in his face. Mark brightened and looked up suddenly, exclaiming that now he remembered the gun more clearly—it wasn't a 9mm semiautomatic, it was a BB gun. As the acute terror diminished, he was also able to remember the make of the car in which the assailants drove off, as well as clear descriptions of the two men. His restitution fantasies of revenge began to take another form as Mark talked about helping the police make an arrest. As his request, Mark spoke with the detective involved in the case to offer the information he had recovered in the course of the interview. Two hours after admission to the emergency room, Mark was discharged.

Mark was seen in two follow-up sessions in which he continued to go over the events. The fantasies of what he should have done were intermingled with talk of the mortification of feeling helpless and of the increasing recognition that there actually was nothing he could have done to alter what had occurred. When his sleeping difficulties and hypervigilant feelings abated, Mark declined further clinical contact. However, over the following several weeks one of the three responding officers stopped in on him regularly for brief chats during the course of their usual patrol. In the last clinical follow-up, six months after the incident, Mark had still not bought a gun and, instead of reciting his numerous violent revenge fantasies, spoke of his latest academic demands and of his new friendships with the cops on his beat. While he had not forgotten the terror or rage associated with his experience, Mark added that his good memory had been instrumental in helping the police arrest the men who had attacked him. And, as he said, "that felt really good."

WAR, COMMUNAL VIOLENCE, AND
THERAPEUTIC IMPLICATIONS

In our work with children exposed to communal violence in the American inner city, we hear frequent references in the popular press to "urban warfare" and to the notion that the experience of random, familial, and gang- or drug-related violence is analogous to the experience of violence associated with civil or international warfare. There are important similarities between the experiences of individuals exposed to warfare and to urban violence in terms of the range of acute and long-term physiological and psychological responses. Both in wartime and in violent city neighborhoods, children are vulnerable to the internal and external factors that place them at greater risk for developmental difficulties or, conversely, tend to protect them from the most adverse effects of their exposure to violence. Regardless of the arena of violence, children's healing and recovery are assisted by such internal attributes as cognitive competence, previously developed range of defensive mechanisms, self-esteem and secure attachments, as well as by external factors, including supportive parents and other adults, security of their physical environment, and continuity of interpersonal relationships and social institutions. Both in wartime and in the city, children can be helped to recover from their experiences of violence through prompt reestablishment of physical safety, family ties, and normal routines; through the provision of accurate information that promotes cognitive understanding; through the availability of opportunities to use imagination to take distance from upsetting memories and to try on different resolutions of the events to which they were exposed; and through the calm, sensitive attention of caring adults, particularly the child's parents.

Not only are there general similarities between children's exposure to warfare and to urban interpersonal violence, there are also important distinctions in the cultural context of children's experiences that can have a significant impact on their adaptation. In addition to the strengths that children and families may find within themselves for coping with exposure to communal violence, there are also protective factors built into cultures. These include a sense of purpose and feeling of belonging to something greater than one's self. When they function well, ideology and the belief in a larger political or religious worldview justify terrible sacrifices and mediate suffering. In many wartime situations, at least where the fighting does not persist for generations, children are also protected by a sense of continuity with a community not torn by violence. In these circumstances, adults who remember a life of prewar stability can transmit to their children a sense that pervasive violence is not the only possible life experience, and that their own lives will return to normal.

Unfortunately for many poor children in urban America, it is precisely this sense of past stability, historical continuity, and hope for the future that is missing from the family and community environments in which their chronic exposure to communal violence takes place. In contrast with the experience of many children in wartime, children in the American inner city live in a world characterized not by consistent reminders of a more stable past but by multigenerational poverty, academic failure, political and economic disenfranchisement, and a pervasive absence of expectations that the future will be better than the present. In communities plagued by random rather than politically or ethnically driven violence, what is also missing is a sense that the suffering of individual children and families has meaning in relation to their belonging to a larger group. These limitations of socioeconomic security and family and community cohesion are likely to have placed inner-city children in developmental jeopardy before their exposure to violent events, and these same factors are likely to compound children's disadvantage in their efforts at restitution in the wake of violence. For these reasons, traditional modes of conceptualizing and delivering mental health and social services are likely to be inadequate to the psychological needs of the children and families who are most vulnerable to the effects of that violence. Professionals who hope to intervene successfully in these children's lives following their experience of traumatic violence must take extraordinary measures to create new external structures that can promote healing and recovery where existing family and community structure is so limited. We must be prepared to sustain these intensive efforts for a very long time if a new generation is to move beyond their traumatic experiences.

EXTENDING COLLABORATIONS

Regardless of their shared concerns, no single group of professionals can address the multiple needs of the children and families subjected to massive environmental stress when the professionals attempt to intervene in isolation from one another. The collaboration between police and mental health professionals in New Haven provides one model of creative interdisciplinary action on behalf of children who are at great developmental risk owing to their exposure to violence and who would be unlikely to receive effective intervention through traditional models of social service delivery. Other collaborative projects around the country also engage mental health professionals in partnerships with other social service professionals and apply principles of child development to interdisciplinary work with disadvantaged children in community settings. These integrative efforts offer possibilities for more efficient and effective service to vulnerable children and families in spite of the potentially overwhelming volume of children's psychological needs.

In one such project, a group of school administrators, teachers, pediatricians, and clinicians in New Haven developed a model for school-based crisis intervention to follow episodes of violence that affect large groups of children in a particular school, such as a death or serious injury to a student or teacher, or a shooting in the school building. By establishing crisis teams in advance, and by planning for possible crisis responses, schools are in a better position to provide children and their families with the stability and clear authority they need to reorganize in the wake of a frightening event; a sense of chaos can exacerbate feelings of fear and helplessness. School-based responses, utilizing personnel familiar to the students and their families, can provide accurate information about the event, afford opportunities for many children to discuss their experience and reactions and to receive emotional support from peers and teachers, and identify those children who need more intensive mental health intervention (Schonfeld and Kline, 1994).

The work of Taylor (1994) in Boston and Garbarino (et al., 1992) in Chicago also link mental health and educational interventions by providing clinical support and consultation to day care centers, nurseries, and elementary schools in inner-city communities experiencing overwhelming levels of violence. In these settings, thoughtful clinical support for teachers and other school personnel can enable school staff to understand and intervene in the symptomatic behavior of many young children suffering as a result of their exposure to the chronic violence around them. Clinically informed and well-supported teachers are also in a position to identify which of the many children exposed to violence are in most urgent need of direct clinical intervention.

Police, juvenile probation officers, and mental health professionals in New Haven have also begun to work together to address some of the inefficiencies and ineffectiveness of the juvenile justice system in attending to the needs of children and adolescents involved in violent activity. Many children arrested for delinquent acts are known to multiple professionals before becoming involved in the juvenile justice system. Arrest can therefore represent an opportunity for collaboration and interdisciplinary problem solving as an alternative to traditional approaches, which emphasize the independence of the court and associated agencies and which often result in the duplication of efforts or in the assignment of court-ordered treatments that are mismatched to the needs of the child. In a pilot project, police and probation officers have begun to share supervision and monitoring of juvenile offenders by relocating probation officers to community substations and by engaging neighborhood officers in supervising community service projects for youth on probation. In addition, the CDCP Program is coordinating a collaboration among local probation, child welfare, and police and mental health services regarding the assessment, disposition, and case supervision of juvenile offenders.

Other collaborative approaches include home-based family support and preservation programs, in which child welfare professionals work to serve children who have been abused or neglected by their families, and children dealing with another war—that of AIDS affecting their caretakers (Adnopoz, 1993; Adnopoz et al., 1991). Home-based approaches can also coordinate clinical services for children with substance-abuse, psychiatric, or medical problems, as well as ensure appropriate treatment for their disabled parents (Adnopoz and Nagler, 1992).

The specifics of these programs vary widely, but they all share a recognition that the volume of children whose psychological development is in jeopardy cannot be served through traditional clinic-based individual psychiatric approaches and that clinicians must move into community settings where the most vulnerable children and families are located and forge new partnerships with other professionals who share their concerns.

CONCLUSION

In this chapter we have considered the needs of children acutely and chronically exposed to communal violence, which has reached epidemic proportions in the United States. We have discussed some of the impediments that professionals face when responding with grave concern: they run the risk of becoming overwhelmed, much like the children they seek to help. Alternatively, we may face and tolerate the disturbing conflicts that are aroused in the areas of love and hate, empathy and sadism, bodily integrity and life-threatening injury, and the like. When this is possible we are in a much stronger position to admit our helplessness and renew our exploration of the phenomena associated with children's exposure to violence and the range of our potential responses. Recognizing both the complexity of human development and the multiple environmental factors that may impede that development, it is clear that our concerns require multifaceted and sustained responses. Those of us in the fields of mental health, law enforcement, and social and legal services do not have solutions for the multiple social problems that undermine the developmental potential of too many of our nation's children. But when we are able to share the burdens of our tasks, the wealth of our experiences, and the frustrating limitations of our knowledge, we can return together, again and again, to the question: What next? It is only then that the volume will not impede our abilities to listen and to attend to the needs of children and families whose present and future we aim to serve and protect.

Part Six **Under Commodious Wings:**

Research and Mentorship

Chapter 11   The Immorality of Not Knowing:

The Ethical Imperative to Conduct Research in

Child and Adolescent Psychiatry (1994)

Ami Klin and Donald J. Cohen

INTRODUCTION

In the past fifteen years there has been an increasing awareness of the value of safeguards and regulations protecting participants of studies in the behavioral and medical sciences. Classic behavioral studies conducted in the 60s and 70s such as Milgram's (1974) research on obedience to authority, Zimbardo's research on role play (Zimbardo et al., 1977), or even Harlow's (Harlow, 1971) and Gallup's studies involving non-human primates (Gallup and McClure, 1971), would probably raise concerns and not be approved by most Institutional Review Boards (IRBs) nowadays. This trend towards "higher standards" for approval of research was given regulatory status by the National Commission for the Protection of Human Subjects of Biomedical and Behavioral Research (1977) defining the basic ethical principles that should guide research involving human subjects. "Respect for per-

First appeared in *Ethics in Child Psychiatry*, ed J. Hattab (Jerusalem: Gefen Publishing House, 1994), 217–232. Copyright © 1994, Gefen Publishing House. All rights reserved.

sons" and the inalienable rights of subjects to privacy, confidentiality and informed consent were established as the necessary requirements protecting individuals from being "used merely as means" to the researcher's goals. In practice, investigators today are required both ethically and legally to assure that subjects provide informed consent, which signifies the participant's volitional embrace of the investigator's scientific goals. Procedures judged as entailing risk of any form or deception, samples which are not demographically representative of the distribution of gender or ethnicity among the general population, and the involvement of particularly vulnerable populations who are not able to fulfill the requirement of "informed consent" (such as children and the mentally impaired), are all particularly scrutinized in order to prevent injustices affronting societal consensus on appropriate norms of scientific conduct.

These moral values are obviously valuable counterweights against thoughtless and potentially dangerous pursuit of studies that may harm individuals or distort the scientific search for truth. Yet, their implementation has not gone without some inadvertent deleterious impact on the field of human research; also, by framing the questions primarily in terms of the protection of individuals, the protagonists of scientific research—the investigators—may be cast, as in science fiction thrillers, as more dangerous than beneficent. Yet, the goal of ethical regulations is not the needless burdening of scientific progress or the elimination of research. Rather, it is the pursuit of an acceptable balance between trying to assure that humans are not endangered or their autonomy reduced, on the one hand, and the quest for understanding the unknown and the benefits that may accrue from knowledge based on empirical, systematic and creative research, on the other. Research is not supposed to be judged as unduly intrusive, nor are investigators to be perceived as in need of scrutiny to prevent them from their unethical pursuit of dehumanized science. Nevertheless, the cultural pendulum may have swung too far and away from the societal commitment to the fundamental value of the scientific enterprise: to probe the unknown—responsibly and respectfully, but also relentlessly—in order to make knowledge the property not only of a given culture, but particularly of those members of society who are most in need of its benefits.

In a field as young and uncharted as child and adolescent psychiatry, the balance between the known and the unknown still tilts heavily toward the latter. Its population is probably the one most in need of protection. Yet, a cultural aversion directed at research with children may leave whole areas of behavior, pathology, and potential treatments barred to systematic examination. An acknowledgment of the extent of the unknown carries with it a responsibility, indeed a moral mandate, to conduct research. The moral dictum "first do no harm" goes hand in hand with "strive to prevent or minimize harm," be it the result of congenital anomaly, disease process, or societal inequities.

The dilemma defined by the equally valid ethical principles of protection of subjects and need for knowledge is nowhere more acute than when subjects of research are children. Here, the uncertainty about the ethical propriety of clinical investigation has led to some ethically untenable results. One extreme example of over-conformance to safety considerations is provided by what Shirkey (Shirkey, 1968) called the "therapeutic orphans of our expanding pharmacopoeia" (p. 119), a situation created by investigators' great reluctance to conduct studies to determine the safety and efficacy of drugs in children. The use of drugs in childhood is often considered an "orphan" indication, as if childhood was an anomalous and rare state of being and the diseases of childhood were of secondary importance. As Levine (1986, pp. 239–241) points out, if we consider the availability of drugs proved safe and effective through the devices of modern clinical pharmacology and clinical trials a benefit, then it is unjust to deprive classes of persons—e.g. children and pregnant women—of this benefit. The practical implication of this void in knowledge is that practitioners often ignore labels that warn of the unknown effects of drugs on these populations. By so doing, a tendency is created to expose children to unknown risks of drugs. This possibly maximizes the frequency of the occurrence of unsuspected side effects in children and minimizes the probability of their early and systematic detection. It should be noted that most drugs proved safe and effective in adults do not produce unexpected adverse reactions in children (Levine, 1978); yet, when they do, the numbers of harmed children may be higher than would be the case had the drugs been researched systematically and their therapeutic dosage and side-effect profiles determined, before their introduction into clinical practice (Cohen, 1977). At times, the use of a medication for an orphan indication may lead to quite surprising side-effects that would not have been risked if the full implications were known beforehand, as was the case when desipramine was associated with sudden death among hyperactive children (Riddle et al., 1993). Also, it is only through the study of children that the long-term effects on maturation and development can be defined (such as ultimate height, eventual appearance of disturbances in blood pressure, alterations in the timing of puberty, or subtle effects on CNS development). When drugs are tested only with adults, the impact on maturation is completely ignored.

Clinical practice and research with children should obviously strive to exemplify a high level of ethical concern. But there is the danger that such principles might serve as self-justification for inaction, reinforced by an often unflattering portrayal of researchers and fear of malpractice litigation. Our ethical sensitivities, however, should be as much aroused by the persistence of acknowledged ignorance as by the wish to avoid unethical research. For the ethical pride we might take in avoiding human investigation with children will bring no solace to children (and their families) afflicted by developmental or psychiatric disorders, or whose lives and development are seriously burdened by disadvantaged circumstances.

In this chapter, we would like to consider illustrations of the price exacted by the lack of knowledge, and the accompanying ethical imperative to conduct research, in the context of two conditions—one congenital and one environmental—which disrupt the developmental process and growth of children. These illustrations exemplify the fallacy entailed in the assumption that protection of subjects and the research enterprise represent confrontative values. These illustrations also argue that research inaction in clinical practice is not an ethically-neutral stance; the lack of serious research may, and often does, signify a willingness for society to consign children to chronic suffering. Unexamined hypotheses about etiology and treatment, even if they represent the "state of the art" and the "standard of care," represent a willingness by clinicians and society to live with ignorance. This complacence belittles the value of those in need of valid knowledge and authenticated treatments.

AUTISM

Autism is the most severe and most researched psychiatric disorder of early onset, and in the fifty years since Kanner's original description of the syndrome (Kanner, 1943), its research literature has grown to voluminous size. The trends in autism research have more often reflected cultural shifts occurring within the behavioral sciences—from psychoanalytic concepts to the more recent computational metaphors of the cognitive sciences—than paradigm shifts resulting from validated scientific discoveries. As a result, even though we may now assert that a great deal more is known about autism than during the 1940s (Cohen and Donnellan, 1987), our understanding of the etiology, pathogenesis, and treatment of autism remains embarrassingly limited. Large areas of the literature appear to be plagued, ironically, by one of the very defining criteria of the disorder, namely insistence on sameness.

In order to break new ground in a field that has been so active and yet has produced so few tangible gains in basic understanding and effective treatment of a disorder, investigators are required not only to depart from their own theoretical preconceptions, but to actively pursue new and more "aggressive" approaches. Such approaches are becoming increasingly available with the technological revolution taking place in the neurobiological sciences, such as neuroimaging, and the increased understanding of brain formation and function provided by molecular biology. To be sure, some of these methodologies carry a price of discomfort for the patients and their families. Invasive procedures, from blood drawing to interviews of the extended family, may raise concerns among child psychiatrists and others involved with children's care. After all, such medical procedures are usually deemed justified only for specific therapeutic indications, for example the diagnosis of suspected brain lesions or treatable diseases.

And yet, few mental health professionals would characterize autism as anything but a medical condition, albeit characterized by an as of yet ill-defined neurologic etiology. Though still diagnosed exclusively in terms of behavioral presentation, few if any disorders of childhood can be as devastating to a child's development and the family's life as autism. But because the condition is still characterized as a behavioral syndrome, the investment of the scientific community is somewhat halfhearted. Had a biological marker been found for the disorder, as in the case of metabolic (e.g. PKU) or infectious (e.g. HIV) diseases, the commitment to new approaches, and willingness to make use of the most recent methodologies available, would probably be of a different order of magnitude.

From an ethical standpoint, acknowledgment of the devastating impact of autism and its medical nature should make us at least as uneasy as one would feel when confronting any other severe, chronic life-disruptive disorder of unknown origin. Unfortunately, there is very little that the practitioner can do in terms of medical workup that is likely to yield results significant enough to justify the discomfort and cost of available procedures in the case of the individual child. This is a message as painful to the child's caregivers as it is to the compassionate mental health professional. With disorders as severe and mysterious as autism, medicine historically has found a sense of self-justification and comfort through the pursuit of new knowledge. But how far are we willing to go, how strong is the ethical mandate justifying research of autism, and what are the safeguards necessary to protect this vulnerable population?

Interestingly, systematic research has done much to dispel one of the most harmful misconceptions of the origins of autism. Based on the prevalent notions of child development at the time, several authors (e.g. Bettelheim, 1967) suggested a potential role of parental psychopathology in the pathogenesis of the disorder. Specifically, the social withdrawal typical of autistic children was hypothesized to be the result of emotionally unresponsive and inadequate parenting. Already burdened by their children's disabilities, caregivers were also faced with the accusation that they actually contributed to, if not caused, the disorder afflicting their child. Terms such as "refrigerator parents" invaded the literature of autism for many years. It was only with the advent of epidemiological studies showing that the disorder did not discriminate in terms of social class or culture, of further studies showing no evidence of increased parental psychopathology, of psychological research demonstrating that the nearly ubiquitous mental retardation was a reality not attributable to "negativism" or non-compliance, of medical research documenting the association of the disorder with a host of medical conditions such as congenital rubella and fragile X syndrome, as well as with a higher risk for seizure disorders and other neurological abnormalities, that this misconception was rectified and autism redefined as a condition of "organic" etiology.

Paradoxically, however, the same approach that served to protect children and their families from cruel misconceptions is often viewed with suspicion when used to explore a different kind of familial link, namely genetics. The early impression that autism had no genetic aspects is now increasingly questioned by research findings (Pauls, 1987) showing that siblings are at a significantly greater risk for also exhibiting autism and other developmental difficulties, and that monozygotic twins are more likely than fraternal twins to be concordant for the disorder (Folstein and Piven, 1991). Familial links in milder forms of autism, such as "Asperger syndrome" (Wing, 1981) appear even more pronounced. Nevertheless, investigators find themselves in a vulnerable position not shared by colleagues researching more "purely medical" conditions such as Alzheimer's disease or heart conditions.

Equally vulnerable is the position of the researcher interested in the pathogenesis of autism. Being a disorder of very early onset, autism has a pervasive impact on the emergence of most developmental processes. And yet, autistic children come to the attention of the specialist only after an average of three to four years from the onset or recognition of the disorder (Siegel et al., 1988), leaving the crucially important early aspects of the syndrome outside the realm of investigation. Though helpful, parental reports and non-traditional sources of information such as home videos made by parents prior to diagnosis are fraught with methodological difficulties. Given the low prevalence of the disorder, prospective studies are economically prohibitive except if carried out with a high-risk population—in this case, with the younger siblings of autistic individuals. Such forms of research require a degree of intrusion and intervention that raises several ethical considerations, including the arousal of inevitable parental concerns (which can, nevertheless, be appropriately addressed with sensitive genetic counseling). A reluctance to conduct such research is probably unmatched in other fields of medicine, where genetic counseling and monitoring are seen as an obligation of the health professional. The prevailing assumption that the intrusion accompanying research in autism is resented by potential participants has so far gone unexamined.

Neurobiological research on autism, with its inevitably invasive methodologies, is also viewed with skepticism, much of which is based on the still limited yield of this research effort. Neurobiological findings vary considerably and are often subtle. For example, neuroanatomical models have placed the "site of lesion" at various points of the neuraxis, from the brain stem and cerebellum to the cortex (Golden, 1987). Neurochemical findings are equally elusive, with serious limitations identified in even the most commonly reported findings such as elevations of peripheral levels of serotonin (Anderson and Hoshino, 1987). Neurobiological research is plagued by the lack of precise and testable mechanisms, poor nosology, and small samples. With the recent advancements in technology and methodology, and refinement in descriptive phenomenology and classification, the need for carefully designed studies of sufficiently large numbers of patients has once again come to the fore. The complexity factor added by the developmental nature of autism signifies that children should also be subjects in neurobiological research. Nevertheless, the constraints posed by the inclusion of children in, say neuroimaging or neurochemical studies, can become nearly insurmountable. The question remains whether by so doing we are protecting them from harmful procedures, or denying them the benefits of an expanding science.

This question would probably have little meaning if a "purely medical" disorder, such as leukemia, was involved. In the 1960s, when leukemia was an almost certainly fatal illness, leukemic children underwent highly experimental treatment trials which promised little benefit and were often associated with a great deal of suffering, discomfort and perhaps even earlier death from drug side effects. Those concerned with the child's rights to die in peace resisted their participation in studies. Yet, as a result of this effort and the sacrifice of families and children who participated in research on anti-metabolite and other drugs, the child oncologist today is able to (happily) inform parents that certain forms of leukemia affecting the large majority of afflicted children are potentially curable. Had overzealous research regulations curbed investigations, would the prognosis for this disorder been so dramatically altered? In other words, if an uncompromising view of unconditional subject protection had been adopted by clinical researchers and the advocates for children, leukemic children would have won the battle against human experimentation and lost their war. But the life-threatening nature of cancer muted ethical objections.

The commitment of medical researchers and funding agencies to leukemia contrasts sharply with autism. This highlights an ethical stance in regard to autism that allows physicians, educators, psychologists, and academic and funding institutions to consider autism a less debilitating condition than leukemia. But in what sense is autism associated with less human suffering than leukemia? More than just a rhetorical muse, this question needs to be addressed in order to justify decisions regarding which disorders should, and which should not, be subject to the best scientific methodology available in medicine.

Research on the etiology and pathogenesis of autism should be scrutinized in terms of its potential contributory value to the understanding of the disorder. Similarly, studies of intervention and treatment should be monitored so that gains can be assessed independently of theoretical biases or cultural ideologies, with only the individual patient's progress in mind. Such systematic follow-up protects the child from unexamined assumptions based on changeable educational currents. In other words, in the area of intervention, research protects the subject. All forms of treatment, pharmacological as well as behavioral, should be properly scrutinized by human investigation committees, and their proponents called upon to justify their actions in terms of empirical information. Let us consider a few illustrations substantiating this ethical stance.

The 1975 (U.S.) Public Law 94–142 (1977) regulations mandating least restrictive placements for individuals with disabilities have often been interpreted as a mandate to provide mainstreaming for all autistic children. However commendable the premises underlying this notion were, the implementation of this approach often escaped careful scrutiny, possibly because the general value was judged to be too important for a rebuttal based on systematic research. Although autism has a wide range of phenotypic expression, both in terms of intellectual level and range of symptom severity, for the large majority of autistic children such a placement may be considered at best unhelpful, and at worst harmful. The little research there is on educational strategies indicates unequivocally that intensive, individual and behavioral approaches provide the conditions for a far more beneficial intervention than could be possible in a regular classroom. When issues such as these are at stake, research is necessary both to document the impact of the intervention technique and to protect the individual child from falling victim to ideologic determinations distant from the child's condition and educational needs.

The danger posed to the individual child and family is tenfold greater in the area of treatment, particularly unconventional forms of treatment. Despite strong claims by partisans of particular treatment approaches and much dedicated effort that has gone into their implementation, no treatment has been demonstrated to produce major alterations in the natural course of the disorder (DeMyer et al., 1981; Rutter, 1985). In the absence of a definitive cure, there are a thousand treatments. With the exception of a few approaches (notably behavior modification and pharmacological intervention, and to a lesser degree, educational guidelines), proposed interventions have not been rigorously studied. Most worrisome are treatments which disrupt educational routines, are costly, make unwarranted claims of success, and discard systematic research as an unsuitable form of evaluation.

In a hundred-mile radius of the Yale Child Study Center, there are over a dozen major unconventional treatment interventions available for children with autism and their families. These include megavitamin therapy, hugging therapy, auditory training, facilitated communication, physical exertion, discipline and group regimentation, patterning of psychomotor skills, round-the-clock stimulation within a confined space, dolphin therapy, and so forth. The propounders of these approaches are invariably hostile to systematic evaluations conducted by independent researchers, aggressively marketing their approach with little if any evidence substantiating their claims of success. Such claims fall on the very vulnerable ears of parents and educators whose hopes and dedication may lead them to embrace the approach with its cost in both material and human terms. Many among the sponsors of these approaches discard researchers' protests, arguing that systematic studies are inherently flawed to measure gains and progress because they imply a disbelief in the approach, interfere with the treatment process, or underestimate the child's potential to the point of compromising the whole enterprise. Desperately in search of a spark of hope, many parents adopt these arguments. They invest their time, feelings and commitment, and often large sums of money, to "give it a try." After all, what caring parent would leave a stone unturned in the hope of finding a cure for their child's devastating ailment?

These circumstances can and have caused a great deal of human suffering. A recent and popular example of an unconventional therapy is that of "facilitated communication" (Prior and Cummins, 1992). Colleagues critical of its approach and doubtful of its validity have often been pressured into conformity or otherwise faced ostracism by those who are true believers in the method; skeptics may be judged incompetent, when their only fault is to feel that their professional responsibility entails not acting by blind belief but to validate the adopted treatment approach. At times, parents who have already mourned for their child's illness and accepted the implications of the disability have been led to believe that their previous acceptance of the diagnosis was the result of a physician misleading them. Legal loopholes and the pressure for a cure have often disarmed investigators concerned with testing the significance of the messages produced through this method. Just as with other non-traditional therapies, however, rigorous research has been blocked by a call to belief.

One widespread ethical stance in need of urgent scrutiny regards the view that behavioral or otherwise non-pharmacological or medical forms of treatment need not be closely examined because there is no risk of chemical, radioactive, or similar side effects. Doctors' experiences with thalidomide ushered in an era of cautionary and regulatory safeguards in pharmacology. No equivalent landmark can be found in the realm of unconventional, behavioral, dietary, etc., treatments. Anatomic anomalies are easily photographed and the medical mistake laid bare in its visual cruelty. Unfortunately, we cannot take photographs of parents' anguish facing accusations of mistreatment of their loved ones, or of the crushing down of their high, spuriously-risen hopes for a cure, or of the stagnation or regression of children's development due to the abandonment of conventional forms of treatment for the sake of miracle cures. Thalidomide-like equivalent landmarks in the realm of non-conventional treatments often go undocumented and unexposed, remaining the private misery of parents and powerless clinicians who are called upon to counsel the parents when things go awry.

CHILDREN FROM DISADVANTAGED BACKGROUNDS

In contrast to autistic children, infants and toddlers growing up in poor inner-city conditions characterized by high levels of crime, social alienation, poor health care and inadequate adult supervision cannot be said to be afflicted with a developmental disorder. In their case, nature may not be at fault, but nurture. When the children are diagnosed as having a medical condition there is the risk of self-fulfilling prophecy, based on early stigmatization. Nevertheless, an alarmingly large number of these youngsters present with very significant language delays and social-emotional symptomatology, which place formidable obstacles to later educational success while fostering self-destructive traits and patterns of interaction and relationships. For the mental health professional accompanying the growth of these children, the fragility of their skills and ubiquity of their delays cannot but impress themselves as a condition, if not in principle, then in reality.

From society's standpoint, including a large portion of the mental health community, the plight of these children is usually seen in the context of perennial, and unresolved, if not "inevitable," social malaise. Once these children's difficulties are defined as almost exclusively social or educational problems, the implication is straightforward: vastly smaller amounts of resources are invested in research and documentation of developmental dysfunctions, the factors perpetuating their condition, and remedial programs devised to address these children's and their families' needs—than is the case with medical disorders. Researchers who are not immediately immersed in the care and study of psychosocial issues may share in this value system; they may believe, along with lay people, that after all there is little to be discovered but the truisms of child development and the devastating impact of poverty, violence and drugs.

In the newborn intensive care unit (NICU) of modern American hospitals, it is common to see very small infants born prematurely to unwed mothers who did not receive prenatal care receive the world's best medical care at enormous cost. Their survival is testimony to the advances of biomedical research. Caring for very small, premature babies may generate hospital bills over $75,000 or $100,000; these bills are paid by insurance companies and the government. Many of these quite small babies experience CNS trauma during the newborn period, such as intra-ventricular hemorrhage, and then return home to stressed families who have difficulty caring for vulnerable babies. A few years later, we can predict, a high proportion will be in need of special educational and clinical services. Society is far less willing to provide for intensive family support and early child intervention than for the high technology medicine that preserved the child's life. Yet, the cost for two or three days during the first week of life in the NICU may equal the cost of the environmental programs for one year. We have felt that when such a vulnerable child is maintained in the NICU, a portion of the costs should be set aside in an escrow fund to later pay for the remedial services he is likely to need. That is, the decision to preserve life entails a respect for the later quality of life.

Following a low-birth-weight baby from NICU to school raises ethical questions involving society's priorities and allocation of resources. Documentation of children's development in disadvantaged situations is at the heart of any discussion of the moral foundations of the mental health research community. Medical and public health students, as well as health providers and social policy analysts, are beginning to reappraise the lopsided society values that emphasize high technology treatment but skimp on prevention and then on early intervention. Increasingly, health professionals are recognizing the medical responsibility to advocate for changes in priorities among the larger community (Adams and Sandfort, 1992; Commission on Behavioral and Social Sciences and Education, 1993).

Today, we can trace a multigenerational, developmental trajectory that defines the life course of hundreds of thousands of poor children (National Center for Health Statistics, 1991). The developmental pathway starts before their birth to mothers (often unwed) who are too young and ill-prepared to assume the parental responsibility. During their gestation, they do not receive adequate prenatal care or nutrition, and as embryos and fetuses are exposed to drugs, alcohol, tobacco, and chronic stress. Often born prematurely and small, these infants start life very vulnerable to medical and neurological complications, including sepsis and brain hemorrhage. The small, premature infants who go home with middle-class parents may do remarkably well; those who go into poor families, and with little family support and structured stimulation, do much worse (National Health/Education Consortium, 1991). Thus, psychobiological vulnerability interacts with environmental provisions, and adversity is quickly compounded. By the first year, these babies are developmentally impaired, and they are clearly behind in social, emotional and cognitive skills by the time they enter preschool programs in the nursery school years (IHDP, 1990). In a city such as ours, the majority of inner-city children are not prepared adequately for school entry and fail the standard tests of school readiness, such as the ability to follow simple instructions (Children's Defense Fund, 1991). Each year, such children fall further behind in school achievement, as behavioral problems such as hyperactivity and conduct difficulties emerge and interfere with attendance and attention. As they enter puberty, at ages as early as ten or eleven, they become involved in sexuality, which often leads to intercourse before age fourteen and the birth of a child by fifteen. Over 1,000,000 children are born out of wedlock annually in the United States, many to teenagers (National Center for Health Statistics, 1991). Again, in our city, school truancy can begin as early as age ten, with a compounding of lack of academic achievement and missed days from school. By age twelve or thirteen, children drop out of school. Today, about 50% of all inner-city children do not finish high school (National Commission of the States, 1990). Without a high school education, they cannot enter the mainstream of employment. Throughout their lives, children from the most impoverished backgrounds are exposed to violence—most often at home, at the hands of those who are supposed to care for them; in the neighborhood; in their day care settings; on the street; and in school. They are often witnesses to people being hurt, then the victims of such injury and, too often, finally the perpetrators. Violence and aggression often permeate their worlds, traumatize their inner lives, and shape their personalities, making them wary and anxious and, finally, angry and retaliatory.

The anthropology of these children's lives has now been well depicted (e.g. Cicchetti and Toth, 1993), although we know far too little about those who escape (the 50% who complete school, for example) and succeed, in spite of trauma. For many, the cycle of poverty continues from one generation to the next. There is a predictable, multigenerational pattern that shapes the lives of children, from conception through procreation. At each step, however, there are possible interventions that may change the pathway into positive directions more likely to lead to success and achievement. Over the years, a host of "intervention" models have been created and tried (Meissels and Schonkoff, 1990). And yet, there is a remarkable paucity of hard information on what inner-city children actually experience and how they represent their experiences; what accounts for individual differences; and what types of interventions, at different phases of child and family development, are able to be useful for which children and families. The magnitude and social costs of some of the specific problems are enormous: for example, over two million children are reported annually for child abuse and neglect, resulting in about 2,000 child deaths and an additional 160,000 cases of serious injuries (Daro and McCurdy, 1990); over 350,000 are in foster care because their families cannot care for them; over 500,000 men are in prison, most having followed developmental trajectories similar to the one just presented (Department of Commerce, Bureau of the Census, 1990b). Given the seriousness of these issues, one might expect a proportionate research response aimed at defining and reducing risk and improving treatment for those who succumb. Yet, there is a paucity of systematic, rigorous research, and the quality of studies is far short of what one finds in other fields of biomedical investigation. For example, hardly anything is known about specific treatments for child abuse (Commission on Behavioral and Social Sciences and Education, 1993).

There are many different factors that may lead to a relative lack of serious research engagement on the interface between social policy, family and community factors, and child development. Three prevailing attitudes deserve special scrutiny in the context of thinking about the ethics of research: (a) research involving disadvantaged children is often deemed relatively unexciting and unchallenging; scientific breakthroughs from laboratory research seem remote; (b) research in this area may be resented; it may question assumptions reflecting vested interests and political balances; and (c) research on children growing up in great psychosocial disadvantage may be feared; shedding light on the unknown may reveal unsettling facts about the inadequacies of present practice and the magnitude of the problems which confront society.

The "Unexciting/Unchallenging" Attitude

While hundreds of articles are published every year on normative and abnormal development of cognitive processes, language, social skills and personality, much less is known about how these processes unfold under the unfavorable circumstances characterizing a large section of the inner-city population. The assumption that all there is to it is to provide an adequate environment masks a lack of knowledge and wishful thinking. The term "developmental delay" may itself convey an overly optimistic sense: even though the acquisition of skills is currently not at a par with expected levels, "delay" suggests that the child will eventually catch up and will have suffered no irreversible harm. But the child with developmental delays is not like the tortoise who finally and unstoppably reaches his goal—normal development. The delayed child may be put off the course.

In its early years, the best-studied and enduring early intervention program in the United States, Head Start, was sometimes promoted as a way of accelerating the development of disadvantaged children and bringing them to the same starting point as the general population by the 1st grade at school (Zigler and Muenchow, 1992). To a remarkable degree, Head Start has achieved broad political acceptance and solid national funding; it has shown itself to be a useful, replicable program. Yet a gap exists in our knowledge. The early optimism about "intervention" gradually has given way to recognition of the need for continuing, intensive interventions, in school, at home, and in the community. The dire statistics characterizing the performance of inner-city children at school, and their later over-representation in both welfare and justice systems, reveal that there is no single program, at one phase of development, that will immunize a child against failure. The early founders of Head Start already knew that cognitive stimulation or short-term interventions alone will not ameliorate the developmental problems of inner-city children, once and for all. Rather, they recognized the importance of parent involvement, health care, and nutrition, as well as child-oriented educational activities. Also, many of the early advocates emphasized not only cognitive skills but the intangibles, such as curiosity, motivation, confidence, expectations from self and from others, attitudes toward learning and play, and patterns of social behavior. All of these are crucial factors determining readiness to start school and gain social competence (National Center for Clinical Infant Programs, 1992). But our knowledge of how these processes unfold under adverse conditions is very limited. Possibly more is known about foreign cultures than about less conspicuous segments of American society. The factors and processes involved in what accounts to growing personality structures have been little researched. The shaping and formative outcome of these structures are little known, though writers of editorials and politicians often have "theories" about the psychology of individuals who are old enough to enter the world of welfare and the justice system.

Consider a 2½-year-old little boy whose typical reaction to the loving approach of his teacher was to become verbally and physically aggressive toward her. This behavior was due to his increasing attachment to her, not the opposite. But his experiences with adults taught him that every time he became attached to a person, a loss ensued or something bad happened to him. Now he combats his own instinct for love as a self-preserving, adaptive reaction. What is going to be the future emotional life of this youngster is unknown to us, nor is the prevalence of such self-destructive traits. By age four this child spent two months in an inpatient psychiatric unit following suicidal gestures. In medicine, case studies are often the catalyst of longer-scale systematic investigations. Conspicuous cases of profound psychosocial disability equally should stimulate major research programs and sustained, systematic, multi-disciplinary research. Why has research of this type been relatively limited?

One possibility is that the impact of early trauma, losses, noise, crowdedness, poor nutrition, inconsistency of caregiving, and a host of other factors are blurred together into rather fatalistic blanket judgments. Researchers, like others, may try to protect themselves from feeling the full brunt of the suffering experienced by young children, by "knowing" the cause of their problems. An appreciation of these various contributory or causal factors may reveal feasible objectives, delineating realistic challenges. Also, research on these phenomena holds virtually untapped sources of information about human development, which are at once fascinating, morally mandated, and of potentially enormous social value. The importance of this challenge should set in motion the typical mechanisms available to the scientific community, such as the delineation of a field of inquiry and creation of forums for discussion. The efforts of one agency, the Zero-to-Three National Center for Clinical Infant Programs, provides a model of interdisciplinary sharing of clinical and research concerns for very young, vulnerable children.

Virtually none of the central psychological processes—such as language acquisition, cognitive development and social-emotional skills—emerges unscathed from adverse environmental conditions. However, this field remains relatively uncharted. Intervention approaches still tend to follow intuitive knowledge, and outcome studies are rare. Yet, there is no reason for researchers to assume a defeatist attitude. Some dire assumptions foreclosing the argument for research and documentation in this field have already collapsed when brought into some degree of systematic scrutiny. For example, the assumption that children exposed prenatally to cocaine were often deemed irreversibly damaged was found to be misleading, as these children were often more susceptible to post-natal than gestational toxicity, implying that correctable caregiving factors were causally implicated in outcome (Mayes et al., 1992). This piece of good news, of course, also carries a corollary, namely that our real task is to research the adverse conditions in which these children grow up. It leaves no room for hiding behind "neurological inevitabilities."

The "Resented" and "Feared" Attitudes

Hand in hand with a need to know what is effective in fostering the development of disadvantaged children goes the need to know how cost-effective are the different interventions. Cost-effectiveness research implies knowledge of developmental processes, obstacles to development, their interaction, typical outcomes, as well as definitions of desirable goals. The lack of operationalization and systematic investigation of risk factors and the paucity of follow-up studies keep this field in a state of gloomy awareness. Ignorance in this respect plays the role of protective mechanism for both decision-makers and service providers. Resentment and fear follow if research begins to reveal what we do not want to see.

The results of cost-effectiveness research usually place a price tag on a desired outcome. Once risk factors are operationally defined and studied over time, and costs carefully documented both in terms of financial and human terms, it becomes reasonable to discuss what is the acceptable cost that society is willing to pay in order to achieve the desired goal. Unprotected by the subterfuge of the unknown, and possibly stripped from the comfort offered by the assumed "inevitability," decision makers would then have to confront decisions which spell to them and society at large what is achieved with x amount of dollars, and what is the cost down the road if these x amount of dollars are not spent. The power of such information cannot be currently estimated, but if the recent resource allocations to Head Start and its newly-achieved prominence in the political agenda is anything to go by, the impact of cost-effectiveness knowledge would be immense. Rather modest follow-up studies proved of great importance in shaping the political process in support of Head Start.

Caring providers of services to children may tend to avoid knowledge of outcome because they fear the worst for the youngsters they work with and the methods and philosophies adhered to in their work. Similarly, administrators who make policy and allocation decisions may also be rather complacent; they may chose to dwell in ignorance (and resent being shown) about the actual effectiveness of current interventions, albeit at a cost. Unwilling accomplices, service providers and decision-makers thus may help, to some extent, to sustain the present scarcity of knowledge. Hence the ethical imperative to conduct research aimed at doing away with protective ignorance, and squarely presenting the facts and decisions at stake. The children we serve and care for deserve no less.

Today, the ethical imperative is not only to do more for children who suffer from psychosocial disadvantage, and for their families. As always, the poorest children and families have enormous, unmet needs: They need more money and better housing, better access to schools and more opportunities in society. They are over-burdened in every sector of life—by poor nutrition and health, chaotic living situations, exposure to violence, the impact of racism. In addition to advocacy to improve the life situation of poor children, there is an ethical responsibility to determine what types of affordable social changes are most likely to be useful and to define the barriers to their implementation within society, the community, and among those who are being served. Knowledge of children's and family's development and of the intersections between policy, social action, and development also is an effective weapon in advocacy.

An aggressive increase in research in this field of inquiry would enhance the position of caregivers as purveyors of a humanized, rational science. Rigorous science and clinical care are synergistic, and their goals converge: to bring the benefits of modern methodologies to the masses of "therapeutic orphans" whose most handicapping vulnerability may lie in being part of a scientifically disenfranchised segment of our society.

SUMMARY

The emergent awareness of the paramount value of safeguards and regulations protecting participants of research studies has been a great accomplishment earned by the mental health community in the past decade and a half. Nevertheless, the view that research and human welfare are at odds contradicts the premises of research in child and adolescent psychiatry. Both rigorous research and clinical care are aimed at reducing human suffering. Autism, a condition of congenital origin with a neurobiological basis, is among the most devastating medical conditions that afflict children; it deserves the same type of rigorous, systematic research that has led to major improvements in the care of children with other biological disorders. The development of vulnerable children who grow up under unbearable psychosocial adversity is unfortunately more easily predicted than many natural phenomena; research on the multiple interacting factors which place children on a high-risk developmental pathway leading to psychosocial maladaptation and on treatments offers hope for creating, sustaining, and funding useful interventions. There is an ethical responsibility to acknowledge ignorance. There is also an ethical mandate to conduct investigations, responsibly and respectfully, but also relentlessly, in order to make knowledge the property of those members of society who are most in need of its benefits, and who are victimized by research inaction.

Chapter 12 Research in Child Psychiatry: Lines of Personal, Institutional, and Career Development (1986)

Donald J. Cohen

Richard Wollheim both begins and ends *The Thread of Life* (1984) with a quotation from Kierkegaard's journal for 1843:

> It is perfectly true, as philosophers say, that life must be understood backwards. But they forget the other proposition, that it must be lived forwards.

Wollheim concludes his study of what it is for a person to live a life—for there to be an actor (a person), a process (living), and a product (a life)—with the observation that "for a person, not only is understanding the life he leads intrinsic to leading it, but for much of the time leading his life is, or is mostly, understanding it."

How does a child understand his life: learn that he is the one who is leading it; that his thoughts are his thoughts, inside of him; and that there are others who have their own thoughts and who, in leading

First appeared in *Clinical Research Careers in Psychiatry,* eds. H. A. Pincus and H. Pardes (Washington, D.C.: American Psychiatric Association, 1986), 51–78. Reprinted with permission from Clinical Research Careers in Psychiatry, copyright © 1986, American Psychiatric Press, Inc. All rights reserved.

their own lives, impinge on his life? For the child psychiatrist and analyst, understanding how child patients understand themselves, or try to understand themselves, is central to the therapeutic task. For me, it has represented a sustained fascination since childhood, in knowing how the mind works, what are its origins, how it derails. The thread between the awkward concerns of a bookish childhood—in large part spent observing an ethnically expressive, extended family, as well as a richly populated fantasy world—and a career in child psychiatry may seem easy enough to follow from this end. It was not so clear when this life was lived forwards.

PERSONAL DEVELOPMENT: A CASE STUDY

Training for this career started before adolescence, in preoccupations about births and deaths, family origins, successes and failures, how the body works: it took early shape with the discovery by chance of philosophy and then theology during an intense adolescence. By the sophomore college year as a philosophy and psychology major, I concentrated on Ryle and then Wittgenstein and Austin, and the philosophy of mind and the mind-body problem. This became the theme of my Fulbright in Cambridge, where after graduation I decided—in the place where my type of philosophy was done better than anywhere in the world—that philosophy was not for me. But the particular seriousness of this philosophical enterprise—its attempt, at any rate, to raise questions in their broadest (and for me, this meant also most conscious and moral) sense—persisted as a model of the intellectual life. Also remaining from those years was the awareness of the transmission of values, from generation to generation, teacher to student, and the belief that life is far more complex than anyone appreciates who tries to lead one. In a way, philosophers succeed when they demonstrate that the simple is far from that, while scientists strive to discover the simplicity underlying complexity. In Cambridge, I felt annoyed by philosophical complexity; later, one aspect of the attraction of psychoanalysis over behaviorism was its appreciation of the layerings upon layerings of the mind.

From early in college, I was fortunate in my teachers. For various reasons, I had the capacity, which some students never develop, of understanding what was needed to elicit the engagement of professors. As a teacher, now, I can see this capacity in even young and naïve students: it is primarily an ease in identification that allows a student to find the teacher's work truly of interest, to desire to take it in, and to be able to express gratitude for this nurturance through work. If the student is lucky, as I was, there are authentically good objects available for this incorporative process, and they are varied enough to provide a well-balanced diet for future, selective metabolism.

During my sophomore summer, Spyridon Alivisatos allowed me to work in his biochemistry laboratory on histamine dinucleotides. His own early work with Wooley on the serotonin hypothesis of schizophrenia aroused curiosity about neuropharmacology. On returning to Brandeis in the autumn, I visited the local state hospital to see schizophrenic patients. There, a staff psychiatrist told me about an "odd psychologist" who was conditioning chronic schizophrenics in the back wards. With no introduction, I wandered in to the Behavior Research Laboratory created by Ogden Lindsley, and for the next several years, he and his work entranced me. In small cubicles, chronic patients pulled plungers on various schedules of reinforcement for candy, cigarettes, and trinkets, while Ogden and a very small group of associates formed the first experimental analyses of psychosis using operant paradigms.

During the very first visit, Lindsley spent hours expansively describing cumulative records, the natural history of clinical exacerbations apparent in them, the effects of drugs that could be seen on various schedules, the mysteries that led patients to continue to respond during hundreds of hours of extinction. This started a transforming experience. He was dramatically a new object: a recent Skinner Ph.D. who was also a tattooed Yankee sailor; a bold empiricist who did away with the mind; an enthusiast who loved to teach. At college, I worked on texts and exercised those analytic talents learned in Talmudic study; in the Behavior Research Laboratory, I manipulated behavior. Lindsley shared himself—from ideas about how science should be done to problems of funding and family—and his students were thus initiated not only into a way of thinking about work but also into a way of being.

What motivates a teacher to take a student into his world? What need is there, in us as teachers, to form this relationship in which we expose ourselves in ways that cannot be fully controlled or predicted? What did Lindsley find in a college junior—a bookish philosopher from another culture with so little to offer? As teachers, we see in the eyes of students something good in us reflected back, hope for the future, and, at times, a buffer against disappointments. Perhaps Lindsley found as much comfort, if not intrigue, in my rootedness in the world of philosophy and religion, as I found excitement in his enthusiasms and freedom to study and do anything.

With Lindsley, and through his introduction, in the Skinner pigeon lab, I felt at the forefront of the science of behavior. We studied social behavior of children (my first papers) and used operant methods to condition autistic chil-

dren, whose behavior never was orderly enough to satisfy the principles of behavior control. We studied pain perception, sleep, hallucinations; we created
and toyed with methods for pleasure and interest. The small cadre of BRL researchers experienced the opportunity to enjoy the playfulness of science and
not to feel, too soon, the need to be productive, efficient, effective (terms I use
too often now). Lindsley was not a good administrator: if he were, he might not
have taken so much time from his work to talk and teach. He didn't publish sufficiently, he didn't get grants in time or finish his annual reports, he loved to talk
until dawn over coffee. He was a heroic figure. He initiated students to the fellowship of doing science, which he treated as a theatrical activity. "We should
paint our own pictures," he would say, "not study the pictures of some dead
artists." And while this iconoclasm may be harmful, for some students it was
also exhilarating and liberating, and it remains an important message for those
who encourage their students to read more than to do.

Going to England to do philosophy following graduation was a morato-
rium, and acceptance to graduate school in psychology and medical school
were left open. By chance, I was invited to spend a good deal of time in the
home of the professor of medicine in Oxford, and, through him, could compare my feelings on clinical rounds with those in philosophy tutorials. One
morning, I asked what he would do in my shoes and, without hesitation, he
prescribed Yale Medical School, since it was so much like Cambridge. While
analytic neutrality has its uses, there are times when a young man needs an au-
thoritarian consultant, and it is good that there are teachers with courage to be
available for such occasions. In a way, though, my mind had already been made
up a year earlier during a visit to Yale when I met, through the intervention of a
fellow behaviorist, Daniel X. Freedman.

At the time, Dr. Freedman was a brilliant young researcher, bubbling with
ideas about neurochemistry, drugs, psychosis, hallucinations, LSD, psychoanalysis, schizophrenia. The leftovers were enough to fuel several careers. He
never stopped working or talking, and I attached myself to his office and laboratory and came under those commodious wings, which have sheltered five or
six generations of students through residencies and into full-blown careers.

Dr. Freedman was unlike Ogden Lindsley in every superficial way, but they
shared the same commitments: to the importance of students, to the possibility
that a teacher can make a difference, to the need for a teacher to encourage the
student to find his own way. Dr. Freedman was willing to accept the burdens of
ambitious, ambivalent, questioning, and critical students, with their mixture of
admiration and withholding. And there were no boundaries on time or topic.

A student cannot wait for appointments but must be present at the right time, when the teacher is ready for companionship and to teach: usually late at night, early in the morning, in the hallway. Those who were willing to be present for Dr. Freedman never were disappointed. Most remarkably, less than any other "famous" teacher, he had no need to assert his own role, to take over, or to take credit. He enjoyed the achievements of young people, encouraging their competitiveness and success even on problems that he had staked out for himself. He admired true experts and forced his students to seek them out, shipping me to Boston to study babies with Peter Wolff and placing me with William Kessen and Ed Zigler to learn about child development and theory. He imparted a love of clinical complexity, since nothing for him was what it seemed; pleasure in doing science related to healing patients, moral seriousness, and a comfort in seeking advice.

He provided funds to build a laboratory to study newborns and watched over my growing interest and competence as a clinical researcher, finding ways to have me present and discuss the work. By medical school graduation, I felt at ease talking with parents, studying babies, working on the wards, and teaching what I had learned to others.

As a pediatrics house officer, I focused on psychosomatic disorders, and especially conditions that make children ugly or difficult to bear or be with, such as childhood eczema. Had there not been a field of child psychiatry, I would have stayed at Children's Hospital and become a pediatrician. Nothing is more suitable for a child psychiatrist, I think, than as much time as possible spent in pediatrics. To enter child psychiatry without pediatrics leaves clinicians at a great disadvantage; they have missed not only the intellectual opportunity to learn about the clinical biology of childhood but, more importantly, the existential, immediate, tactile engagement with children and their families at critical moments. Pediatrics remains the most authentic road into child psychiatry, even more relevant, I think, than general psychiatry.

During residency in psychiatry, I continued a research clinic for eczema and other skin disorders at Children's, through the support of the senior pediatricians and dermatologists who allowed a psychiatric resident the chance of continuing to admit and treat patients and do clinical studies. This was crucial to my continued identity as a child investigator, but may have contributed to my not becoming more involved in the study of adult disorders. Research, in any case, was not much valued during my residency in general psychiatry. I entered psychoanalysis at this time, with a child analyst, and returned to Children's to do child psychiatry.

Two years at the National Institute of Mental Health, in the Section on Twin and Sibling Studies with William Pollin, were critical for at least two reasons. First, NIMH was the hub of biological research in psychiatry, which had not then permeated into residency. Second, much of my time was spent in the politically heady world of child development policy (as special assistant to Ed Zigler, who was then the first Director of the Office of Child Development); academic knowledge about children and families could make a national difference.

The choice of Yale for a first academic job was based on three factors: the presence of teachers, senior clinicians who were thoroughly child psychiatrists and would be models; a history of scholarship; and the offer of protection to develop. Today, young investigators often are eager to have their "own shop" and accept offers that are "too good to turn down." For me, the presence of experienced senior faculty was more tempting. We anticipated a stay of a few years on the road back to Boston.

On coming to Yale in 1972, I planned to study autism and other serious disorders. These clinically enigmatic conditions were the bedrock of the field—they defined the major mission of child psychiatry, I felt, and I had learned of the suffering of their parents as their advocate in Washington. But perhaps more fundamental in my motivation was the sense that here one could learn about those questions—mind and its origins in, and connections with, the body. Clinical investigators do not choose their areas of study by chance, however much our lives are shaped by accidents.

The freedom to engage in relatively invasive research with children with autism and other serious disorders in an institution that was not accustomed to such work was the result of at least several converging factors. These included the pediatric background and interests of the senior faculty; their enthusiasm for new knowledge; and the credibility of the biomedical investigators (myself and then J. Gerald Young) as clinicians and child analysts. Having come from NIMH, I was enthusiastic about the new biological psychiatry and sought links with the scientific program (initiated by Daniel X. Freedman) in the Department of Psychiatry. It was especially good fortune to be welcomed by Malcolm Bowers who, along with my closest collaborator, Bennett Shaywitz, chief of pediatric neurology, made possible the studies on CSF metabolites in autism and other disorders.

During the past decade, research in which I have been engaged has been in tune with the spirit and methods of the times, and has included biomedically oriented, multidisciplinary studies of the serious neuropsychiatric disorders of childhood. But its tone has been set most clearly by its center: clinical concern about children and their families, and a fascination with their inner lives. For young clinical investigators (and tiring older ones), having a belief in their value as clinicians is extremely important; it helps them survive the failures, competition, and aggression of science and to maintain a sense of personal integrity in the process of doing and reporting their work. Analysis affirmed my gifts and primary clinical identity.

The path between childhood preoccupations, college and medical school interests, and the career I have so far lived may seem straighter than it was experienced in its living. Perhaps this is a fundamental fact, in retrospect: That the shaping of a career, when it is authentic, is an expression of all that goes into living a life, and that the accidents along its path are as over-determined as are its most important experiences. Or, that what we mean as a career, a profession, is not intelligible—if it is real—outside of the context of all that goes into life. It forms the backbone of our lives, along with the few sustaining friendships and loves, with which it too often may be in competition, but from which it takes a great deal of its resiliency. In this sense—to which I will return—the teacher who allows himself to meet the student in the real, lived world between them must accept responsibility for helping the student in leading his life, as a whole person.

In emphasizing the role of teachers—and more recently, of colleagues—in my career, I think I am expressing one of the fundamental analytic contributions to our understanding of human development. At this point, personal and institutional histories become intertwined and so I will turn to consideration of the institutional worlds in which professional lives and careers are lived.

A PROFESSION AND ITS INSTITUTIONS

Professional lives—careers—are lived in time and in particular places. They are shaped by broad intellectual, economic, social, and political forces as these are mediated by institutions. There are overarching institutions that define the nature of the profession, at any particular historical moment. The profession of child psychiatry is only decades old. Before the 1920s or so (and in many parts of the world even today), there was no serious consideration that children had mental disorders and that these could be understood and treated scientifically. There are also the smaller, geographically definable institutions, the workplaces in which professionals carry out daily tasks. The definition of a profession and the nature of its workplace evolve hand-in-hand, as the profession defines its mission, values, and appropriate activities. Child psychiatry is such a young profession that the history of the profession and its various institutions can be recounted by founders and second-generation leaders. It is mature enough, however, that there are child psychiatrists who cannot envision it as being much different from the way they saw it practiced during training.

Careers, the core of the lives of professionals, are lived in institutions. Careers shape and are shaped by institutions. The creation and transformation of institutions are also the major ways in which the careers of one generation impact on the next, the medium through which teachers transmit their values and skills to their students. Not only the practice but the nature and approach to questions for study are defined by the definition of a profession and its workplace.

Today, it may seem self-evident that child psychiatry is taught and practiced as it is: with an emphasis on hearing the child's point of view, its use of individual psychotherapy, concern for inner life, work within the context of the playroom, emphasis on family dynamics, attempts to define disorders and specific syndromes, particular administrative relationship to adult psychiatry (almost always as a section in a larger department of psychiatry), and the like. But each of these, and the many other defining characteristics of the field, has only recently evolved, and there are many countries in the world where these ideas remain unsettled. Similarly, we may take for granted the style, methods, and questions of currently practiced clinical research, but these too are new, evolving, and multiply determined.

Professional self-understanding requires awareness of the assumptions of a field—assumptions that guide child psychiatry's conception of who are its patients, what are its legitimate treatments, what is in need of further study, and how it should be organized for training, service, and research. Researchers are expected to raise questions about just these issues, about ideas that others accept as given. Their mission is to study critically ideas and activities that are central to a profession and its status. As a result, investigators may at times be unpopular or threatening, as today when clinical researchers try to determine efficacy of psychological therapies and the short- and long-term dangers of medications.

PERSPECTIVE

The broad institutions that shape what we call a profession are related to the smaller institutions, workplaces, which have a geographical locus and internal politics; people shape and are shaped by institutions; theories and methods change because of intrinsic development and external influences; lives are lived in institutions and have as one of their results further changes in institutions. Of most relevance, these institutions—broad and local—define what we mean by a career in clinical investigation and, more specifically, by a successful career. These institutions provide the criteria (and the rewards) for what should be studied and how. An historical perspective reveals that these standards are relative and that what we call state-of-the-art won't be; it warns us not to be too proud of today's paradigms and suggests reasons for some degree of conservatism and modesty. We still read with interest and insight some marvelous papers from the '50s and '60s written by analysts and others, based on individual cases, which would never be accepted for publication in our leading journals today. We don't know what "hot" work being published today will survive the next year or two.

This historical narrative can also be used to draw a trajectory. Teachers use such trajectories, consciously or not, to make decisions for their own careers and to guide the careers of others. The history reveals two important forces. First, that what has endured during the three-quarters of a century of professional development is the importance of young professionals being deeply engaged in and acquiring expertise about individual children and their psychological difficulties. And second, that clinical researchers have always tried to relate the most interesting, new theories and methods with actual services to children and families. Young clinical investigators today often wonder about the importance of maintaining this immersion in phenomenology and this core identity, as a clinician—as someone who cares for children while trying to better understand how they understand themselves; there are major centers of investigation that have placed less emphasis on clinical credibility or authenticity than on the pursuit of increased scientific research sophistication. The historical review suggests the wisdom for the child psychiatrist beginning a career as a clinical investigator to be firmly rooted in clinical work while he or she masters the most advanced new methods that are available. But this idea, as well, requires critical scrutiny, and it is subject to change as the profession understands and defines itself differently.

TIME: THE DEVELOPMENTAL LINE FROM
STUDENT TO CHILD PSYCHIATRIC RESEARCHER

Lives are lived in time, and the process of change in a person over time is the basic subject matter of child development and child psychiatry. The process of becoming a clinical investigator in child psychiatry takes time—three to five years, formally, and many years before and after. As with other developmental lines, there are fixations and regressions, as well as precocity; not all individuals will see the line to its very end and some will reach the developmental goals long before others.

Today, among the issues that confront a young investigator are the numerous options that become available for types of research in child psychiatry—from study of society and epidemiology; through meticulous investigation of behavior, language and fundamental psychological processes; to neurochemical organization and genetic regulation. He or she must decide on what age child to study and at what level of biological or psychological organization. Without knowing enough to be certain the decision is correct, the young investigator must decide whether the research should focus on a disorder (such as schizophrenia), a process (such as socialization), a mechanism (such as receptor modulation), a method (such as epidemiology), a treatment (such as psychotherapy), or some combination of these, and still other possibilities. Selecting where to do clinical and research training will be a function of this fundamental decision and will greatly shape what options are available in actuality.

Child psychiatrists will follow many different lines into becoming clinical investigators, and this variety of developmental pathways surely should be encouraged. Further empirical research about modes and points of entry into a clinical research career—as well as points of exit and reasons for leaving one—might usefully guide policy. Based on my own experiences and observations of perhaps two or three generations following me, two points seem to stand out as critical. Individuals must be engaged with children as early as possible, and for this, pediatrics is the most suitable route into child psychiatry; also, doing research must be accessible even before individuals are "fully trained" as clinicians, let alone as child psychiatrists. It has struck me, in pessimistic moments, that individuals who have not done research of some type by college will not actively and naturally do research later. They may do research as part of "building a career," but not as intrinsic to living a career, in the sense portrayed earlier.

But even those who have experienced the pleasure of discovering something new and teaching it to others through writing can easily be diverted into clinical work and practice. These individuals are the most precious natural resources for clinical research careers. To foster such careers, the "potential investigator" must be invited into close, personal working relationships with teachers who are more established but are still actively determining and living their research lives. This type of relationship—in which teaching, friendship, counseling and collaboration are fused, to varying degrees—must have continuity over time and sufficient intensity. It can be successful only if there is a mutual commitment, with all the dangers of self-exposure and hurt that such a relationship entails. Not all established investigators, even those who are good collaborators, are suited for or interested in being mentors, and some gifted mentors, capable of helping a number of students into a career of research and teaching, may not themselves be the most gifted and hard-working scientists or investigators. There are special attributes of mentors, and there are special characteristics of the fit between mentor and student at different phases of each of their development. For these and many other reasons, the process I will now describe cannot be condensed into a curriculum of training, although the availability of such research training programs and curricula in various departments throughout the country is surely to be welcomed.

During the process of development as a clinical researcher, the mentor must intuitively or consciously understand the process and its normative crises. Just as the parent sees where the child is heading, long before the child even dimly perceives the next stages, the mentor must have a very long-sighted perspective on where the young investigator can hope to reach, and when, and with what skill.

There are 13 explicable but overlapping steps that young investigators have tended to take during the past several years, as they mature into clinical researchers in child psychiatry in our Center and elsewhere:

1. Review the literature in order to write a chapter with the mentor, usually one that the senior investigator has been asked to write;

2. Write a further research review and analysis chapter or two as they try to decide on an area in which they wish to make their own special investment;

3. Analyze and write up data that are already available from some older study that nobody has gotten around to writing;

4. Through steps 1–3, the individual begins to work with a senior investigator who owns the data and who receives the invitations to write and to speak. At this point, the individual has become a member of a research group and feels a sense of pride in and responsibility for its work;

5. Begin work on a research project, usually taking increasingly broad responsibility for its functioning;

6. Develop a special technique that the individual knows better than anyone else;

7. Plan a study, using the techniques and focusing on a special clinical research group of patients, usually ones who are involved in other studies;

8. Write a research protocol and have it approved through the Human Investigation Committee, usually after several difficult revisions;
9. Present a paper at a local meeting and a national conference;
10. Write a paper for publication based on the new study and deal with the first rejections and the need for revisions;
11. Write a grant application and deal with rejection, misunderstandings and lack of sympathy of the review "pink sheet";
12. Plan for a career and major lines of work;
13. Deal with the needs of spouse and children while planning a move.

During this process, which may last up to five years, the individual young investigator must be helped by those who have survived and are more secure, to achieve six major tasks of adult development.

First, and most critically, a young investigator must develop coping skills to deal with the frustration, rejection, competition, and success that he will experience. He will feel the rivalry of peers as well as of those who are older and younger; he will find that he is not as appreciated as he should be; he will be left to sink-or-swim in front of site visit committees and audiences before he is fully up to the task; and when he finally receives a prize award, he will discover that the pleasure of success is less powerful and enduring than the pain of rejection.

Second, if his mentors have been satisfactory, he will be socialized into being honest. He will learn that it is acceptable to report his results, which are usually negative and uninteresting, without shame or guilt. The examples of fraud in science—a big fraud that becomes headlines and a little fraud that becomes a publication about which we all wink knowingly—suggest that the temptation to confabulate is in all of us. Those who succumb most grandly are not, in general, the relatively incompetent investigators who may feel they must cheat to survive or the ordinary investigators (like most of us) who accept their fate in life. Instead, the most painful aspect of big fraud is that it is so often the work of young men who are competent, even gifted, and who need more admiration than they can possibly obtain from busy, distant mentors. They gain this love through dazzling performances on the scientific highwire.

The third developmental task is to be socialized into collaboration and community. Especially for child psychiatrists at this point in the intellectual history of the field, research is social and depends on being able to accept the help of others and then to help others. Much of the work of the clinical investigator involves communication and negotiation, from the point of designing a study, through the use of consultants in methodology, to sharing laboratory procedures and patients. Learning how to navigate through the jungle of academic departments—who works with whom, how to deal with rivalries about methods and findings, what should one do about co-authorship—requires intuition and guidance. Those who are unfamiliar with the intellectual and social geography of academic settings cannot appreciate fully the intensity and energy invested in preserving territorial prerogatives dealing with the question of whose name should appear (or where it should appear) on a publication, and recognizing the "real friends" and the unsuspected "enemy." Individuals entering into this world easily may be hurt in crossfire not of their own making and may be offended by local customs. Mentors must serve as guide and protector and help to rescue younger investigators from traps into which they may wander (or help dig for themselves).

Fourth, the young investigator will have to learn how to balance many balls at once: his personal needs and the needs of his family and children for his time as well as for the practicalities of life (money, stability), on one hand, and the demands of his work, his ambitions, and his clinical responsibilities, on the other. Nobody will be completely happy with him, and he will often be least happy with himself for not doing well enough in any area of his life that he could if he were fully devoted to it.

Fifth, the young investigator will develop a sense of personal identity that is based on his own area of special skills within the research group and the broader community. Through presentations at meetings he will learn how he measures up to the national standards and gain an increasingly realistic picture of his worth and what matters most to him. His mentor will play critically important roles in allowing him or her the opportunities to move ahead in his experience of giving lectures, joining committees, and entering the broader world as his own person. In these ways, he will gain an increasingly satisfying fit among his abilities, ambitions, values, and actual achievements.

If mentorship goes well, the young investigator will achieve these developmental tasks in part through his identification with the teacher as the mentor shares his experience with pain at rejection and criticism and his pleasure with successes.

If the environment is reasonably facilitating and the individual is fortunate, the young investigator will avoid too early and too traumatic a series of rejections or hurt pride; too much administrative responsibility, which will take him from creative work; too early demands for self-support through grants and patient care; and too much self-serving. That is, he will be allowed to develop internally and personally, and at a reasonable pace.

At many stages of this process, the mentor and student (that is, the slightly older investigator and the younger colleague) will have to deal with painful feelings arising from within their relationship. These feelings will concern disappointments with each other, hurt feelings, annoyances, and jealousies. At some point they will have to face the process of separation and individuation and the angry and the other feelings that arise during termination. These processes of distancing may, and must, occur when the mentor and the colleague remain in the same institution. This maturational step also can be a source of pleasure for both teacher and student. The older investigator (perhaps only six or seven years older) can take pride in the relationship and the achievements of the younger person, while muting his occasional thoughts of infanticide; the younger investigator can free himself of no longer needed dependencies, preserve what is useful in the relationship, while muting his patricidal feelings. The process is most likely to go well if the mentor had dealt maturely, thoughtfully, and graciously with his own mentors: if he continues to be able to make use of them and even to begin moving towards caring for them, as their needs arise. The waning of the Oedipus in the scientific mentor-student relationship can thus result in lifelong, sustaining friendships and collaborations that are remodeled on the basis of mutual respect and interdependence during the course of maturation.

When all has gone reasonably well over three to five years, the younger investigator is ready in all senses for the sixth development task, to be a professor: a teacher, clinician, and investigator capable of independent work and of taking care of the next generation. The student who has the capacity to be parented—to appreciate the nurturance and to show this through his own growth—will develop the ability to parent: to be loyal to the values of his teachers by conveying them to his own students. This process of development can be disrupted at many points, including immersion in full-time clinical work and the decision to leave the Academy, entirely.

For the field of child psychiatry, an important diversionary force is the long training in general psychiatry that precedes training in child psychiatry. During this process, talented individuals can be siphoned off into research and academic careers in general psychiatry. This possibility is increased by the greater resources, including job opportunities, controlled by general psychiatry. However, in my experience, the major disruptions along the developmental line leading to a career in clinical research are not financial or other realistic concerns, serious though they are. Instead, people leave the academic research line after feeling or being hurt in just those areas of our lives where our deepest emotions are felt, in relation to narcissism, feeling loved and feeling fully engaged and actualized. Mentorship, if it is authentic, must include acceptance and appreciation of these feelings. This is easiest when the mentor himself or herself is relatively comfortable with life, and with the career he has and is living.

There are thus many threats to the developmental line leading from student to clinical researcher. Some of these are becoming more virulent as universities face the so-called realities of the "new medical economies." With financial stringencies, all feelings become heightened, and it is possible for cruelty to be displayed more openly when it is rationalized as "good administration." Pressures from deans, chairmen, clinical directors—from all of us—to maintain tight economic control are likely to be compounded with less availability of funding for research and training from any source. In this circumstance, there are dangers to both the very young and the old. But even the most seasoned teachers and investigators are not immune, regardless of the level of their prior exposure: even they may feel exploited or in danger. The greatest worries for the future texture of student-teacher relationships may arise from the form of our adaptation, as communities of scholars and physicians, to the challenges posed by balancing values and finances.

PERSON, PLACE, TIME, SUMMING UP

Child psychiatry is an increasingly exciting field for clinical research, with broader interest in the disorders of children and new methods available for their study. The clinical researcher plays critical roles in directing what to study, in understanding the whole child and the nature of his or her disorder, in appreciating development, and in retaining a skepticism about easy answers. In part, the clinician's role will be as moderator; he can correct the quick generalization with the specifics of today's case, and he can use the last several cases to make a convincing point that may run against the exciting new hypothesis, regardless of its statistical p value. In turn, new hypotheses will come from immersion in the clinical material; the clinical researcher will need to know how to extract from the richness of phenomenology what can be studied rigorously and generalized.

The process of development of child psychiatric researchers will precede by many years their actual work as child psychiatrists. Often, the process will have started in childhood, with their own curiosity about the mind and children's problems, with their desire to understand life as it is lived. It is important for those individuals who have a proclivity to clinical research in child psychiatry to experience the actual process of doing research—to do studies—as early as possible in college and medical school. If Ogden Lindsley had sent me back to Brandeis until I learned more psychology, I never would have returned to become an operant researcher. The good mentor must accept the risk of allowing the student to get in over his head and then be around to help out in a way that makes the student feel like he is swimming quite well on his own.

There will be no single training process or curriculum for child psychiatrists who wish to become researchers—individuals who wish for such a career cannot tolerate too much systematic teaching, in any case. For the next years, at least, there will be multiple different styles of research, and this will also include different mixtures of clinical work and research. There must be institutions in which the developmental process can proceed. These institutions require senior clinical and nonclinical faculty, committed to the process of education; clinical and laboratory resources; and sufficient financial and administrative security to allow for the protection and long-term development of young investigators.

This chapter only barely touches on fundamental questions of concern to younger investigators, such as the relevance of psychoanalytic training or continued clinical work to research careers; the best way of fashioning a life that balances individual needs; the need for independent centers for child psychiatry; and what the new economics of health care will mean for those concerned about academic investigation and the life of the university. The case studies offered in this chapter exemplify only some of the concepts and principles that can be applied in fostering and understanding the development of young clinical investigators in child psychiatry.

Two important areas have not been dealt with at all and are noted here to highlight their importance. First, I have not dealt with questions concerning the later phases of natural history of clinical research—burnout, administer-out, national lead-out and other unnatural and premature ends, as well as normal maturation into "senior" research roles in addition to mentorship.

Second, and more critically, I have not discussed questions concerning the facilitation of careers of creative individuals who are out of the current "mainstream" but who represent the tradition of scholarship exemplified by D. W. Winnicott, Anna Freud, Erik Erikson, Rene Spitz, Sally Provence, and others who have sat with, watched, and thought about how children understand themselves and their worlds. One might wonder about the fate of their papers (and those of many others whom we read with continuing interest) if they were submitted today by a young child psychiatrist to our leading journals and granting agencies. We can easily predict the thrashing they might receive and how we in the reviewing establishment might try to be helpful with suggestions about design, sampling, methodology, hypothesis testing, and the like. "The author presents a major theoretical system on the basis of limited observations of babies and blankets, but he fails to adequately specify the population, methods for formal psychiatric assessment of children and their parents, and the precise physical characteristics of the soft objects he used. If he is interested in pursuing this line of work, I would suggest . . ." Given this current ideology and tone, as well as economic realities, which one of the pioneers in our broad field would be hired today, let alone move up the tenure line? There are some in the research world today who might not be concerned about this situation and who might look with some scorn at the papers I find admirable. Yet, it seems to me to be especially critical, perhaps just for this reason, to find the time and space in the university to allow gifted clinicians to mature and find their own voices as clinical scholars.

In telling the developmental story of clinical research careers in child psychiatry from the perspective of one person and one place, I have emphasized the centrality of the close, enduring, mutually enriching relationships that develop between teacher and student, and the time this process takes. As a society, we need to ensure the continued existence of academic environments for such relationships.

Postscript: Inner Life

Matthew Isaac Cohen

ALWAYS GO FOR THE OBJECTS

I recall accompanying my father on a visit to a state facility for juvenile offenders. I am unsure of the precise year. Most likely it was in the early 1990s when I was starting graduate school in anthropology and my father was beginning his work on children and violence that resulted in the Child Development/Community Policing Program in New Haven, and in a series of collaborations with clinicians and researchers in Israel on the relations of violence with depression, suicide, and trauma among Palestinian and Israeli civilians, and among Israeli military personnel. My father interviewed one of the residents at this facility, an African-American boy with a history of violence with guns, drug use, and sexual misconduct. Minutes into the interview, the boy revealed a vivid fantasy about an imaginary younger brother to whom he taught lessons he had learned from his hard life on the streets. The facility's attending mental health worker was present during the interview, which lasted perhaps a quarter of an hour. Before this he had never heard a peep about such an imaginary relative, and was agog at the vein of fantasy my father had tapped.

We left the facility, and my father and I were on the way back to the car when I asked him how he had managed to unveil such a guarded aspect of the boy's private life. "Always go for the objects," he replied with more than a trace of machismo pride. The boy had been disarmed by unexpected questions regarding his relationship with his parents, without allusions to the boy's misdeeds. It was axiomatic that what followed in the interview would emerge through the aperture to inner life pried open by the discomfiture of self-reflection. There *are* royal roads to the psyche.

WRITER'S LIFE

The essays collected in this volume speak in the languages of a number of intersecting disciplines—psychoanalysis, child psychiatry, developmental psychology, social policy, and others. My father wrote many other articles at the same time, reporting findings of experiments in neural imaging, biochemistry, and genetics. One catches the occasional glimpse of this biological child psychiatrist in passing references to the cerebral cortex and serotonin reuptake inhibitors. The essays here are not centrally concerned with advances in the medical treatment of autism, Tourette's syndrome, or the other disorders that my father investigated; faddish therapies are dealt with critically. Rather, the concern is with enduring truths of the inner life, and with the profound insights that children and adults who have not followed normal developmental pathways provide into the human condition. Certain messages and themes chime repeatedly. We learn how a capacity for imagining and play is useful insofar as it allows for the deepening of enduring relations, while conversely an overly stimulated imagination (one overridden by realistic fears, unrealistic forebodings, and pathological suspicions) can cripple a person's social development. We develop a respect for aggression and see both how aggressive impulses lead to individuation and how real communal violence can lead to psychological disaster. Our attention is drawn to those impaired by bodies and minds locked in war, to people with inexplicable compulsions, individuals with bizarre fantasies; and we recognize in these people commonalities with our own selves. We learn how some children and adults are naturally good psychologists of themselves. Others, particularly people with autism, lack a capacity for self-reflection and analysis.

Behind all these essays, and particularly in the more autobiographical pieces, is a philosophy of and a practical guide to life. The happy and sad moments of life are not meant to be experienced alone, but in the company of a small number of friends and family. A social life and a career should be intertwined in the deepening of feelings of sympathy, love, and mutual engagement that are the hallmarks of deep and enduring relationships. A good student does not feign interest in the enthusiasms of a teacher; she takes on a mentor's values and passions as her own. The ultimate goal of the therapeutic process is the development of a capacity to share one's life, to love and be loved. A good therapist understands each patient as presenting opportunities to learn something about the operations of the psyche, and to rectify faults in the therapist her- or himself: in my father's case, the decades-long therapeutic engagement with bullish "Abe" (Chapter 1 and 5) was an antidote to his own constitutional bookishness.

It is not incidental, in this regard, that most of these pieces are co-authored with other researchers. They are actuations of a belief that writing is an eminently social practice that serves to fortify relations in a community of research. I know from being witness to his countless hours in front of typewriter and computer that my father was the sole author of many of the articles with multiple names attached to them. But he took more pride in the mentoring and career building that emerges from co-authorship than in the accolades contingent to publishing as a sole author. And he was as prodigious a correspondent as anyone I have ever known. Many, many people around the world counted him as their dearest friend, and still hold him inside.

INNER LININGS

My father always had lining stitched inside his pants. This was not in order to prevent wrinkles or stretching at the knees, but because he did not like the feel of the pants' fabric against his skin.

The inner linings of his jackets were typically mottled with pen marks, caused from carrying pens without tops in his inner pockets. I used to fantasize that these marks were caused by patients who had attacked him with pens.

My father understood that the worlds of fantasy and actuality are not so distant. We maintain autonomous fantasy systems and we live our lives according to beliefs that are little more than conjectural and hypothetical. The fantasies are properly rehearsals for reality. (It is a sad fact of the human condition that traumatic environmental and psychic events can reverse this relation.) The inner lining beneath the social skin—the ego functions that serve to maintain self-cohesion—is a work of culture. My mother—who always purchased my father's clothes—was responsible for ensuring that my father's clothes were properly lined. They both recognized the need for pants lining as *meshugas*—Yiddish for craziness—but also recognized that it was *meshugas* worth respecting for the strength of character it evoked. Pant linings for my father were what cigars were for Freud. My own fantasy about the attack on my father's jacket lining by his patients was an articulation of family culture. Inner lining is a remarkable dramaturgical invention, a concealed structure to be enacted together as a company.

PRIVATE LIFE

The broad strokes of the career of Donald J. Cohen are outlined in this volume in three autobiographical essays. This career was built on the bedrock of deep engagements with professional collaborators—teachers, students, patients, parents of patients, philanthropists, fellow scholars and researchers, advocates, professionals in allied fields, policy makers. Many collaborators, probably most, could be categorized by two or more of these affiliative labels. For example: parents of patients commonly were advocates and philanthropic supporters. Some of these parents were also instrumental in shaping policy and representing mental illness in the mass media. A few of these parents wrote books and articles on mental health and would send manuscript drafts to my father for commentary.

Professional ethics meant that a notional screen was drawn separating the consulting room from our family's private life. This barrier was never absolute. Rather, life with a community of clinical research was seamlessly articulated with one spent engaged with family and friends. My mother is a clinical child psychologist and was my father's colleague at the Yale Child Study Center. My sister Rachel met her husband Allan (who is now a pediatric surgeon at Harvard) through the latter's bursary job at the center. My sister Rebecca's husband is a faculty member at the center as well as one of the editors of this book. My brother Joe studied philosophy as an undergraduate at Yale, and through him, my father vicariously revisited texts he had studied at Brandeis and as a Fulbright scholar at Cambridge. I pursued undergraduate studies in psychology at Harvard, which brought me into direct contact with scholars who were my father's professional colleagues and collaborators. I also spent summers doing laboratory work at the center, consulted on various projects as an anthropologist, and contributed to volumes my father edited. These family connections were not nepotistic, but rather realizations of a social ethos in which personal and professional lives are integrally connected. Telephone calls from Abe and a Hollywood executive, family holidays that were also business trips, and late-night meetings in our house with professional colleagues were salient features of life when I was a child. Students and colleagues gathered at our house to read D. W. Winnicott's *The Piggle* (an annotated edition was planned but never written). Some of my father's collaborators remain the closest of family friends.

The interarticulation of the personal and professional was evident to anyone who knew my father, but aspects of my father's own imaginative life were unknown to all but the most intimate. There were multitudinous murals, wooden sculptures, and collages in the 1960s and early 1970s. Few know that my father was a prolific but unpublished children's author, in the form of serialized stories about the semifictional Chicago gangster Mashie Bear and his sidekick Potsie. Some of the stories, dealing with improbable schemes such as the theft of Lake Michigan, were initially rehearsed as bedtime tales. Later, versions of these stories arrived in the form of typed letters sent to my sisters and me at summer camp. These tales probably played a therapeutic function for my father—they allowed him to revisit and romance the scenes of his childhood in a playful mode and assuage feelings of separation anxiety from us. My father was also a playwright, annually churning out plays that friends read aloud to celebrate the Jewish holiday of Purim. His Purim plays were always farcical in tone, rife in sexual innuendo, and tuned to political events in New Haven, the United States, Israel, and the world. Purim became a high point in the religious calendar for the regular group of reader-actors who congregated at our house. It was probably this annual exposure to Purim plays, more than anything else, that stimulated my own interest in performance.

These sundry creative activities were all keyed to particular social exchanges. The early visual artifacts were presented as "gifts" to family and friends. The Mashie Bear stories were manifestly intended to stimulate the imagination of my sisters and me and enlighten us on the culture of a partially imagined Chicago. The Purim festivities were offered primarily to members of the "*Shabbes* group," an informal Bible study group that met weekly in houses of Westville Jewish families. Our house was not in walking distance from Westville, and we thus were unable to host group gatherings on the Sabbath. On Purim, however, when the religious proscription against driving was not in effect, our house became a liminal staging ground for a reflexive transformation of community.

WALKING LIKE TOM CRUISE

My father was once in a documentary on a child psychiatric issue. One shot showed him walking outside the Child Study Center. He agreed to the shot, but on the condition that the director first instruct him on how to walk like Tom Cruise, whose macho strut was perceived in those days as the epitome of cool. Being in a "movie" evoked desire for a movie star's signature body technique. It took many takes and much time to get the shot right, but finally the director and my father were satisfied.

Reading these essays, which overlap in theme and concern, is an exercise in learning how to walk in the style of other people. We begin reading as an "anthropologist on Mars" and end in lockstep with the style of a diverse group of pathological and normal others, including the author. Reading Donald Cohen's words does not make us Donald Cohen, any more than my father became Tom Cruise on film because he was instructed in his gait. Internalizing the discourse or behavior of another does not magically transform you into another person. It does allow you, however, to acquire a portion of that other person's grace.

LIFE IN SOCIETY

My father's father, Joe Cohen, sold used bakery equipment and was successful enough to put three sons through graduate school, though he was an elementary school dropout himself. Papa Joe read Mickey Spillane, smoked cigars, ate garlic and *schmaltz,* and played cards with members of his childhood gang. Much of my father's early adulthood was an attempt to distance himself from a childhood culture of perceived inerudition. He read voraciously and hobnobbed with intellectuals at Brandeis, Cambridge, Yale, and Harvard; he tried to learn how to play a classical instrument (the cello, unsuccessfully) and cultivated an appreciation of the arts (wisely purchasing an early Brice Marden); he "married up" to my mother; he purchased a house with a swimming pool in the elite New Haven suburb of Woodbridge. Years of psychoanalysis fostered an appreciation of the past and reconciliation with and renewed love for his father. Years of practice as a child psychiatrist brought him into contact with a diverse cross-section of society, from the most ordinary to the most affluent of children and families.

Living a life in full social intercourse entails a relinquishment of control. A responsible and responsive member of Yale University must confront daily the reality of the impoverished citizens of New Haven, and deal respectfully with a population scarred by urban violence, prostitution, drug dealing, and worse. An image pops into mind from a videotape my father's research group made in the early 1990s of an "Oedipal child" around age 4 or 5 playing with dolls with a psychoanalyst. A small spider had made its home in the analyst's dollhouse and was spotted by the child, who reacted with astonishment and fear. The analyst thought the child was only pretending to see a spider and began to interpret this as a fantasy until her attention was drawn to the presence of a real spider in her office. The psychoanalyst also gave a noticeable start, and in this moment of recognition the playing child, analyst, and observers of the videotape understood that there *are* such things as spiders in dollhouses—ones that are really scary, and potentially dangerous. What matters are which tools we have to deal with those spiders, the fonts of wisdom and sources of support we can draw upon in moments of crisis. This book provides a set of such tools for life with others.

Notes

1. Hobson (1991) presents a cogent argument that what children acquire is not a "theory" or set of hypothetical constructs about others' minds, but rather that through early experiences with others, children develop a knowledge of minds and such mental states as feelings and beliefs. Hobson places, as we shall also, the beginnings of the ability to understand beliefs and feelings in the earliest interactions between mother and infant and in how the infant's earliest sensory/perceptual capacities allow him to respond to such interactions. Throughout this paper, we use the phrase "theory of mind" to refer to children's developing understanding of how feelings, beliefs, and thoughts are related to the actions and language of others.

CHAPTER 8. THE DEVELOPMENT OF A CAPACITY FOR IMAGINATION IN EARLY CHILDHOOD

1. *Editors' Note.* A substantial part of this section and another one in its entirety ("Understanding the Concept of the Mental World and Mental States") have been deleted, as their contents are reviewed in depth in Chapters 3 and 4.

CHAPTER 9. THE SOCIAL MATRIX OF AGGRESSION

1. As in other areas of psychoanalytic concern, terminological issues often have clouded the discussion of aggression. We shall try to distinguish the three major domains of psychoanalytic thinking in relation to aggression as (a) what can be *observed;* (b) what the individual is *experiencing,* not always consciously; and (c) what can be *inferred* and theoretically explained about the child's mental functioning.

   Thus, we will refer to (a) *aggressivity* (or aggressive acts and behavior) in relation to what is observable as assertive, destructive, hurtful, etc., in a child's ongoing behavior; (b) to *aggressive feelings,* and *mental states* (including fantasies, affects, wishes, thoughts, motives, and intents) in relation to what the child clearly or apparently is experiencing; and (c) to *aggression* (including aggressive drives, instincts, forces, impulses, striving, derivatives and the like) in relation to the psychoanalytic theory of mental organization and functioning.

   We hope that the context, as well, will make the domain of discussion clear. There is obviously, and for good reasons, a slippery slope connecting these three domains of discourse; behavior, feelings, and inferred processes are intimately related, and it is easy to switch from one level of discourse to another. Yet, we are especially interested in describing apparent paradoxes and discontinuities in the relations among these domains during the course of development and at particular moments for individual children.

2. Note the critical difference in this position and that, for example, of Klein (1957a), who placed aggression at the center of character formation but gave almost singular responsibility to the infant with his individual level of hunger and greed (real and fantasied) and his recognition of the consequences of his insatiable needs on the mother. In this view, the mother's reaction plays little role in shaping and channeling the infant's experience in fantasy of his aggressive, assertive desires (Cohen, 1990).

Bibliography

Abraham, K. 1921. Contributions to the theory of the anal character. In *Selected papers*. London: Grant A. Allan, Maresfield Reprints, pp. 370–392.

———. 1923. Contributions to the theory of the anal character. *International Journal of Psychoanalysis,* 4:400–418.

———. 1925. Influence of oral erotism on character formation. *International Journal of Psychoanalysis,* 6:247–258.

Abrams, S. 1988. The psychoanalytic process in adults and children. *Psychoanalytic Study of the Child,* 43:245–261.

Adams, G., and Sandfort, J. R. 1992. *State investment in child care and early childhood education.* Washington, D.C.: Children's Defense Fund.

Adnopoz, J. 1993. Reaching out: The experiences of a family support agency. In *Development in jeopardy: Clinical responses to infants and families,* ed. E. Fenichel and S. Provence. Madison: International Universities Press, pp. 119–166.

Adnopoz, J., Grigsby, R. K., and Nagler, S. 1991. Multiproblem families and high-risk children and adolescents: Causes and management. In *Child and adolescent psychiatry: A comprehensive textbook,* ed. M. Lewis. 3d ed. Baltimore: Williams and Wilkins, pp. 1059–1066.

Adnopoz, J., and Nagler, S. 1992. Supporting HIV infected children in their own families through family-centered practice. In *Advancing family preservation practice,* ed. R. Grigsby and S. Morton. Newberry Park: Sage, pp. 119–128.

Alpert, J., Cohen, D. J., Shaywitz, B. A., and Piccirillo, M. 1981. Neurochemical and behavior organization in disorders of attention, activity and aggression. In *Vulnerabilities to delinquency,* ed. D. O. Lewis. New York: S. P. Medical and Scientific Books, pp. 109–171.

Anderson, G. M., and Hoshino, Y. 1987. *Neurochemical studies of autism.* New York: Wiley.

Apter, A., Pauls, D. L., Bleich, A., Zohar, A. H., Kron, S., Ratzoni, G., Dycian, A., Kotler, M., Weizman, A., and Cohen, D. J. 1992. A population-based epidemiological study of Tourette syndrome among adolescents in Israel. *Advances in Neurology,* 58:61–65.

Association, American Psychiatric. 1994. *Diagnostic and statistical manual of mental disorders.* 4th ed. Washington, D.C.: American Psychiatric Press.

Astington, J. W., and Gopnik, A. 1991. Theoretical explanations of children's understanding of mind. *British Journal of Development,* 9:7–31.

Astington, J. W., Harris, P. L., and Olson, D. R. 1988. *Developing theories of mind.* Cambridge: Cambridge University Press.

Bandura, A. 1973. *Aggression.* New York: Holt.

Banks, M. S., and Salapatek, P. 1983. Infant visual perception. In *Infancy and developmental psychobiology: Handbook on child psychology,* ed. M. M. Haith and J. J. Campos. New York: Wiley, pp. 435–572.

Baron-Cohen, S. 1989a. Are autistic children "behaviorists"? An examination of their mental-physical and appearance-reality distinctions. *Journal of Autism and Developmental Disorders,* 19:579–600.

———. 1989b. The autistic child's theory of mind: A case of specific developmental delay. *Journal of Child Psychology and Psychiatry,* 30:285–297.

———. 1991a. Do people with autism understand what causes emotion? *Child Development,* 62:385–395.

———. 1991b. Precursors to a theory of mind: Understanding attention in others. In *Natural Theories of Mind,* ed. A. Whiten. Oxford: Blackwell.

———. 1993. From attention-goal psychology to belief-desire psychology: The development of a theory of mind, and its dysfunction. In *Understanding other minds: Perspectives from autism,* ed. S. Baron-Cohen, H. Tager-Flusberg, and D. J. Cohen. Oxford: Oxford University Press, pp. 59–82.

Baron-Cohen, S., Leslie, A. M., and Frith, U. 1985. Does the autistic child have a "theory of mind"? *Cognition,* 21:37–46.

Baron-Cohen, S., Tager-Flusberg, H., and Cohen, D. J. (eds.). 1993. *Understanding other minds: Perspectives from autism.* Oxford: Oxford University Press.

———. 2000. *Understanding other minds: Perspectives from developmental cognitive neuroscience,* 2nd ed. New York: Oxford University Press.

Bartsch, K., and Wellman, H. 1989. Young children's attribution of action to beliefs and desires. *Child Development,* 60:946–964.

Bemporad, J. R. 1979. Adult recollections of a formerly autistic child. *Journal of Autism and Developmental Disorders,* 9:179–197.

Beres, D. 1960a. Imagination and reality. *International Journal of Psychoanalysis,* 41:327–334.

———. 1960b. The psychoanalytic psychology of imagination. *Journal of the American Psychoanalytic Association,* 8:252–269.

Bettelheim, B. 1967. *The empty fortress.* New York: Free Press.

Bibring, E. 1941. The development and problems of the theory of instincts. *International Journal of Psychoanalysis,* 21:102–131.

Bliss, J. 1980. Sensory experiences of Gilles de la Tourette syndrome. *Archives of General Psychiatry,* 37:1343–1347.

Bowlby, J. 1969–1982. *Attachment and loss.* New York: Basic Books.

Braverman, M., Fein, D., Lucci, D., and Waterhouse, L. 1989. Affect comprehension in children with pervasive developmental disorders. *Journal of Autism and Developmental Disorders,* 19:301–316.

Brenner, C. 1971. The psychoanalytic concept of aggression. *International Journal of Psychoanalysis,* 52:137–144.

Bretherton, I. 1985. Attachment theory. Monograph Society for Research in *Child Development,* 50:3–35.

Bruner, J. 1975. The ontogenesis of speech acts. *Journal of Child Language,* 2:1–19.

Buber, M. 1947. *Tales of the Hasidim: The early masters.* New York: Schocken.

Bullowa, M. 1979. *Before speech: The beginnings of interpersonal communication.* Cambridge: Cambridge University Press.

Buss, A. H. 1961. *The psychology of aggression.* New York: Wiley.

———. 1966. Instrumentality of aggression, feedback, and frustration as determinants of physical aggression. *Journal of Personality and Social Psychology,* 3:153–162.

Caparulo, B. K., and Cohen, D. J. 1977. Cognitive structures, language, and emerging social competence in autistic and aphasic children. *Journal of the American Academy of Child and Adolescent Psychiatry,* 16:620–645.

———. 1983. Developmental language studies in the neuropsychiatric disorders of childhood. In *Children's language,* ed. K. E. Nelson. New York: Gardner Press, pp. 423–463.

Caparulo, B. K., Cohen, D. J., Rothman, S. L., Young, J. G., Katz, J. D., Shaywitz, S. E., and Shaywitz, B. A. 1981. Computed tomographic brain scanning in children with developmental neuropsychiatric disorders. *Journal of the American Academy of Child and Adolescent Psychiatry,* 20:338–357.

Commission on Behavioral and Social Sciences and Education. 1993. National Research Council. In *Understanding child abuse and neglect.* Washington, D.C.: National Academy Press.

Chase, T. N., Friedhoff, A. J., and Cohen, D. J. (eds.). 1992. *Advances in neurology, volume 58. Tourette's syndrome: genetics, neurobiology and treatment.* New York: Raven Press.

Children's Defense Fund. 1991. *The state of America's children.* Washington, D.C.: Children's Defense Fund.

Chandler, M., Fritz, A. S., and Hala, S. 1989. Small-scale deceit: Deception as a marker of two-, three-, and four-year-olds' early theories of mind. *Child Development,* 60:1263–1277.

Cicchetti, D., and Cohen, D. J. (eds.). 1995a. Perspectives on developmental psychopathology. In *Developmental psychopathology: Volume 1. Theory and methods.* New York: Wiley, pp. 3–20.

———. 1995b. *Developmental psychopathology: Volume 2. Risk, disorder and adaptation.* New York: Wiley.

———. 1995c. *Developmental psychopathology: Volume 1. Theory and methods.* New York: Wiley.

Cicchetti, D., and Toth, S. 1993. *Child maltreatment, child development, and social policy.* Norwood: Ablex.

Cohen, D. J. 1962. Justin and his peers: An experimental analysis of a child's social world. *Child Development,* 33:697–717.

———. 1972. *Serving school age children.* Child Development Series No. 4. Washington, D.C.: U.S. Government Printing Office.

———. 1974. Competence and biology: Methodology in studies of infants, twins, psychosomatic disease, and psychosis. In *The child in his family: Children at psychiatric risk,* ed. E. J. Anthony and C. Koupernik. New York: Wiley, pp. 361–394.

———. 1980a. Constructive and reconstructive activities in the analysis of a depressed child. *Psychoanalytic Study of the Child,* 35:237–266.

———. 1980b. The pathology of self in primary childhood autism and Gilles de la Tourette syndrome. *Psychiatric Clinics of North America,* 3:383–402.

———. 1990. Enduring sadness. Early loss, vulnerability, and the shaping of character. *Psychoanalytic Study of the Child,* 45:157–178.

———. 1991a. Finding meaning in one's self and others: Clinical studies of children with autism and Tourette's syndrome. In *Contemporary constructions of the child: Essays in honor of William Kessen,* ed. F. Kessel, M. Bornstein, and A. Sameroff. Hillsdale: Lawrence Erlbaum Associates, Chapter 10, pp. 159–175.

———. 1991b. Tourette's syndrome: A model disorder for integrating psychoanalytic and biological perspectives. *International Review of Psychoanalysis,* 18:195–209.

———. 2001a. Into life: Autism, Tourette's syndrome and the community of clinical research. *Israel Journal of Psychiatry and Related Sciences,* 38:226–234.

———. 2001b. Tourette's syndrome: A model disorder for integrating psychoanalysis and biological perspectives. *International Journal of Psychoanalysis,* 18: 195–209.

Cohen, D. J., Bruni, R. D., and Leckman, J. F. 1988. *Tourette's syndrome and tic disorders: Clinical understanding and treatment.* New York: Wiley.

Cohen, D. J., Caparulo, B., and Shaywitz, B. 1976. Primary childhood aphasia and childhood autism: Clinical, biological, and conceptual observations. *Journal of the American Academy of Child and Adolescent Psychiatry,* 15:604–645.

Cohen, D. J., Detlor, J., Shaywitz, B. A., and Leckman, J. F. 1982. Interaction of biological and psychological factors in the natural history of Tourette syndrome: A paradigm for childhood neuropsychiatric disorders. *Advances in Neurology,* 35:31–40.

Cohen, D. J., Detlor, J., Young, J. G., and Shaywitz, B. A. 1980a. Clonidine ameliorates Gilles de la Tourette syndrome. *Archives of General Psychiatry,* 37:1350–1357.

Cohen, D. J., and Donnellan, A. 1987. *Handbook of autism and pervasive developmental disorders.* New York: Wiley.

Cohen, D. J., Marans, S., Dahl, K., Marans, W., and Lewis, M. 1987. Analytic discussions with oedipal children. *Psychoanalytic Study of the Child,* 42:59–83.

Cohen, D. J., Shaywitz, B. A., Caparulo, B., Young, J. G., and Bowers, M. B., Jr. 1978. Chronic, multiple tics of Gilles de la Tourette's disease. CSF acid monoamine metabolites after probenecid administration. *Archives of General Psychiatry,* 35:245–250.

Cohen, D. J., Shaywitz, B. A., Young, J. G., and Bowers, M. B., Jr. 1980b. Cerebrospinal fluid monoamine metabolites in neuropsychiatric disorders of childhood. In *Neurobiology of cerebrospinal fluid,* ed. J. H. Wood. New York: Plenum Publishing Corp. pp. 665–683.

Cohen, D. J., Shaywitz, B. A., Young, J. G., Carbonari, C. M., Nathanson, J. A., Lieberman, D., Bowers, M. B., Jr., and Maas, J. W. 1979a. Central biogenic amine metabolism in children with the syndrome of chronic multiple tics of Gilles de la Tourette: Norepinephrine, serotonin, and dopamine. *Journal of the American Academy of Child and Adolescent Psychiatry,* 18:320–341.

Cohen, D. J., Towbin, K., Mayes, L. C., and Volkmar, F. R. 1995. Precursors, emergence, and continuity of the self: Developmental follow-up of multiplex developmental disorder. In *Developmental follow-up: Concepts, genres, domains, and methods,* ed. S. L. Friedman and H. C. Haywood. Orlando: Academic Press, pp. 155–179.

Cohen, D. J., Young, J. G., Nathanson, J. A., and Shaywitz, B. A. 1979b. Clonidine in Tourette's syndrome. *Lancet,* 2:551–553.

Cohen, P., and Cohen, M. 1993. Conceptual worlds: Play, theatre and child psychoanalysis. In *The many meanings of play in child psychoanalysis,* ed. A. Solnit. New Haven: Yale University Press, pp. 75–98.

Cohen, S. N. 1977. Development of drug therapy for children. *Federal Process,* 36:2356–2358.

Cummings, E. M., Hollenbeck, B., Iannotti, R. J., Radke-Yarrow, M., and Zahn-Waxler, C. 1986. Early organization of altruism and aggression. In *Altruism and aggression,* ed. C. Zahn-Waxler, E. M. Cummings, and R. J. Iannotti. New York: Cambridge University Press, pp. 165–188.

Cummings, E. M., Iannotti, R. J., and Zahn-Waxler, C. 1989. Aggression between peers in early childhood: Individual continuity and developmental change. *Child Development,* 60:887–895.

Daro, D., and McCurdy, K. 1990. *Current trends in child abuse reporting and fatalities: The results of the 1990 Annual Fifty-State Survey.* Chicago: National Committee for Prevention of Child Abuse.

DeCasper, A. J., and Fifer, W. P. 1980. Of human bonding: Newborns prefer their mothers' voices. *Science,* 208:1174–1176.

DeMyer, M. K., Hingtgen, J. N., and Jackson, R. K. 1981. Infantile autism reviewed: A decade of research. *Schizophrenia Bulletin,* 7:388–451.

Department of Commerce, Bureau of the Census (DC/BC). 1990a. *Current population reports,* Ser. P-60, No. 168: *Money, income, and poverty status in the United States, 1989.* Washington, D.C.: U.S. Government Printing Office.

Department of Commerce, Bureau of the Census (DC/BC). 1990b. Households and family characteristics: March 1990 and 1989. *Current population reports.* Washington, D.C.: U.S. Government Printing Office.

Dodge, K. A. 1980. Social cognition and children's aggressive behavior. *Child Development,* 51:162–170.

———. 1986. Social-information processing variables in the development of aggression and altruism in children. In *Altruism and aggression,* ed. C. Zahn-Waxler, E. M. Cummings, and R. J. Iannotti. New York: Cambridge University Press, pp. 280–302.

Dodge, K. A., and Coie, J. D. 1987. Social-information-processing factors in reactive and proactive aggression in children's peer groups. *Journal of Personality and Social Psychology,* 53:1146–1158.

Dollard, J., Doob, L. W., Miller, N. E., Mowrer, O. H., and Sears, R. R. 1939. *Frustration and aggression.* New Haven: Yale University Press.

Downey, T. W. 1984. Within the pleasure principle: Child analytic perspectives on aggression. *Psychoanalytic Study of the Child,* 39:101–136.

———. 1987. Notes on play and guilt in child analysis. *Psychoanalytic Study of the Child,* 42:105–125.

Ekstein, R., and Caruth, E. 1969. Levels of verbal communication in the schizophrenic child's struggle against, for, and with the world of objects. *Psychoanalytic Study of the Child,* 24:115–137.

Ekstein, R., and Wallerstein, J. 1954. Observations on the psychology of borderline and psychotic children. *Psychoanalytic Study of the Child,* 9:344–369.

Erikson, E. 1987. *A way of looking at things.* New York: W. W. Norton.

Estes, D., Wellman, H. M., and Wooley, J. D. 1989. Children's understanding of mental phenomena. In *Advances in child development and behavior,* ed. H. Reese. New York: Academic Press, pp. 41–87.

Etzel, B. C., and Gewirtz, J. L. 1967. Experimental modification of caretaker-maintained high-rate operant crying in a 6- and a 20-week-old infant (Infans tyrannotearus): Extinction of crying with reinforcement of eye contact and smiling. *Journal of Experimental Child Psychology,* 5:303–317.

Feinman, S., and Lewis, M. 1983. Social referencing at ten months: A second-order effect on infants' responses to strangers. *Child Development,* 54:878–887.

Fenichel, O. 1945. *The psychoanalytic theory of neurosis.* New York: Norton.

Feshbach, S. 1964. The function of aggression and the regulation of aggressive drive. *Psychology Review,* 71:257–272.

Flavell, J. H., Flavell, E. R., Green, F. L., and Moses, L. J. 1990. Young children's understanding of fact beliefs versus value beliefs. *Child Development,* 61:915–928.

Folstein, S. E., and Piven, J. 1991. Etiology of autism: Genetic influences. *Pediatrics,* 87:767–773.

Fraiberg, S., and Adelson, E. 1973. Self-representation in language and play: Observations of blind children. *Psychoanalytic Quarterly,* 42:539–562.

Freedman, D. X. 1992. The search: Body, mind, and human purpose. *American Journal of Psychiatry,* 149:858–866.

Freud, A. 1945. Indications for child analysis. In *The writings of Anna Freud, volume V.* London: Hogarth Press, pp. 3–38.

———. 1957. The Hampstead child-therapy course and clinic. In *The writings of Anna Freud, volume V.* London: Hogarth Press, pp. 3–8.

———. 1965. *Normality and pathology in childhood.* New York: International University Press.

———. 1972a. Comments on aggression. In *The writings of Anna Freud, volume VIII.* London: Hogarth Press, pp. 151–175.

———. 1972b. Comments on aggression. *International Journal of Psychoanalysis,* 53:163–171.

————. 1973. A psychoanalytic view of developmental psychopathology. In *The writings of Anna Freud, volume VIII.* London: Hogarth Press, pp. 57–74.

Freud, S. 1905. Three essays on the theory of sexuality. *The standard edition of the complete works of Sigmund Freud,* volume 7, ed. J. Strachey. London: Hogarth Press, pp. 125–243.

————. 1909. Character and anal erotism. In *The standard edition of the complete works of Sigmund Freud,* volume 19, ed. J. Strachey. London: Hogarth Press, pp. 169–175.

————. 1920. Beyond the pleasure principle. In *The standard edition of the complete works of Sigmund Freud,* volume 18, ed. J. Strachey. London: Hogarth Press, pp. 3–64.

————. 1924. The economic problem of masochism. In *The standard edition of the complete works of Sigmund Freud,* volume 19, ed. J. Strachey. London: Hogarth Press, pp. 159–170.

————. 1926. Inhibitions, symptoms and anxiety. In *The standard edition of the complete works of Sigmund Freud,* volume 20, ed. J. Strachey. London: Hogarth Press, pp. 77–174.

————. 1930. Civilization and its discontents. In *The standard edition of the complete works of Sigmund Freud,* volume 21, ed. J. Strachey. London: Hogarth Press, pp. 59–145.

————. 1937. Analysis terminable and interminable. In *The standard edition of the complete works of Sigmund Freud,* volume 23, ed. J. Strachey. London: Hogarth Press, pp. 216–253.

————. 1953. Case 2, Frau Emmy von N. In *The standard edition of the complete works of Sigmund Freud,* volume 2, ed. J. Strachey. London: Hogarth Press, pp. 48–105.

Friedhoff, A. J., and Chase, T. N. 1982. *Gilles de la Tourette's syndrome.* New York: Raven Press.

Fromm, E. 1955. *The sane society.* New York: Holt, Rinehart, and Winston.

Gallup, G. G., Jr., and McClure, M. K. 1971. Preference for mirror-image stimulation in differentially reared Rhesus monkeys. *Journal of Comparative and Physiological Psychology,* 75:403–407.

Garbarino, J., Dubrow, N., Kostelny, K., and Pardo, C. 1992. *Children in danger: Coping with the consequences of community violence.* San Francisco: Jossey-Bass.

Gay, P. 1988. *Freud: A life for our time.* New York: Norton.

Gillespie, W. H. 1971. Aggression and instinct theory. *International Journal of Psychoanalysis,* 52:155–160.

Glare, P. G. W. 1982. *Oxford Latin dictionary.* Oxford: Clarendon Press.

Golden, G. 1987. Neurological functioning. In *Handbook of autism and pervasive developmental disorders,* ed. D. J. Cohen and A. Donnellan. New York: Wiley, pp. 133–147.

Goodenough, F. L. 1931. *Anger in young children.* Minneapolis: University of Minnesota Press.

Green, E. H. 1933. Friendships and quarrels among preschool children. *Child Development,* 4:236–252.

Greenacre, P. 1967. The influence of infantile trauma on genetic patters. In *Emotional growth.* New York: International University Press, pp. 260–299.

————. 1971. Notes on the influence and contribution of ego psychology to the practice of psychoanalysis. In *Separation-individuation,* ed. J. B. McDevitt. New York: International University Press, pp. 171–200.

Greenberg, D. 2001. Commentary on "Into life": What is a teacher. *Israel Journal of Psychiatry and Related Sciences,* 3–4:240–241.

Gunnar, M. R., and Stone, C. 1984. The effects of positive maternal affect on infant responses to pleasant, ambiguous, and fear-provoking toys. *Child Development,* 55:1231–1236.

Haith, M. M., Bergman, T., and Moore, M. J. 1977. Eye contact and face scanning in early infancy. *Science,* 198:853–855.

Harcherik, D. F., Leckman, J. F., Detlor, J., and Cohen, D. J. 1984. A new instrument for clinical studies of Tourette's syndrome. *Journal of the American Academy of Child and Adolescent Psychiatry,* 23:153–160.

Harlow, H. F. 1971. *Learning to love.* San Francisco: Albion.

Harlow, H. F., and Harlow, M. K. 1965. The affectional systems. In *Behavior of nonhuman primates,* ed. A. M. Schrier, H. F. Harlow, and F. Stollnitz. New York: Academic Press, pp. 287–334.

Harris, P. 1988. *Children and emotion.* Oxford: Blackwell.

Hartmann, H. 1948. Comments on the psychoanalytic theory of instinctual drives. *Psychoanalytic Quarterly,* 17:287–334.

Hartmann, H., Kris, E., and Loewenstein, R. M. 1949. Notes on the theory of aggression. *Psychoanalytic Study of the Child,* 3:9–36.

Hartmann, H., and Loewenstein, R. M. 1962. Notes on the superego. *Psychoanalytic Study of the Child,* 17:42–81.

Hartup, W. W. 1974. Aggression in childhood: Developmental perspectives. *American Psychologist,* 29:336–341.

Hay, D. F. 1984. Social conflict in early childhood. In *Annals of child development,* ed. G. Whitehurst. London: JAI, pp. 1–44.

Hertzig, M. E., Snow, M. E., and Sherman, M. 1989. Affect and cognition in autism. *Journal of the American Academy of Child and Adolescent Psychiatry,* 28:195–199.

Hobson, R. P. 1986. The autistic child's appraisal of expressions of emotion: A further study. *Journal of Child Psychology and Psychiatry,* 27:671–680.

———. 1989. On sharing experiences. *Development and Psychopathology,* 1:197–203.

———. 1990a. On psychoanalytic approaches to autism. *American Journal of Orthopsychiatry,* 60:324–336.

———. 1990b. On the origins of the self and the case of autism. *Development and Psychopathology,* 2:163–181.

———. 1991. Against the theory of "theory of mind." *British Journal of Developmental Psychology,* 9:33–51.

Hornik, R., Risenhoover, N., and Gunnar, M. R. 1987. The effects of maternal positive, neutral, and negative affective communications on infant responses to new toys. *Child Development.,* 58:937–944.

IHDP. 1990. Infant Health and Development Program: Enhancing the outcomes of low-birth weight, premature infants. *Journal of the American Medical Association,* 263:3035–3042.

Jacobson, E. 1954. The self and the object world. *Psychoanalytic Study of the Child,* 9:75–127.

Justice, United States Department of. 1994. *Crime in the United States: 1993 uniform crime reports.* Washington, D.C.: U.S. Government Printing Office.

Kanner, L. 1943. Autistic disturbances of affective contact. *Nervous Child,* 2:217–250.

Kaufman, P., and Frase, M. J. 1990. *Dropout rates in the United States: 1989.* Washington, D.C.: U.S. Department of Education.

Kessen, W., Levine, J., and Wendrich, A. 1979. The imitation of pitch in infants. *Infant Behavior and Development*, 2:93–100.

Kidd, K. K., Prusoff, B. A., and Cohen, D. J. 1980. Familial pattern of Gilles de la Tourette syndrome. *Archives of General Psychiatry*, 37:1336–1339.

Klein, M. 1930. The importance of symbol-formation in the development of the ego. *International Journal of Psychoanalysis*, 11:24–39.

———. 1932. *The psycho-analysis of children.* New York: Delacorte Press/Seymour Lawrence.

———. 1957. Envy and gratitude. In *Envy, gratitude, and other works.* London: Hogarth Press, pp. 176–235.

Klin, A., Volkmar, F., and Sparrow, S. 1992. Autistic social dysfunction: Some limitations of the theory of mind hypothesis. *Journal of Child Psychology and Psychiatry*, 33:861–876.

Kohut, H. 1971. *The Analysis of the self.* New York: International University Press.

———. 1977. *The Restoration of the self.* New York: International University Press.

Leckman, J. F., Cohen, D. J., Gertner, J. M., Ort, S., and Harcherik, D. 1984. Growth hormone response to clonidine in children ages 4 to 17: Tourette's syndrome vs. children with short stature. *Journal of the American Academy of Child and Adolescent Psychiatry*, 23:174–181.

Leckman, J. F., Cohen, D. J., Price, R. A., Riddle, M. A., Minderaa, R. B., Anderson, G. M., and Pauls, D. L. 1986. The pathogenesis of Gilles de la Tourette's syndrome: A review of data and hypotheses. In *Movement disorders,* ed. N. S. Shah and N. B. Shah. New York: Plenum Press, pp. 257–272.

Leckman, J. F., Dolnansky, E. S., Hardin, M. T., Clubb, M., Walkup, J. T., Stevenson, J., and Pauls, D. L. 1990. Perinatal factors in the expression of Tourette's syndrome: An exploratory study. *Journal of the American Academy of Child and Adolescent Psychiatry*, 29:220–226.

Leckman, J. F., Goodman, W. K., Anderson, G. M., Riddle, M. A., Chappell, P. B., McSwiggan-Hardin, M. T., McDougle, C. J., Scahill, L. D., Ort, S. I., Pauls, D. L., et al. 1995. Cerebrospinal fluid biogenic amines in obsessive compulsive disorder, Tourette's syndrome, and healthy controls. *Neuropsychopharmacology*, 12:73–86.

Leckman, J. F., Hardin, M. T., Riddle, M. A., Stevenson, J., Ort, S. I., and Cohen, D. J. 1991. Clonidine treatment of Gilles de la Tourette's syndrome. *Archives of General Psychiatry*, 48:324–328.

Leckman, J. F., and Mayes, L. C. 1998a. Understanding developmental psychopathology: How useful are evolutionary accounts? *Journal of the American Academy of Child and Adolescent Psychiatry*, 37:1011–1121.

———. 1998b. Maladies of love: An evolutionary perspective on some forms of obsessive-compulsive disorder. In *Advancing research in developmental plasticity: Integrating the behavioral science and neuroscience of mental health,* ed. D. M. Hann, L. Huffman, I. Lederhendler, and D. Meinecke. Rockville: National Institute of Mental Health, National Institutes of Health, pp. 134–152.

Leckman, J. F., Peterson, B. S., Anderson, G. M., Arnsten, A. F., Pauls, D. L., and Cohen, D. J. 1997. Pathogenesis of Tourette's syndrome. *Journal of Child Psychology and Psychiatry*, 38:119–142.

Leckman, J. F., Riddle, M. A., Hardin, M. T., Ort, S. I., Swartz, K. L., Stevenson, J., and Cohen, D. J. 1989. The Yale Global Tic Severity Scale: Initial testing of a clinician-rated scale of tic severity. *Journal of the American Academy of Child and Adolescent Psychiatry,* 28:566–573.

Leckman, J. F., Walker, D. E., and Cohen, D. J. 1993. Premonitory urges in Tourette's syndrome. *American Journal of Psychiatry,* 150:98–102.

Leckman, J. F., Walker, D. E., Goodman, W. K., Pauls, D. L., and Cohen, D. J. 1994. "Just right" perceptions associated with compulsive behavior in Tourette's syndrome. *American Journal of Psychiatry,* 151:675–680.

Lee, H. B. 1949. Creative imagination. *Psychoanalytic Quarterly,* 18:351–360.

Lester, B. M., and Boukydis, C. F. Z. 1984. *Infant crying.* New York: Plenum Press.

Levine, R. J. 1978. Appropriate guidelines for the selection of human subjects for participation in biomedical and behavioral research: The Belmont Report. In *Ethical principles and guidelines for the protections of human subjects of research.* DHEW Publication No. (OS) 78–0013. Washington, D.C.: U.S. Department of Health, Education, and Welfare, pp. 4.1–4.103.

———. 1986. *Ethics and regulation of clinical research,* 2nd ed. Baltimore: Urban and Schwarzenberg.

Lewis, M., and Goldberg, S. 1969. Perceptual-cognitive development in infancy. *Merrill-Palmer Quarterly,* 15:81–100.

Lila, M. 2002. A battle for religion. *New York Review of Books,* 49;19: http://www.nybooks.com/articles/15888 (last accessed January 17, 2005).

Loewald, H. W. 1960. Internalization, separation, mourning, and the superego. In *Collected papers.* New Haven: Yale University Press, pp. 257–276.

———. 1971. On motivation and instinct theory. In *Papers on psychoanalysis.* New Haven: Yale University Press, pp. 102–137.

———. 1972a. Freud's conception of the negative therapeutic reaction. In *Papers on psychoanalysis.* New Haven: Yale University Press, pp. 315–325.

———. 1972b. Perspectives on memory. In *Papers on psychoanalysis.* New Haven: Yale University Press, pp. 148–173.

———. 1973. Comments on some instinctual manifestations of superego formation. In *Papers on psychoanalysis.* New Haven: Yale University Press, pp. 326–341.

———. 1977. Instinct theory, object relations, and psychic structure formation. In *Papers on Psychoanalysis.* New Haven: Yale University Press, pp. 207–218.

———. 1978a. *Psychoanalysis and the history of the individual.* New Haven: Yale University Press.

———. 1978b. On motivation and instinct theory. *Psychoanalytic Study of the Child,* 26:91–128.

———. 1979. Reflections on the psychoanalytic process and its therapeutic potential. *Psychoanalytic Study of the Child,* 34:155–167.

———. 1988. *Sublimation.* New Haven: Yale University Press.

Lorenz, K. 1966. *On aggression.* New York: Harcourt, Brace and World.

Mahler, M. S. 1958. Autism and symbiosis, two extreme disturbances of identity. *International Journal of Psychoanalysis,* 39:77–83.

———. 1971. A study of the separation-individuation process and its possible application to borderline phenomena in the psychoanalytic situation. *Psychoanalytic Study of the Child,* 26:403–424.

———. 1974. Symbiosis and individuation: The psychological birth of the human infant. *Psychoanalytic Study of the Child,* 29:89–106.

Mahler, M. S., and Furer, M. 1968. *On human symbiosis and the vicissitudes of individuation.* New York: International University Press.

Mahler, M. S., and McDevitt, J. B. 1982. Thoughts on the emergence of the sense of self, with particular emphasis on the body self. *Journal of the American Psychoanalytic Association,* 30:827–848.

Mahler, M. S., Pine, F., and Bergman, A. 1975. *The psychological birth of the human infant.* New York: Basic Books.

Marans, S. 1994. Community violence and children's development: Collaborative interventions. In *Children and violence,* ed. C. Chiland and G. Young. Northvale: Jason Aaronson, pp. 109–124.

Marans, S., and Cohen, D. J. 1993. Children and inner-city violence: Strategies for intervention. In *Psychological effects of war and violence on children,* ed. L. Leavitt and N. Fox. Hillsdale: Lawrence Erlbaum, pp. 218–301.

Marans, S., Mayes, L., Cicchetti, D., Dahl, K., Marans, W., and Cohen, D. J. 1991. The child-psychoanalytic play interview: A technique for studying thematic content. *Journal of the American Psychoanalytic Association,* 39:1015–1036.

Marans, S., and Pastore, N. 1995. *The police-mental health partnership: A community-based response to urban violence.* New Haven: Yale University Press.

Marcovitz, E. 1982. Aggression. *Psychoanalytic Inquiry,* 2:11–20.

Martinez, P., and Richters, J. E. 1993. The NIMH community violence project: II. Children's distress symptoms associated with violence exposure. *Psychiatry,* 56:22–35.

Mayes, L. C., and Carter, A. S. 1990. Emerging social regulatory capacities as seen in the still-face situation. *Child Development,* 61:754–763.

Mayes, L. C., and Cohen, D. J. 1992. The development of a capacity for imagination in early childhood. *Psychoanalytic Study of the Child,* 47:23–47.

———. 1994. Experiencing self and others: Contributions from studies of autism to the psychoanalytic theory of social development. *Journal of the American Psychoanalytic Association,* 42:191–218.

———. 1995. Constitution. In *Psychoanalysis: The major concepts,* ed. B. E. Moore and B. D. Fine. New Haven: Yale University Press, pp. 271–292.

———. 1996a. Children's developing theory of mind. *Journal of the American Psychoanalytic Association,* 44:117–142.

———. 1996b. Anna Freud and developmental psychoanalytic psychology. *Psychoanalytic Study of the Child,* 51:117–141.

Mayes, L. C., Cohen, D. J., and Klin, A. 1993. Desire and fantasy: A psychoanalytic perspective on theory of mind and autism. In *Understanding other minds: Perspectives from autism,* ed. S. Baron-Cohen, H. Tager-Flusberg, and D. Cohen. New York: Oxford University Press, pp. 450–465.

Mayes, L. C., Granger, R. H., Bornstein, M. H., and Zuckerman, B. 1992. The problem of prenatal cocaine exposure: A rush to judgment. *Journal of the American Medical Association,* 267:406–408.

Meissels, S., and Schonkoff, J. P. 1990. *Handbook of early childhood intervention.* New York: Cambridge University Press.

Milgram, S. 1974. *Obedience to authority: An experimental view.* New York: Harper and Row.

Moran, G. S. 1987. Some functions of play and playfulness: A developmental perspective. *Psychoanalytic Study of the Child,* 42:11–29.

Moses, L. J., and Flavell, J. H. 1990. Inferring false beliefs from actions and reactions. *Child Development,* 61:929–945.

Nachman, P. A., and Stern, D. A. 1984. Affect retrieval. In *Frontiers in infant psychiatry,* ed. J. D. Call, E. Gelenson, and R. Tyson. New York: Basic Books, pp. 95–100.

National Center for Clinical Infant Programs (NCCIP). 1992. *Head Start: The emotional foundations of school readiness.* Washington, D.C.: The Zero to Three National Center for Clinical Infant Programs.

National Center for Health Statistics (NCHS). 1988. *Vital statistics of the United States.* Washington, D.C.: National Center for Health Statistics, Public Health Services.

———. 1991. *Vital statistics of the United States. Volume 1. Natality.* Washington, D.C.: National Center for Health Statistics, Public Health Services.

National Commission for the Protection of Human Subjects of Biomedical and Behavioral Research. 1977. *Research involving children: Report and recommendations.* DHEW Publication No. (OS) 77–0004. Washington, D.C.: U.S. Department of Health, Education, and Welfare.

National Commission of the States (NCS). 1990. *Interactional assessment of educational progress.* Denver: National Commission of the States.

National Health/Education Consortium (NC/EC). 1991. *Healthy brain development: Precursors to learning.* Washington, D.C.: National Health/Education Consortium.

Nelson, C. A. 1987. The recognition of facial expressions in the first two years of life: Mechanisms of development. *Child Development,* 58:889–909.

Neubauer, P. B. 1987. The many meanings of play. Introduction. *Psychoanalytic Study of the Child,* 42:3–9.

———. 1993. Playing: Clinical implications. In *The meaning of play in child psychoanalysis,* ed. A. Solnit. New Haven: Yale University Press, pp. 44–53.

New Haven Public Schools (NHPS). 1992. Report on the SAHA. In *Social development project evaluation, 1991–92: Final report.* New Haven: New Haven Public Schools, Office of the Superintendent, pp. 179–196.

Olson, G. M., and Sherman, T. 1983. Attention, learning and memory in infants. In *Infancy and developmental psychobiology,* ed. M. M. Haith and J. J. Campos. New York: Wiley.

Oxford English Dictionary. 1989. Oxford: Clarendon Press.

Parens, H. 1979. *The development of aggression in early childhood.* New York: Jason Aronson.

Parke, R. D., and Slaby, R. G. 1983. The development of aggression. In *Handbook of child psychology,* ed. E. M. Hetherington. New York: Wiley, pp. 547–641.

Paul, R., Cohen, D. J., and Caparulo, B. K. 1983. A longitudinal study of patients with severe developmental disorders of language learning. *Journal of the American Academy of Child and Adolescent Psychiatry,* 22:525–534.

Pauls, D. 1987. The familiarity of autism and related disorders: A review of the evidence. In *Handbook of autism and pervasive developmental disorders,* ed. D. Cohen and A. Donnellan. New York: Wiley, pp. 192–198.

Pauls, D. L., Cohen, D. J., Heimbuch, R., Detlor, J., and Kidd, K. K. 1981. Familial pattern and transmission of Gilles de la Tourette syndrome and multiple tics. *Archives of General Psychiatry,* 38:1091–1093.

Pauls, D. L., and Leckman, J. F. 1986. The inheritance of Gilles de la Tourette's syndrome and associated behaviors: Evidence for autosomal dominant transmission. *New England Journal of Medicine,* 315:993–997.

Pauls, D. L., Towbin, K. E., Leckman, J. F., Zahner, G. E., and Cohen, D. J. 1986. Gilles de la Tourette's syndrome and obsessive-compulsive disorder: Evidence supporting a genetic relationship. *Archives of General Psychiatry,* 43:1180–1182.

Peretz, M. 2001. New Haven diarist interrupted. *The New Republic,* October, p. 46.

Perner, J., Frith, U., Leslie, A. M., and Leekam, S. R. 1989. Exploration of the autistic child's theory of mind: Knowledge, belief, and communication. *Child Development,* 60:688–700.

Peterson, B. S., and Cohen, D. J. 1998. The treatment of Tourette's syndrome: Multimodal, developmental intervention. *Journal of Clinical Psychiatry,* 59:62–72; discussion 73–74.

Peterson, B. S., and Leckman, J. F. 1998. The temporal dynamics of tics in Gilles de la Tourette syndrome. *Biological Psychiatry,* 44:1337–1348.

Peterson, B. S., Leckman, J. F., and Cohen, D. J. 1995. Tourette's syndrome: A genetically predisposed and an environmentally specified developmental psychopathology. In *Developmental psychopathology: Volume 1. Risk, disorder, and adaptation,* ed. D. Cicchetti and D. J. Cohen. New York: Wiley, pp. 213–242.

Peterson, B. S., Riddle, M. A., Cohen, D. J., Katz, L. D., Smith, J. C., and Leckman, J. F. 1993. Human basal ganglia volume asymmetries on magnetic resonance images. *Magnetic Resonance Imaging,* 11:493–498.

Peterson, B. S., Skudlarski, P., Anderson, A. W., Zhang, H., Gatenby, J. C., Lacadie, C. M., Leckman, J. F., and Gore, J. C. 1998. A functional magnetic resonance imaging study of tic suppression in Tourette syndrome. *Archives of General Psychiatry,* 55:326–333.

Piaget, J. 1929. *The child's conception of the world.* New York: Harcourt Brace.

———. 1937. *The construction of reality in the child.* New York: Basic Books.

Price, R. A., Kidd, K. K., Cohen, D. J., Pauls, D. L., and Leckman, J. F. 1985. A twin study of Tourette syndrome. *Archives of General Psychiatry,* 42:815–820.

Prior, M., and Cummins, R. 1992. Questions about facilitated communication and autism. *Journal of Autism and Developmental Disorders,* 22:331–337; discussion 337–338.

Public Law 94–142. 1977. The Education for All Handicapped Children Act of 1975. Federal Register, August 23, 42(163).

Putnam, M. G., Rank, B., Pavenstedt, E., Anderson, I. N., and Rawson, I. 1948. Case study of an atypical two-and-a-half-year-old. *American Journal of Orthopsychiatry,* 18:1–30.

Pynoos, R. 1993. Traumatic stress and developmental psychopathology in children and adolescents. In *American Psychiatric Press review of psychiatry,* ed. J. Oldham, M. Riba, and A. Tasman. Washington, D.C.: American Psychiatric Press, pp. 205–238.

Pynoos, R. S., Frederick, C., Nader, K., Arroyo, W., Steinberg, A., Eth, S., Nunez, F., and

Fairbanks, L. 1987. Life threat and posttraumatic stress in school-age children. *Archives of General Psychiatry,* 44:1057–1063.

Pynoos, R. S., and Nader, K. 1989. Children's memory and proximity to violence. *Journal of the American Academy of Child and Adolescent Psychiatry,* 28:236–241.

Pynoos, R. S., Steinberg, A. M., and Wraith, R. 1994. A developmental model of childhood traumatic stress. Unpublished manuscript.

Quiggle, N. L., Garber, J., Panak, W. F., and Dodge, K. A. 1992. Social information processing in aggressive and depressed children. *Child Development,* 63:1305–1320.

Rank, B., and MacNaughton, D. 1950. A clinical contribution to early ego development. *Psychoanalytic Study of the Child,* 5:53–65.

Rapin, I. 1979. Effects of early blindness and deafness on cognition. In *Congenital and acquired cognitive disorders,* ed. R. Katzman. New York: Raven Press.

Reich, W. 1933. *Character analysis.* New York: Simon and Schuster.

Riddle, M. A., Geller, B., and Ryan, N. 1993. Another sudden death in a child treated with desipramine. *Journal of the American Academy of Child and Adolescent Psychiatry,* 32:792–797.

Rimland, B. 1964. *Infantile autism: The syndrome and its implications for a neural theory of behavior.* New York: Prentice Hall.

Ritvo, S. 1978. The psychoanalytic process in childhood. *Psychoanalytic Study of the Child,* 33:295–305.

Ritvo, S., and Provence, S. 1953. Form perception and imitation in some autistic children: Diagnostic findings and their contextual interpretation. *Psychoanalytic Study of the Child,* 8:155–161.

Ritvo, S., and Solnit, A. J. 1958. Influences of early mother-child interaction on identification processes. *Psychoanalytic Study of the Child,* 13:64–85; discussion 86–91.

Rochlin, G. 1982. Aggression reconsidered. *Psychoanalytic Inquiry,* 2:121–132.

Rosen, V. H. 1960. Some aspects of the role of imagination in the analytic process. *Journal of the American Psychoanalytic Association,* 8:229–251.

Rosenzweig, F. 1971 [1930]. *The star of redemption.* Trans. William W. Hallo (from the second edition of 1930). New York: Holt, Rinehart and Winston.

Rotenberg, K. J. 1980. Children's use of intentionality in judgements of character and disposition. *Child Development,* 51:282–284.

Roth, A., and Fonagy, P. 2004. *What works for whom? A critical review of psychotherapy research.* 2nd ed. New York: Guilford Press.

Rovee-Collier, C. K. 1987. Learning and memory in infancy. In *Handbook of infant development,* ed. J. D. Osofsky. New York: Wiley, pp. 98–148.

Rovee-Collier, C. K., and Fagan, J. W. 1981. The retrieval of memory in early infancy. In *Advances in infancy research,* ed. L. P. Lipsitt. Norwood: Ablex, pp. 226–254.

Rovee-Collier, C. K., Sullivan, M. W., Enright, M., Lucas, D., and Fagen, J. W. 1980. Reactivation of infant memory. *Science,* 208:1159–1161.

Rule, B. G., Nesdale, A. R., and Mcara, M. J. 1974. Children's reactions to information about the intentions underlying an aggressive act. *Child Development,* 45:794–798.

Rutter, M. 1985. The treatment of autistic children. *Journal of Child Psychology and Psychiatry,* 26:193–214.

Samet, J. 1993. Autism and theory of mind: Some philosophical perspectives. In *Understanding other minds: Perspectives from autism,* ed. S. Baron-Cohen, H. Tager-Flusberg, and D. J. Cohen. Oxford: Oxford University Press, pp. 427–449.

Sandler, J., Kennedy, H., and Tyson, R. L. 1980. *The technique of child analysis.* London: Hogarth Press/Karnac Books.

Schonfeld, D., and Kline, M. 1994. School-based crisis intervention: An organizational model. *Crisis Intervention and Time-Limited Treatment,* 1:155–166.

Schorr, L. B. 1988. *Within our reach: Breaking the cycle of disadvantage.* New York: Doubleday.

Schwab-Stone, M., Chen, C., Greenberger, E., Silver, D., Lichtman, J., and Voyce, C. 1999. No safe haven. II: The effects of violence exposure on urban youth. *Journal of the American Academy of Child and Adolescent Psychiatry,* 38:359–367.

Schwab-Stone, M. E., Ayers, T. S., Kasprow, W., Voyce, C., Barone, C., Shriver, T., and Weissberg, R. P. 1995. No safe haven: A study of violence exposure in an urban community. *Journal of the American Academy of Child and Adolescent Psychiatry,* 34:1343–1352.

Shantz, D. W., and Voydanoff, D. A. 1973. Situational effects on retaliatory aggression at three age levels. *Child Development,* 44:149–153.

Shapiro, A. K., and Shapiro, E. 1968. Treatment of Gilles de la Tourette's syndrome with haloperidol. *British Journal of Psychiatry,* 114:345–350.

Shapiro, A. K., Shapiro, E. S., Bruun, R. D., and Sweet, R. D. 1978. *Gilles de la Tourette syndrome.* New York: Raven Press.

Shapiro, T. 1977. The quest for a linguistic model to study the speech of autistic children: Studies on echoing. *Journal of the American Academy of Child and Adolescent Psychiatry,* 16:608–619.

Shapiro, T., and Hertzig, M. E. 1991. Social deviance in autism: A central integrative failure as a model for social non-engagement. *Psychiatric Clinics of North America,* 14:19–32.

Sherman, M., Shapiro, T., and Glassman, M. 1983. Play and language in developmentally disordered preschoolers: A new approach to classification. *Journal of the American Academy of Child and Adolescent Psychiatry,* 22:511–524.

Shirkey, H. 1968. Therapeutic orphans. *Journal of Pediatrics,* 72:119–120.

Shotter, J., and Gregory, S. 1976. On first gaining the idea of oneself as a person. In *Life sentences: Aspects of the social role of language,* ed. R. Harre. New York: Wiley, pp. 3–9.

Siegel, B., Pliner, C., Eschler, J., and Elliott, G. R. 1988. How children with autism are diagnosed: Difficulties in identification of children with multiple developmental delays. *Journal of Developmental and Behavioral Pediatrics,* 9:199–204.

Solnit, A. J. 1972. Aggression: A view of theory building in psychoanalysis. *Journal of the American Psychoanalytic Association,* 20:435–450.

———. 1987. A psychoanalytic view of play. *Psychoanalytic Study of the Child,* 42:205–219.

———. 1993. From play to playfulness in children and adults. In *The many meanings of play in child psychoanalysis,* ed. A. Solnit. New Haven: Yale University Press, pp. 29–43.

Sorce, J., Emde, R. N., Campos, J. J., and Klinnert, M. 1985. Maternal emotional signaling. *Developmental Psychology,* 21:195–200.

Spitz, R. A. 1965. *The first year of life.* New York: International University Press.

———. 1969. Aggression and adaptation. *Journal of Nervous and Mental Disorders,* 149:81–90.

Stechler, G., and Halton, A. 1987. The emergence of assertion and aggression during infancy: A psychoanalytic systems approach. *Journal of the American Psychoanalytic Association,* 35:821–838.

Stepansky, P. E. 1977. A history of aggression in Freud. *Psychological Issues.* Monograph 39. New York: International University Press.

Stone, L. 1971. Reflections on the psychoanalytic concept of aggression. *Psychoanalytic Quarterly,* 40:195–244.

Tager-Flusberg, H. 1989. A psycholinguistic perspective on language development in the autistic child. In *Autism: New directions on diagnosis, nature, and treatment,* ed. G. Dawson. New York: Guilford Press, pp. 92–116.

Taylor, L. 1994. Witnessing violence by young children and their mothers. *Developmental and Behavioral Pediatrics,* 15:120–123.

Taylor, L., Zuckerman, B., Harik, V., and McAlister-Groves, B. 1992. Exposure to violence among inner-city parents and young children. *American Journal of Disorders of Children,* 146:487–494.

Terr, L. 1991. Childhood traumas: An outline and overview. *American Journal of Psychiatry,* 148:10–20.

Towbin, K. E., Riddle, M. A., Cohen, D. J., and Leckman, J. F. 1988. The clinical care of individuals with Tourette's syndrome. In *Tourette's syndrome and tic disorders: Clinical understanding and treatment,* ed. D. J. Cohen, R. D. Bruun, and J. F. Leckman. New York: Wiley, pp. 329–352.

Tronick, E., Als, H., Adamson, L., Wise, S., and Brazelton, T. B. 1978. The infant's response to entrapment between contradictory messages in face-to-face interaction. *Journal of the American Academy of Child and Adolescent Psychiatry,* 17:1–13.

Tustin, F. 1983. Thoughts on autism with special reference to a paper by Melanie Klein. *Journal of Child Psychotherapy,* 9:199–131.

Ungerer, J., Brody, I., and Zelazo, P. 1978. Long-term memory for speech in 2 to 4-week old infants. *Infant Behavior and Development,* 1:177–186.

U.S. Congress, House of Representatives, Select Committee on Children, Youth and Families. 1989. *Children and their families: Current conditions and recent trends.* Washington, D.C.: U.S. Government Printing Office.

Volkmar, F. R., and Cohen, D. J. 1985. The experience of infantile autism: A first person account by Tony W. *Journal of Autism and Developmental Disorders,* 15:47–54.

———. 1988. Classification and diagnosis of childhood autism. In *Diagnosis and assessment,* ed. E. Schopler and G. Mesibov. New York: Plenum, pp. 71–89.

Volkmar, F. R. 1987. Social development. In *Handbook of autism and pervasive developmental disorders,* ed. D. J. Cohen and A. M. Donnellan. New York: Wiley, pp. 41–60.

Waelder, R. 1932. The psychoanalytic theory of play. *Psychoanalytic Quarterly,* 2:208–224.

———. 1956. Critical discussion of the concept of an instinct of destruction. *Bulletin of the Philadelphia Association of Psychoanalysis,* 6:97–109.

Walker, A. S. 1982. Intermodal perception of expressive behaviors by human infants. *Journal of Experimental Child Psychology,* 33:514–535.

Weil, A. 1953. Certain severe disturbances of ego development in children. *Psychoanalytic Study of the Child,* 8:271–287.

Weil, A. P. 1970. The basic core. *Psychoanalytic Study of the Child*, 25:442–460.

Weiland, H., and Rudnick, R. 1961. Considerations of the development and treatment of autistic childhood psychoses. *Psychoanalytic Study of the Child*, 16:549–563.

Wellman, H. M. 1988. First steps in the child's theorizing about the mind. In *Developing theories of mind*, ed. P. H. Astington and D. Olson. Cambridge: Cambridge University Press, pp. 64–92.

———. 1990. *The child's theory of mind*. Cambridge: MIT Press.

Wellman, H. M., and Estes, D. 1986. Early understanding of mental entities: A reexamination of childhood realism. *Child Development*, 57:910–923.

Wellman, H. M., and Woolley, J. D. 1990. From simple desires to ordinary beliefs: The early development of everyday psychology. *Cognition*, 35:245–275.

Wimmer, H., and Perner, J. 1983. Beliefs about beliefs: Representation and constraining function of wrong beliefs in young children's understanding of deception. *Cognition*, 13:103–128.

Wing, L. 1981. Asperger's syndrome: A clinical account. *Psychological Medicine*, 11:115–129.

Winnicott, D. W. 1945a. Primitive emotion and development. *International Journal of Psychoanalysis*, 26:137–143.

———. 1945b. Primitive emotional development. In *Through pediatrics to psychoanalysis*. New York: Basic Books, pp. 145–156.

———. 1950. Aggression in relation to emotional development. In *Collected papers*. New York: Basic Books, pp. 204–218.

———. 1956. Primary maternal preoccupation. In *Through pediatrics to psychoanalysis*. New York: Basic Books, pp. 300–305.

———. 1958. The capacity to be alone. *International Journal of Psychoanalysis*, 39:416–420.

———. 1960. Ego distortion in terms of true and false self. In *The Maturational processes and the facilitating environment*. London: Hogarth Press, pp. 140–152.

———. 1969. The use of an object. *International Journal of Psychoanalysis*, 50:711–716.

———. 1971. *Playing and reality*. London: Tavistock Publications.

———. 1977. *The Piggle*. Madison: International University Press.

Wollheim, R. 1984. *The thread of life* (William James lectures). Cambridge: Harvard University Press.

Young, A. B., and Penney, J. B. 1984. Neurochemical anatomy of movement disorders. *Neurologic Clinics*, 2:417–433.

Zborowski, M., and Herzog, E. 1995 [1952]. *Life is with people: The culture of the shtetl*. New York: Schocken.

Zigler, E., and Muenchow, S. 1992. *Head Start: The inside story of America's most successful educational experiment*. New York: Basic Books.

Zill, N., and Schoenborn, C. A. 1988. Developmental, learning, and emotional problems of our nation's children, United States, 1988. Advance data from *Vital and health statistics*, No. 190. Hyattsville: U.S. Department of Health and Human Services, National Center for Health Statistics.

Zimbardo, P. G., Ebbesen, E. B., and Maslach, C. 1977. *Influencing attitudes and changing behavior*, 2nd ed. Reading: Addison-Wesley.

Contributors

Miriam Berkman, J.D., M.S.W., Assistant Clinical Professor of Social Work, Yale Child Study Center, New Haven, Connecticut

Matthew Isaac Cohen, Ph.D., Senior Lecturer, Department of Drama and Theatre, Royal Holloway, University of London, London, England

Peter Fonagy, Ph.D., F.B.A., Freud Memorial Professor of Psychoanalysis, Director, Sub-Department of Clinical Health Psychology, University College London, Chief Executive, Anna Freud Centre, London, England

Robert A. King, M.D., Professor of Child Psychiatry and Psychiatry, Yale Child Study Center, New Haven, Connecticut

Ami Klin, Ph.D., Harris Associate Professor of Child Psychiatry and Psychology, Yale Child Study Center, New Haven, Connecticut

James F. Leckman, M.D., Neison Harris Professor of Child Psychiatry, Psychology, and Pediatrics, Director of Research, Yale Child Study Center, New Haven, Connecticut

Steven Marans, Ph.D., Professor of Child Psychoanalysis and Psychiatry, Yale Child Study Center, Director, National Center for Children Exposed to Violence, New Haven, Connecticut

Andrés Martin, M.D., M.P.H., Associate Professor of Child Psychiatry and Psychiatry, Yale Child Study Center, New Haven, Connecticut

Linda C. Mayes, M.D., Arnold Gesell Professor of Child Psychiatry, Psychology, and Pediatrics, Yale Child Study Center, New Haven, Connecticut

Martin Peretz, Editor-in-Chief, *The New Republic,* Washington, D.C.

Index

Abraham, K., 123, 163

Adnopoz, Jean, xxi, 202

Adolescents, 197–99. *See also* Juvenile offenders

Aggression: in animals, 167; attribution of aggressive intent, 170–71, 177; and biological processes, 166; and character, 123, 125–27, 165; clinical illustration of, 173–75; definition of, 250*m*; definitional issues regarding, 167–68; domains of psychoanalytic thinking regarding, 250*m*; and fantasy, 161, 166, 173, 176; and frustration, 167; goals of, in young children, 168, 169–70; hostile versus instrumental aggressivity, 169; and individuation, 161, 165; observational studies of, in children, 166–71, 176; psychoanalytic view of, xiii, 162–66; social cognition model of, 167; so-cial learning theory of, 168; social matrix of, in first years of life, 159–78; summary and research implications for, 176–78; theories of mind and modulation of, 171–73

Aggressive feelings and mental states, 250*m*. *See also* Aggression

Aggressivity, 166–67, 169, 173–78, 180–82, 250*m*. *See also* Aggression

AIDS, 202

Alexander, Duane, 35–36

Alivisatos, Spyridon, 31–32, 227

Analysis. *See* Child analysis; Psychoanalysis

Anderson, George, 19, 26, 37, 45

Anger. *See* Aggression

Apter, Alan, 91

Asperger syndrome, 212

Attachment, 55, 71

Augustine, 4, 16, 17

Autism: and absence of desire for the
other, 60–61; Asperger syndrome, 212;
case histories on, 52–54; characteristics
of, xvii, xxiii, 21, 43–44; definition of,
62; diagnostic criteria for, 39–40, 211;
and echolalia, 68–69; educational
strategies for autistic children, 214–15;
and experiencing self and others, 65–
79; and facilitated communication,
215–16; and false-belief tasks, 78; family collaboration in research on, 38; and
fantasy, 51, 69; federal legislation and
policy on, 35–36; genetic studies on,
212; and language, 39, 67; longitudinal
studies of, 51–52; negative research
findings on, 38–39; neurochemistry
and neurobiology of, 19, 21–22, 33, 37–
39, 213; neuroimaging for study of, xix, ·
21, 38–39, 41, 211, 213; and parental
psychopathology, 212; pathogenesis of,
212–13, 214; patient-focused approach
to, xviii–xix; research on, 28–46, 51–
52, 86, 210–16, 224, 230; Rimland on
biological basis of, 32; and serotonin,
19, 33, 39; and social cognition, 40–41;
and social relations, 21–22, 31, 39, 44,
50–52, 60–61, 67–70, 73–74, 127;
studies of normal development and
studies of, 41–42; and theory of mind,
40–41, 49–64, 66–67; unconventional forms of treatment for, 215–16

Baron-Cohen, Simon, xvii, 41, 45, 62, 66,
78, 100, 171

Behaviorism. See Operant conditioning

Berkman, Miriam, 179–203

Biological child psychiatry, 34, 37, 91, 243

Bowers, Malcolm, xvi, 37, 230

Brain imaging. See Neuroimaging

Bristol, Marie, 36

Bruun, Ruth D., 85

Buber, Martin, xv, 24

Caparulo, B. K., 51, 67, 68–69, 92

Catastrophic circumstances. See Violence

CDCP. See Child Development/Com-
munity Policing (CDCP) project

Character, 108, 122–27, 163, 165

Charcot, Jean-Marie, 83

Chase, Thomas N., 91

Child abuse and neglect, 219

Child analysis: analyst's role in, 129–30;
of boy with enduring sadness, 108–13,
121–22; countertransference in, 111–12;
developmental urgency of, 128–29; of
five-year-old hyperactive boy, 134–37,
139–41; interpretation in, 129–31, 139,
154; Loewald on, xxii, xxiii; play in,
129–41; of three-year-old girls with
stool withholding and separation-distress, 131–34, 136–37, 139–41, 173–75;
transference in, 139, 140, 160. See also
Play; and specific child analysts

Child Development/Community Policing (CDCP) project, xiii, xxi–xxii, 10,
184–99, 202

Children. See Infants; Mother-child relationship

Chomsky, Noam, xxiii, 18

Cicchetti, Dante, xiii, 85, 92, 101, 219

Circumcision, 19

Clomipramine, 93

Clonidine, xix, 23, 90–91

Cocaine, 222

Cognitive behavior therapy, xii, 102

Cohen, Donald: academic achievements
of and awards for, xxi, 5–6, 25–28; art-
work by, 246; career and contributions
of, xi–xiv, xv–xxiv, 4–6, 20, 34–37, 39,
230–31, 245; childhood of, 4, 28–29,
43, 226; children of, 244–45; children's
books by, 246; clothing of, 244–45; as
collector of antiquities, 9; conceptual
perspective of, xvi–xvii; death of, 4;
in documentary on child psychiatry,
246–47; education of, 4, 8, 16–20, 31–

34, 226–29, 247; family background
and family relationships of, 3–4, 6,
29–30, 245–46, 247; final illness of, 7,
9, 11–12, 25; grandchildren of, 6; international work of, xxi, 6, 10, 12; and Israel, xxi, 6, 9, 12, 30, 242; Judaism of,
xxiv, 8–12, 24–25, 26, 246; last speech
of, xv–xvi; marriage of, 4, 27, 244–45,
247; mentors of, xvi, xx, 4, 19, 24, 31–
33, 226–29, 231, 240; mentorship by,
xiii–xiv, xx; patients and patients' families as collaborators with, xviii–xix, 38,
245; personal dealings of, with students
and colleagues, xiv, 245–46; psychoanalyses experienced by, xxii, 17, 247;
Purim plays by, 246; as social being,
xvi, 245–46; writings by, xvii, xxi, 5, 32,
41, 243–44, 246; Yiddish read by, 9. See
also Yale Child Study Center
Cohen, Howard, 4, 27
Cohen, Joseph, 9
Cohen, Matthew Isaac, 242–48
Cohen, Phyllis, 4, 27, 139, 244–45, 247
Cohen (Donald J.) National Child Trau-
matic Stress Initiative, xxii
Comer, James, xxi
Comings, David E., 91
Competence model, 62
Consciousness, xxiii
Constipation, 131–34
Cost-effectiveness research, 222–23
Countertransference, 111–12
Crimes, 181, 192–99

Day care, xx–xxi, 35
Death instinct, 160
Depression: case history of adult male
with, 107, 113–22; case history of boy
with, 107, 108–13, 121–22; developmental psychoanalytic approach to, xii,
107–27; and exposure to violence, 180;
of mothers, 108, 114, 117, 121
Descartes, Rene, xvii, xxiii, 4, 18

Desire: absence of, in autism, 60–61; development of desire for the other, 57–
60; emergence of, and falling in love,
54–57, 78; and fantasy, 49–50; and internalization, 59, 60; psychoanalytic
view of, 55–57; and theory of mind,
49–50, 67. See also Love
Developmental delay, 220–22
Developmental Disabilities Act, 35
Developmental psychopathology, xii–xiii,
xxiii, 23, 101
Dibble, Eleanor, 5
Disadvantaged backgrounds. See Poverty
Downey, T. W., 161
Dreams: of adult male suffering from depression, 115–18, 120, 121; bedwetting
dream, 117
Dropouts, 181, 218–19

Echolalia, 68–69
Eczema, 20, 229
Education. See headings beginning with
School
Ego. See Self
Emerson, Ralph Waldo, 142, 159
Erenberg, Gerald, 86
Erikson, Erik, 137, 240
Ethics: of autism research, 210–16, 224;
and character, 125, 127; informed con-
sent and research, 208; and research,
207–24; of research on children from
disadvantaged backgrounds, 216–24

Facilitated communication, 215–16
False-belief tasks, 78, 172
Families: and autism, 38; collaboration
with, in Yale Child Study Center research, xviii–xix, 38; impact of violence
on, 184–85; and Tourette's syndrome,
97
Fantasy: and aggression, 161, 166, 173, 176;
and autism, 51, 69; of boy with enduring sadness, 109–10; and caring for self,

Fantasy (*continued*)
59–60; and character, 125–26; of Cohen's son, 244, 245; and desire for others, 49–50, 59–60; and falling in love
and emergence of desire, 55–56, 78; intervention fantasies, 191; masturbation
fantasy, 115–16, 120; on mind-body
connections, 124; oedipal phase fantasies, 146, 153–54; and separation from
parents, 74–75; and theory of mind,
49–64. *See also* Imagination; Play
Father-child relationship, 112–13, 114,
120–21, 135–36
Fonagy, Peter, xi–xiv
Foster care, 219
Freedman, Daniel X., xvi, xx, 3–5, 19, 24,
33, 228–30
Freeman, Roger, 86
Freud, Anna: on aggression, 162, 164, 182;
career of, 240; on child analysis, 111,
128, 130, 138, 160; on imagination, 146;
on play, 130, 138
Freud, Sigmund: on aggression, 160, 162,
163; *Beyond the Pleasure Principle* by,
145–46, 160, 163; on character, 123, 124,
125, 127; and hysteria, 83–84, 88; on
imagination, 145–46; and instinct theory, 160, 162; as Jewish physician and
philosopher, 11; and Tourette's syndrome, 83–84, 85, 88; on traumatic situation, 184
Friedhoff, Arnold J., 86
Frustration: and aggression, 167; in
mother-child relationship, 57–58, 70–
71, 147
Furer, M., 59, 65, 67, 68, 147, 148

Gallup, G. G., Jr., 207
Garbarino, J., 201
Genetic studies: of autism, 212; of
Tourette's syndrome, 89–90, 92
Gershon, Elliot, 5
Gesell, Arnold, 18

Gilles de la Tourette, Georges, 83, 84, 85
Glatstein, Jacob, 9
Goetz, Christopher C., 91
Golden, Gerald S., 85
Grief. *See* Sadness

Haloperidol, 84, 85, 88, 93
Harlow, H. F., 167, 207
Harris, Irving B., xxii, 27, 45
Hartmann, H., 125, 164, 175
Hartup, W. W., 168, 169
Hay, D. F., 168
Head Start, 220–21
Hobson, R. P., 57, 59, 65–69, 249*m*
Hysteria, 84, 88

Imagination: development of capacity for,
in early childhood, 142–55; developmental line for imaginative capacity,
153–54; functions of, 143–44; general
meanings of, 142–43; and internalization, 148; memory distinguished from,
155; and mother-child relationship,
147–48; and oedipal phase, 143, 144–
45, 153–54; origin of term, 145; in play
of five-year-old girl, 143–44; preverbal
roots of mental capacity for, 145–53;
psychoanalytic meaning of, 143; and relationships, 145; summary on, 154–55.
See also Fantasy; Play
Individuation, 147, 161, 165. *See also* Self
Infants: aggression of, 164–66; and attachment, 55, 71; capacities of, for social relationships, 56–57, 71–72, 149–
50; circumcision of, 19; and creating
internal sense of self and attributing
meaning to others, 70–75; development of desire for the other by, 57–60;
falling in love and emergence of desire
in, 54–57, 78; infant-mother matrix,
57, 123, 126, 147; intrapsychic experiences of, 62, 63–64, 70; and joint attention, 72–73, 149–50; memory of,

148–49; in newborn intensive care unit (NICU), 217–18; and social referencing, 150–51, 165; sucking by, 19; of unwed mothers, 180, 218. *See also* Mother-child relationship

Informed consent, 208

Instincts theory, 160, 162, 165

Internalization, 59, 60, 71, 127, 147, 148

International Association of Child and Adolescent Psychiatry and Allied Professions, xxi, 5–6

Interpersonal relationships. *See* Relationships; Social development

Interpretation in child analysis, 129–31, 139, 154

Intervention fantasies, 191

Intrapsychic experiences of infants, 62, 63–64, 70

Israel, xxi, 6, 9, 12, 30, 242

Jacobson, E., 126

Jankovic, Joseph, 91

Juvenile offenders, 181, 202, 242–43

Kanner, Leo, xvii, 29, 67, 210

Kessen, William, xvi, 4, 19, 24, 71, 149, 229

Kessler, David, 27

Kierkegaard, Søren, 225

King, Robert, 27

Klawans, Harold H., 86

Klein, Melanie, 59, 67, 124, 126, 138, 164, 166, 173, 250*n*2

Klin, Ami, 26, 37, 41, 43, 45, 49–64, 207–24

Korczyn, Amos D., 91

Kurlan, Roger, 91

Lang, Anthony E., 91

Language, xxiii, 16–17, 18, 39, 67

Laor, Nathaniel, xxi, 45

Law enforcement. *See* Child Development/Community Policing (CDCP) project; Juvenile offenders

Leckman, James F., xviii, xix–xx, 3–7, 22–23, 27, 39, 42, 45, 83–103

Leibovitz, Yehoshua, 11

Lettick, Amy, 34, 36

Leukemia, 213–14

Levin, Richard, 27

Levine, R. J., 209

Libidinal drives, xxiii, 125, 126, 159–62, 164, 173, 175, 176

Lindsley, Ogden, xvi, xvii, 32, 227–28, 240

Loewald, Hans: on aggression, 126, 161, 166; on character, xii, 121, 123, 125, 126; as Cohen's mentor, xvi, 4; on definition of self, 175; on desire and self, 17, 59; on instincts theory, 165; on mother-child relationship, xxiii, 17, 57, 70, 71, 126, 147–48, 161; on psychoanalysis, 127; psychoanalysis of Cohen by, xxii, 17

Lombroso, Paul, 27, 45

Loss and enduring sadness, 107–27

Love: attachment distinguished from, 55; definition of, 54; and development of desire for the other in infants, 57–60; falling in love and emergence of desire in infants, 54–57; and grief and mourning, 60; and self-awareness, 60. *See also* Desire; Mother-child relationship

Mahler, M. S., 59, 65, 67, 68, 70, 71, 147, 148, 161

Maimonides, 10–11

Marans, Steven, xxi, 144, 178, 179–203

Martin, Andrés, 45

Marsden, C. D., 85–86

Masochism, 125

Masturbation fantasy, 115–16, 120

Mayes, Linda C.: on aggression, 159–78; on autism, xiii, 26, 45, 49–79; on imagination, 142–55; on play, xxii, 128–41; on prenatal exposure to cocaine, 222; on social development, 65–

Mayes, Linda C. (*continued*)
79; on theory of mind, xiii, 49–64, 84;
on Tourette's syndrome, 85, 100, 103
Medications: research on, for children,
209; for Tourette's syndrome (TS), xix,
23, 84, 85, 88, 90–91, 93, 98, 102
Memory: imagination distinguished
from, 155; of infants, 148–49
Mentorship: Cohen's mentors, xvi, xx, 4,
19, 24, 31–33, 226–29, 231, 240; developmental viewpoint on, xiii–xiv, xx,
225–41; and young investigators, 237–
39
Milgram, S., 207
Mind, theory of. *See* Theory of mind
Mother-child relationship: and attachment, 55, 71; and attunement, 126; and
child's gesture, 123; and creating internal sense of self and attributing meaning to others, 70–75; and depressed
mothers, 108, 114, 117, 121; development of desire for the other by infants,
57–60; and falling in love and emergence of desire in infants, 54–57, 78;
frustration in, 57–58, 70–71, 147; and
good-enough breast, 126, 127; and
I-Thou relationships, 17; and imagination, 147–48; infant-mother matrix,
57, 123, 126, 147; infants' capacities for
social relationships, 56–57, 71–72,
149–50; and internalization, 59, 60, 71,
147, 148; and joint attention, 72–73,
149–50; Loewald on, xxiii, 17, 57, 70,
71, 126, 147–48, 161; and mirroring,
126; and social referencing, 150–51, 165;
and unwed mothers, 180, 218

National Center for Children Exposed to
Trauma, xxii
National Commission for the Protection
of Human Subjects of Biomedical and
Behavioral Research, 207–8
National Institute of Child Health and

Human Development (NICHD), 35–
36, 45
National Institute of Mental Health
(NIMH), xx, 4, 5, 34, 36, 45, 230
National Institutes of Health, xviii, 11, 39
National Society for Autistic Children
(NSAC), 34–35
Neubauer, P. B., 130, 137, 138
Neuroimaging: and autism research, xix,
21, 38–39, 41, 211, 213; of integrated
neuronal systems in brain, 100; and
Tourette's syndrome, 92
NICHD. *See* National Institute of Child
Health and Human Development
(NICHD)
NIMH. *See* National Institute of Mental
Health (NIMH)
Nomura, Yishiko, 86
Nordhaus, Barbara, xxi
NSAC. *See* National Society for Autistic
Children (NSAC)
Nuland, Sherwin, 11

Obsessive-compulsive disorder, 89, 92, 93,
98, 102, 103. *See also* Tourette's syndrome (TS)
Oedipal phase, 124, 143, 144–45, 153–54,
171
Office of Child Development, xx–xxi, 4,
20, 34, 230
Operant conditioning, 17–18, 32

Parent-child relationship. *See* Father-child
relationship; Mother-child relationship
Pasteur, Louis, xvi
Pastore, Nicholas, xxi, 179–203
Paul, Rhea, 26, 45, 67
Pauls, David, 26, 27, 45, 89, 92, 212
Peretz, Martin, 4, 7, 8–12
Peterson, Bradley, 27, 92, 100, 101
Piaget, Jean, 75, 146–47
Pimozide, 93
Play: of boy with enduring sadness, 109–

10; in child analysis, 129–41; child analyst's role in, 129; of children following exposure to violence, 195, 196; emergence of, in oedipal phase, 143, 144–45, 153–54; of five-year-old hyper boy, 134–37, 139–41; functions of, 138; and imagination in five-year-old girl, 143–44; and interpretation in child analysis, 129–31, 139, 154; meanings of, for children, 137–38; psychoanalytic theory of, 137–38; Rosen on, 146; and self-understanding, 139–40; and spider in dollhouse, 247–48; of three-year-old girls with stool withholding and separation-distress, 131–34, 136–37, 139–41, 173–75. *See also* Child analysis; Imagination

Police. *See* Child Development/Community Policing (CDCP) project; Juvenile offenders

Pollin, William, 34, 230

Potashnik, Michael, 28, 29

Poverty, 180–81, 200–201, 216–24

Proust, Marcel 160

Provence, Sally, xvi, 4, 24, 26, 37, 65, 67, 240

Psychoanalysis: of adult male with depression, 113–21; of Cohen, xxii, 17, 247; Loewald on, 127; termination phase of, 120–21. *See also* Child analysis

Psychoanalytic psychotherapy of children, 194–97

Public Health Service, U.S., xx–xxi, 20, 34–35

Public Law 94-142, 214

Pynoos, R., 183, 190, 191

Reich, W., 123, 126, 163

Relationships: and autism, 21–22, 31, 39, 44, 50–52, 60–61, 67–70, 73–74, 127; Cohen's early interest in, 29–31; development of desire for the other, 57–60; end of, 24; falling in love and emergence of desire, 54–57, 78; forming and sustaining, 16; I-Thou relationships, 3, 17; and imagination, 145; of preschool children, 43; psychoanalytic theory of social development and studies of autism, 65–79. *See also* Father-child relationship; Mother-child relationship

Research in child and adolescent psychiatry: aggression, 176–78; autism, 28–46, 51–52, 86, 210–16, 224; children from disadvantaged backgrounds, 216–24; cost-effectiveness research, 222–23; developmental delay, 220–22; developmental line from student to researcher, 233–41; ethical imperative for, 207–24; Head Start, 220–21; and informed consent, 208; later phases of career in, 240; mentors for young investigators, 237–39; options for investigators in, 234–35; personal development and training for, 226–31; pioneers in, 240–41; profession and institutions of child psychiatry, 231–33; resented/feared attitudes, 222–23; role of clinical researchers, 239; steps of young investigators for maturing into clinical researchers, 235–36; tasks of adult development for young researchers, 236–38; Tourette's syndrome, 22–23, 26–27, 85–92; unexciting/unchallenging attitude, 220–22. *See also* Yale Child Study Center

Richmond, Julius, xvi

Riddle, Mark, 27

Rimland, Bernard, 32, 34

Ritvo, Edward, xvii, 37, 39–40

Ritvo, Samuel, xvi, 4, 24, 65, 67, 130, 147

Robbery at gunpoint, 197–99

Robertson, Mary M., 91

Rosen, David, 27

Rosen, V. H., 143, 146

Rosenzweig, Franz, xvi, xxiv, 12, 24–25, 26

Rothenberger, Ari, 91

Rutter, Michael, 40

Sadism, 163

Sadness: case history of adult male with, 107, 113–22; case history of boy with, 107, 108–13, 121–22; developmental psychoanalytic approach to, xii, 107–27. *See also* Depression

Sanberg, Paul R., 91

Scahill, Lawrence, 27, 45

Schizophrenia, 227

School placement of autistic children, 214–15

School problems, 181, 218–19

School-based crisis intervention, 201–2

Schultz, Robert, 26, 41, 45

Schwab-Stone, Mary, xxi

Segawa, Masaya, 86

Self: and brain functions, 100; creating sense of self and attributing meaning to others, 70–75; development and maintenance of, 65–79, 99–101; emergence of, 59; Loewald on definition of, 175; and loss of loved one, 60; in normal and autistic children, 65–79; origins of, 123; self-other differentiation and theories of mind, 78–79; therapeutic process and coherence of self for children with Tourette's syndrome, 102–3; Tourette's syndrome and self under siege, 101–2

Self-understanding, 25, 60, 139–40

Senn, Milton, 18

Separation-distress, 58, 73, 131–34, 150–51, 173–75, 195

Serotonin, 19, 31–32, 33, 39, 227

Shapiro, Arthur, xvii, 84, 85, 87

Shapiro, Elaine, 84

Shaywitz, Bennett, 20, 36, 37, 230

Shirkey, H., 209

Singer, Harvey S., 86

Skinner, B. F., xxiii, 17–18, 32

Slayman, Carolyn, 27

Social development: creating internal sense of self and attributing meaning to others, 70–75; interpersonal world of autistic individuals, 67–70; psychoanalytic theory of, and studies of autism, 65–79; self-other differentiation and theories of mind, 78–79; understanding concepts of mental world and mental states, 75–78. *See also* Mother-child relationship; Relationships

Social learning theory of aggression, 168

Social referencing, 150–51, 165

Solnit, Albert J.: on aggression, 161, 162, 173; as Cohen's mentor, xvi, xx, 4, 20, 24, 127; on mother-child relationship, 147; on play, 138, 153; and Yale Child Study Center, xx, xxi, 20, 24, 36, 45

Sparrow, Sara, 26

Spiegel, Shalom, 8–9

Spitz, Rene, 160, 164, 240

Stepansky, P. E., 160, 162

Stool withholding, 131–34, 173–75

Stranger-anxiety, 58, 73, 150–51

Street shooting, 192–97

Sullivan, Ruth, 34

Superego, 125, 164

Tager-Flusberg, Helen, 41, 45, 51, 67

Taylor, L., 180, 201–2

Theory of mind: and aggression, 171–73; and autism, 40–41, 49–64, 66–67; cognitive perspective on, 50, 62; definition of, 66, 249*n*; and desire for others, 49–50, 67; and development and maintenance of the self, 99–100; and development of desire for the other, 57–60; and interpersonal intersubjectivity, 57; and psychoanalytic models of self-other differentiation, 78–79; psychoanalytic perspective on, 49–64

Tics, 93. *See also* Tourette's syndrome (TS)

Tourette Syndrome Association (TSA), 84–85, 91

Tourette's syndrome (TS): brain imaging for study of, 92; case examples on, 23,

94–96; characteristics of, xvii–xviii, 22, 87; clinical understanding of and care for, 94–99; Cohen's early interest in, 22; diagnosis of, 93; genetic studies on, 89–90, 92; history of, 83–84; and integration of biology and psychology, 84–87; and loss of self-control, 22; medications for, xix, 23, 84, 85, 88, 90–91, 93, 98, 102; neurochemistry of, 88; and obsessive-compulsive disorder, 89, 92, 93, 98, 102, 103; parents of children with, 97; patient-focused approach to, xviii–xix; prognosis for, 97–98; psychobiology of, 88–93; research on, 22–23, 26–27, 85–92; and self under siege, 101–2; therapeutic process for, and coherence of self, 102–3

Transference, 139, 140, 160

Trauma. *See* Violence

TS. *See* Tourette's syndrome (TS)

TSA. *See* Tourette Syndrome Association (TSA)

Vaccarino, Flora, 27, 42, 45

van Amerongen, Suzanne, xxii, 17

van de Wetering, Ben J. M., 91

Violence: acute and long-term effects of, 182–83, 194–98; adolescent's exposure to, 197–99; and aggressivity in children, 177–78, 180–82; children's exposure to, 179–83, 190–91; children's immediate responses to, 191, 193–94; collaborative responses to, 201–3; conclusion on, 203; cycle of, 184; developmental context of children's exposure to, 181–82, 191–99; home-based responses to, 202; impact of, on families and communities, 184–85; and juvenile offenders, 181, 202, 242–43; and poverty, 180–81, 200–201, 219; psychoanalytic psychotherapy of children exposed to, 194–97; robbery at gunpoint, 197–99; school-based crisis interven-

tion for, 201–2; statistics on, 179–80; street shooting, 192–97; war compared with urban violence, xxi, 199–201. *See also* Child Development/Community Policing (CDCP) project

Vitiello, Benedetto, 36

Volkmar, Fred, xviii, 26, 36, 37, 43, 45, 50–53, 63, 67

Vulnerability and enduring sadness, 107–27

War, xxi, 199–201. *See also* Violence

Wildstein, Shana, 27

Winnicott, D. W.: on aggression, 125, 161, 164, 165, 166, 173, 175; career of, 240; on imagination, 154; on mother-child relationship, 57, 123, 126; Piggle case of, 175, 246; on play, 138

Wittgenstein, Ludwig, xxiii, 4, 16–17, 18, 31, 83, 226

Wolff, Peter, xvi, 33, 229

Wollheim, Richard, 225

Yale Child Study Center: autism research by, xviii, 36–39, 42–43, 86, 230; clinical perspective of, xviii, 18, 34, 38, 43, 86–87; Cohen's hiring by, 4, 230; family collaboration in research by, 38; interdisciplinary staff of, 86; and mentorship, xx; Tourette's syndrome research by, xviii, 5, 26–27, 86–92; training program of, xix–xx. *See also* Child Development/Community Policing (CDCP) project

Yale Children's Clinical Research Center, 39

Yale Medical School, 6, 19, 33, 228

Young, J. Gerald, 26, 37, 45, 230

Zero-to-Three National Center for Clinical Infant Programs, 222

Zigler, Edward, xvi, xx–xxi, 4, 18, 20, 34, 36, 45, 229, 230

Zimbardo, P. G., 207